Modernity, Islam,
and Secularism
in Turkey

T0337912

PUBLIC WORLDS

Series Editors: Dilip Gaonkar and Benjamin Lee

A L E V   Ç I N A R

Modernity, Islam,

and Secularism

in Turkey

Bodies, Places, and Time

PUBLIC WORLDS, VOLUME 14

UNIVERSITY OF MINNESOTA PRESS

MINNEAPOLIS   LONDON

An earlier version of parts of the last three sections in chapter 3 was previously published as "Refah Party and the City Administration of Istanbul: Liberal Islam, Localism, and Hybridity," *New Perspectives on Turkey* 16 (Spring 1997): 23–40.

Chapter 4 was previously published as "National History as a Contested Site: The Conquest of Istanbul," *Comparative Studies in Society and History* 43, no. 2 (April 2001): 364–91. Reprinted with the permission of Cambridge University Press.

Published by the University of Minnesota Press
111 Third Avenue South, Suite 290
Minneapolis, MN 55401-2520
http://www.upress.umn.edu

Library of Congress Cataloging-in-Publication Data

Çınar, Alev.
    Modernity, Islam, and secularism in Turkey : bodies, places, and time / Alev Çınar.
        p.   cm. — (Public worlds ; v. 14)
    Includes bibliographical references (p.   ) and index.
    ISBN 978-0-8166-4410-0 (alk. paper) — ISBN 978-0-8166-4411-7 (pbk. : alk. paper)
    1. Islam and secularism—Turkey.   2. Islam and state—Turkey.   I. Title.
    II. Series.
    BP190.5.S35C56 2005
    322'.1'09561—dc22

                                                                                    2004023012

Printed in the United States of America on acid-free paper

The University of Minnesota is an equal-opportunity educator and employer.

12 11 10 09 08   10 9 8 7 6 5 4 3 2

Contents

Acknowledgments

I find writing acknowledgments a most difficult task due to the impossibility of acknowledging all the input, feedback, and assistance that went into
the preparation of this book. Regretting that what I say will inevitably be
partial, I want to first thank all those people whose names I cannot remem-
ber or have never learned but whose views and comments that might have
popped up in some random conversation, on a panel, or in a class discussion have inspired me in developing the ideas written here.

I feel very fortunate to have had the chance to work with Anne Norton,
who has supervised this work since its earliest phases and has been a great
inspiration to me not only in this study but in opening up new ways of
seeing, well, just about everything. I also feel indebted to Ian Lustick and
Tom Callaghy, who patiently read very early and raw versions of this
study and wholeheartedly supported my initial explorations in the dark.
I owe special thanks to my friends and colleagues at the University of
Pennsylvania, especially to Beshara Doumani and Rita Barnard, who read
earlier versions and provided invaluable input; to friends in the women's
studies program and the political science department; and particularly to
Hillary Appel and Joe Glicksberg, with whom I shared some of the most
difficult phases of this study. I owe a lot to Srirupa Roy for being such a
good and intelligent friend, for approaching everything so positively and
enthusiastically, and for having read through several versions of different
sections of this work and shared with me her keen insights.

I want to extend most sincere gratitude to Tom Bender for having created such supportive, congenial, and intellectually inspiring conditions at the International Center for Advanced Studies at New York University (ICAS/NYU), where I had an invaluable experience toward developing new perspectives and expanding the scope of my research. The seminars at ICAS/NYU where I had the chance to develop and present different parts of this study have been very beneficial. I am particularly grateful for the feedback I received in these seminars from Tom Bender himself, as well as from Janet Abu-Lughod and Timothy Mitchell. I also feel very fortunate to have shared this experience at ICAS with such good friends as Camilla Fojas, Benglan Goh, Abidin Kusno, and Maha Yahya, who read and commented on earlier versions of sections of this study.

I am most fortunate to have met Amrita Basu at the Five College Women's Studies Research Center and grateful for the opportunities I found there to bring in new perspectives, particularly in developing chapter 3. I want to thank Dale Eickelman for the support he extended and for the encouraging review he provided this work. I am also indebted to Roxanne Euben for the close reading and valuable feedback she provided not once, but twice.

I want to thank Carrie Mullen and Jason Weidemann of the University of Minnesota Press for the support and assistance they extended. I thank Irfan Çiftçi, Hatice Öncül, Osman Özsoy, and particularly Hüseyin Besli of the Istanbul city administration for their friendly cooperation and assistance and for sharing with me their knowledge, archives, and documents.

My work would not have been what it is if it were not for my son, Derya, who brought into my life such inspiration and joy.

Funding and support for the research and writing of this work has been provided by the Ford Foundation Predissertation Summer Grants at the University of Pennsylvania; the United States Institute of Peace Scholarship for Dissertation Research; the University of Pennsylvania Women's Studies Dissertation Writing Grant; the Mellon Foundation/ Sawyer Seminar Postdoctoral Fellowship at the International Center for Advanced Studies, New York University; and the Ford Associateship at the Five College Women's Studies Research Center.

Introduction

Modernity is perhaps one of the most controversial terms in scholarly literature, and to it is ascribed many, sometimes contradictory, meanings. The
fact that it has been and continues to be such a constitutive part of social,
political, cultural, and economic life all over the world compels scholars
of different disciplines to address the term, serving to further proliferate
its meaning and complicate its usage. *Modernity* may refer to a lifestyle, a
culture, a discourse, a historical epoch, a movement, a project, a mind-set,
an intellectual trend, to capitalism, industrialization, democracy, constitu-
tionalism, or secularism. Sometimes it is generalized to mean all of these
at once, running the risk of overloading the term to the point of analytical
uselessness, and sometimes one of its narrower meanings is privileged over
others at the cost of oversimplifying the term and overlooking its other
unexpected manifestations.

Whether *modernity* is referred to as a concept, as a historical, social, or
cultural process, or as an epoch with characteristic institutions, employing
the term as an analytical category is even more challenging for scholars
of non-European contexts[1] due to the complexity of the experience of
modernity in these places. In places outside of Europe, as a consequence
of colonialism and globalization, conditions have mostly evolved under
European influences, even in countries like Turkey, which has never been
directly colonized. Therefore, in these places it is possible to observe that
most of the institutions and practices established in the name of modernity have been modeled after their European counterparts. However, this

adoption does not change the fact that these non-European modernities have their own unique trajectories, creatively combining European influences with local practices and institutions to yield innovative, unique, and often much more complex forms and processes. Observing the experience of modernity in different non-Western contexts, Gaonkar notes that "modernity is more often perceived as lure than as threat, and people (not just the elite) everywhere, at every national or cultural site, rise to meet it, negotiate it, and appropriate it in their own fashion."[2]

However, the widely held assumption that the origins of both modernity and the conceptual tools with which to study it are located in Europe presents a daunting dilemma for scholars studying these unique and contrary modernities. On the one hand, if they unquestioningly accept the European model, they run the risk of slavishly adopting a Eurocentric perspective and disregarding original and unique ways in which modernity has taken root in the context they study. Until the emergence of postcolonial criticism, a large body of literature had already been produced in this mode employing variants of classical modernization theory that took modernity as an exclusively European experience. On the other hand, if the claim to European origins is rejected altogether, scholars run the risk of overlooking the ways in which local conditions have been altered and transformed by European influences. Such scholarship, which has "gone native," so to speak, often takes up defensive anti-Western and anti-modern stances that tend to uncritically exalt local practices and institutions. This perspective has often been cultivated by ultra-nationalist, fundamentalist, or "Third Worldist" ideologies.

It has been postcolonial criticism that has responded to this dilemma and started to produce new ways of approaching the study of modernity in non-European contexts. Devoting a special issue of the Millennial Quartet to "Alternative Modernities," *Public Culture* addressed this dilemma head-on. Studies of alternative modernities presented in this issue suggest that the pervasive presence of modernity in non-Western contexts is the result of neither servile imitation nor an inorganic imposition from outside or above, but rather the product of "creative adaptation."[3]

As such, in a country like Turkey, modernity can be adequately studied only if the creative adaptations of European influences are given due recognition and if both the Eurocentric and the nativistic extremes are avoided. In this study I seek to find such middle grounds through a close analysis of the trajectory of modernity in Turkey, examining both its adoption as official ideology by the founding state and challenges to it by the Islamists of the 1990s, who started to produce the ideology of an

Islamic mode of modernization. This task requires a reexamination of the term *modernity* and the development of an operational definition that will allow the investigation of the locally specific dynamics by which Turkish modernity took shape.

Unfortunately, however, Eurocentric perspectives still dominate scholarship in different disciplines, particularly in political science, economics, and history. Studies of modernity in non-European contexts that stay clear of postcolonial criticism tend to examine only institutions and trends that are characteristic of modernity in Europe, at the expense of a closer analysis of the unique circumstances of those non-European contexts. Practices and institutions that may very well be regarded as "modern" in their own contexts but do not have counterparts in the European experience are not recognized as part of modernity, nor are analytical tools and concepts sufficiently developed to study them. The possibility of an "Islamic modernism" that may be attributed to trends developing within the Islamist movement in Turkey is a case in point. The claim that modernity is an exclusively European product becomes a self-fulfilling hypothesis, because other forms of modernity that do not comply with European norms either are conveniently categorized as belonging to the realm of the pre-modern or traditional or are simply disregarded as anomalies altogether.

Modernity and Contending Modernization Projects in Turkey

Perhaps because Turkey was not a part of the colonial world, relevant academic disciplines in Turkey have been hesitant to incorporate postcolonial criticism in their studies of modernity and therefore have not benefited sufficiently from such critical perspectives. As a result, apart from a very few exceptions, scholarship on Turkey is still producing work that views Turkish modernity from a Eurocentric perspective. A great majority of scholars of Turkish studies unquestioningly assume that modernity in Turkey did not start as an organic process evolving out of local social, economic, and cultural dynamics, but rather was introduced from above by the Ottoman state in the early nineteenth century and later more authoritatively imposed by the new state after 1923.[4] Institutions and practices that constitute modernity in Turkey are more readily thought of as imports from Europe and therefore not as authentic products of the local context. Turkish modernity is seen as an imitation that has never really taken root in society and has always suffered from incongruity with local practices and lack of popular support.[5] These studies overlook unconventional claims made about Turkish modernity, such as one made by

Şerif Mardin, who has shown that modernity, understood as the development of a pragmatic rationality in administrative practices and diversions from the Islamic code, had started to take root in the Ottoman administrative system as early as the sixteenth century.[6]

Regardless of how it is understood, modernity has had an immense transformative and constitutive power in the ongoing formation of the social-political order in Turkey. For many, being modern is a deeply cherished ideal that is held very much as a religion, with its own shrines, rituals, sacred spaces, and mantras. Indeed, for some, routinely going to a Western classical music concert at the Atatürk Cultural Center (Atatürk Kültür Merkezi, or AKM) in Taksim Square in Istanbul has a meaning far beyond the immediate function of experiencing musical pleasure: it is a reaffirmation of a modern and European lifestyle. Perhaps because of this devotion and to preserve the sanctity of the AKM Concert Hall as a sacred site of modernity, which is identified with secularism, the presence of patrons with Islamic attire is met with extreme annoyance and is certainly unwelcome. Similarly, the most significant monument of the nation, Mustafa Kemal Atatürk's mausoleum, Anıtkabir, which is celebrated as a distinguished mark of Turkish secularism and modernity, is a site of nationalist pilgrimage. It is in the devout way in which such monuments of Turkish modernity and secularism are upheld that the official project of modernity has acquired a religious and untouchable status.[7]

In Turkey, *modernity* not only is about a particular lifestyle, institution, practice, or culture, but also is a widely used word in daily popular discourse. Being a "modern woman," having a "modern marriage," abiding by "modern principles," or putting forth "modern thoughts"—all have specific meanings that are frequently evoked in daily talk and the media. There are popular and active associations such as the Modern Journalists Association, the Modern Women Association, or the Support for Modern Life Association, which has a Modern Children club and a Modern High-School Girls project. Therefore, studying modernity in Turkey not only requires the identification of instances, practices, and institutions that are deemed modern, but also necessitates due attention to the meaning of the term as it is used in daily discourse.

It is important to acknowledge that even if a particular conceptualization of modernity becomes dominant in a given time period, it is by no means the only one. The meaning of *modernity* illustrated earlier is the dominant meaning, congruent with the official state ideology founded by Mustafa Kemal Atatürk in the 1920s, which took secularism, Turkish nationalism, and a West-oriented modernity as constitutive principles upon which societal and political institutions were formed and the public and private spheres evolved. As the basis of the founding ideology of the new state, at that time *modernity* was understood as the adoption of what was seen as a universal norm of civilization, but what was in fact French bourgeois culture. On this note, Atatürk said,

> There are a variety of countries, but there is only one civilization. In order for a nation to advance, it is necessary that it join this civilization. If our bodies are in the East, our mentality is oriented toward the West. We want to modernize our country. All our efforts are directed toward the building of a modern, therefore Western, state in Turkey. What nation is there that desires to become a part of civilization, but does not tend toward the West?[8]

Reflecting the dominant understanding at that time, Atatürk's words show how modernity, civilization, and Westernism were seen as one and the same thing, understood primarily as a way of life and a universal norm that all modernizing countries were expected to adopt. This understanding of modernity has been the foundational principle upon which the Turkish Constitution, state institutions, a new sense of nationhood, and a new social order were built, and it continues to dictate the general direction of societal and political transformation to this day.

Nevertheless, the state's official version of modernity based on a West-oriented, secular nationalist ideology has never been the only project. Since the start of the Ottoman modernization efforts in the early nineteenth century, there have always been alternative projects of modernization that have understood and exploited the term in different ways. It was only one of these projects that overpowered others and came to be the founding ideology of the state under the leadership of Atatürk, but the institutionalization of this particular view did not entail the complete elimination of its rivals. Throughout the course of the twentieth century, several alternative conceptualizations have emerged, inspired by a range of different intellectual traditions and ideological movements including Bolshevism and Marxism, Islam, variants of ethnic nationalism, nativism, or laissez-faire liberalism. These have been formulated and deployed not only by different political parties and movements but also by forces of civil society such as the media, intellectuals, business associations, or religious groups, which have interacted with one another and sometimes even come to power, altering the official discourse in important respects.

Hence, even though secularism, Westernism, and Turkish nationalism have been sustained as the core principles of modernity in Turkey, the original conceptualization has substantially changed in the meantime, especially in the ways in which these core principles have been interpreted and reinstitutionalized. These changes came about as a result of important changes of regime and ensuing shifts in the ruling ideology. During the course of the twentieth century, two significant shifts have been worth mentioning. One of these was the rise of the Democrat Party regime in the 1950s when a notion of modernity that took technological and economic development as the primary defining mark of modernization was institutionalized, replacing the former understanding articulated by Atatürk.[9] Starting with this period, the meaning of "the West" also shifted from Europe to North America. France was dethroned as the bearer of the "universal" norm of civilization as the mark of modernity, and was replaced by the United States, which was idealized as the bearer of the ultimate form of an industrialized capitalist society, which had become the new mark of modernity. Indeed, one of the Democrat Party's catchy slogans in the 1950s was that they were going to make Turkey into a "Little America."

The second shift came in the 1980s with the advent of the Motherland Party under the leadership of late president Turgut Özal, who implemented policies based on an understanding that saw modernity primarily as liberal economics, consumerism, and a combination of local elements with global trends. At the turn of the century a third shift seems to be in order with the rising popularity of political projects inspired by Islam that culminated in the electoral victory of the Adalet ve Kalkınma (AK) (Justice and development) Party, which won an overwhelming majority in the parliament in 2002 under the leadership of Istanbul's former mayor Recep Tayyip Erdoğan.

This study compares and contrasts only two periods within this trajectory of modernity in Turkey. First, it examines the initial years of the republic and the techniques and methods employed toward the institutionalization of its main components, secularism and nationalism. The second period was the 1990s, which marked the rise of political Islam with the birth of the Islamist Refah (Welfare) Party, which won its first significant electoral victory in the local elections of 1994, when it came to power in the city administrations of several major cities in Turkey, including Istanbul and Ankara.[10] Examining the activities of the Islamist city administration in Istanbul under the mayoralty of Tayyip Erdoğan until 1998, when he was removed from office, this study analyzes the political ideology developed by the Refah Party and implemented by the city administration to trace its interventions in public life, and it argues that this ideology was as modernist as its secularist counterpart.

In the midst of such alternative projects, modernity can be thought of as a ruling metanarrative or a larger discursive field wherein contending ideologies challenge and seek to overpower each other, ultimately serving to reaffirm modern discourse. According to Connolly, the interactions between such contending views and ideologies "establish a loosely bounded field upon which modern discourse proceeds" and where "adversaries sustain each other."[11]

What makes these different views and ideologies constitutive of modernity is their common goal to transform society toward an ideal future. As is discussed in more detail later, the common element in these projects is the specific attitude toward society, its present and future, that constructs the present as deficient and in need of remedial intervention that will transform it toward the future. On the other hand, the difference between these projects lies in their specific ideological positions, which dictate different visions of the future and also a different sense of "society." In other words, alternative modernization projects not only have different visions of the present and the future, but also have different notions of the "nation." Under conditions of the modern nation-state system, the "society" in question is the nation.

Hence, it is also important to acknowledge that the ideological bases for contending projects of modernization are invariably nationalist. I use the term *nationalism* here to mean any political project that conjures up a particular notion of the nation that is projected upon the community over which it seeks to rule. Broadly defined as such, a nationalist ideology need not take ethnicity as the constitutive basis of the nation; it can be based on a different unifying bond, such as a common culture, a common history, a sense of territorial unity, a common ideology or political ideals (as in the United States), or even a common religion. When religion appears as the basis of a nationalist ideology, the community in question is not the larger transnational or global religious community, as in the *umma* of Islam, but rather the specific national community of the modern nation-state over which the state rules. In other words, a political ideology is nationalist to the extent that it operates on the assumption that there is a monolithic nation with a single, linear history and over which the unitary state is to rule, which can be summed up in the formula "one state = one nation = one history." The fact that the core principle that unites the nation is defined on the basis of ethnicity, language, culture, or religion does not make the ideology any less or more nationalist.

If nationalism is defined as an ideology that builds on the basic assumption that there is a community of people with some common characteristic constituting a unified nation, then all modernization projects also operate through a nationalist ideology that defines the nation in a particular way. In other words, all modernization projects involve the creation of a particular sense of nationhood and the construction of a specific national identity, regardless of whether the unifying characteristic is defined around ethnicity, race, religion, culture, civilization, language, or some other similar primordial bond.

In sum, this work starts with the assumption that modernity is the product of not one, but many, contending ideas and modernization projects, with different notions of nationhood and different ideals projected into the future, which either fight, tolerate, cooperate, imitate, or even merge with each other, though all seek to transform society along a set of social and political ideals. The Turkish case clearly illustrates that modernity is neither exclusively Western nor Eastern, neither foreign nor local, neither universal nor particular, neither historical nor atemporal, neither old nor new, but at times it can be all of these at once, or it can emerge in the ambiguous space in between these binary opposites. Turkey is a country where modernity as Westernism exists simultaneously with modernity as Easternism or where modernity as an unmarked universalism coexists with modernity as a heavily marked particularism. There are those who locate modernity in producing and consuming Western high culture, such as the patrons of the AKM Concert Hall in Istanbul, for whom *modernity* means being learned and cultured in the ways of the West. Others locate modernity in a mixture of local things with Western or global forms, such as fast-food chains that sell typically local food, like the chains that sell *lahmacun* (pastry with ground meat, also called the "Turkish pizza"). Or the apparel chain Mavi Jeans ("blue" jeans), which brings together things Turkish (labor, textiles, and the *Mavi* in its label) with things Western or global (the design, the *jeans*, marketing techniques, etc.). Or hybrid musical genres that have combined hip-hop and dance rhythms and instruments with Turkish folk or classical styles and forms. Or the new beverage Cola Turca, released in 2003 by a Turkish food company that prides itself in producing a soda that looks and tastes exactly like its American counterparts, the formula for which was developed by Turkish researchers in Turkey. Still others locate modernity in forging a national culture that is purely local and authentic, one that has been purified of Western influences. The Çamlıca restaurant managed by the Islamist city administration of Istanbul is an example of this latter case, where everything from the interior design and background music to the food and beverages served are styled to display a "purely local" and "authentically Turkish" culture. I seek to establish here that the latter is also a modern undertaking, because it is part of an Islamist modernization project that seeks to transform Turkish society toward a more prosperous and happy life by tapping into the creative potential immanent in its "authentic" culture that has been suppressed by the Westernizing, imitative state.

As discussed in more detail later, *modernity* is understood here as an intervention related to bodies, space, and time that constructs their present as corrupt in order to induce a need for transformation toward a better future. In other words, bodies (the construction of the national subject), places (the making of national space), and time (the construction of national history) emerge as the sites for modernizing interventions by contending projects. In order to investigate these sites, this study takes the public sphere as the object of analysis and develops an understanding of the public sphere as a visual field that is constituted by performance and visibility rather than debate and dialogue. Through its interventions in the public sphere, the intervening subject constructs itself as the agent of modernity that is to save the nation from its current malady and guide it toward an ideal future. In particular, this study examines the formation and negotiation of Turkish modernity by comparing and contrasting Kemalism, the founding ideology of the republic, which is based on the ideals of secularism, nationalism, and progress promoted by Mustafa Kemal Atatürk, with one of its main contenders, Islamism. Islamism emerged in the 1990s as a new political ideology developed by the main Islamist political party, the Refah Party, which challenged the Westernist and secularist ideology of the state and developed an alternative national ideology that takes an East-oriented Ottoman-Islamic nationalism as its constitutive base. I argue that in the hands of the Refah Party Islamism turned into an equally modernizationist movement that uses the same strategies and techniques as those of the modernizing state to produce and institutionalize its own version of an equally totalizing national project that seeks to transform society toward an ideal future.

Islamism, Fundamentalism, and Islamic Modernism

Throughout the text the terms *secularism* and *Islamism* are used as ideologies or political projects that seek to transform and reinstitute a sociopolitical order on the basis of a set of constitutive norms and principles. As an ideology, Islamism uses selective postulates from Islam so as to constitute its political project, especially in the formulation of an alternative national identity and the assertion of a new sense of nationhood. Even though there is a general tendency in scholarly literature and a presumption in the Western media that Islamism is against the modern and secular values of the West, not all Islamist ideologies are anti-modernist or anti-Western.[12] Since scholarly literature tends to discount particularities within non-European experiences of modernity as belonging to the domain of the "traditional" or the "pre-modern," the study of political Islam has been marked by such a bias, which tends toward framing Islam-based movements as either outside of modernity or against it. Often the word *fundamentalism* is used as a qualifying mark of Islamism that posits Islamist movements as anti-modernist and anti-secularist. Bruce Lawrence notes that "Islamic fundamentalists, like other fundamentalists, are anti-modernist moderns. They are moderns because they accept the instrumental benefits of modernity."[13] They are anti-modernist because they "oppose modernism and its proponents."[14] Furthermore, Lawrence notes that for these movements, religion is mainly a façade, fundamentalism basically operates as an ideology, and "fundamentalist leaders are . . . in reality ideologues."[15] Martin Marty and Scott Appleby point out that the word *fundamentalist* is used to describe such movements because fundamentalists, in their war against modernism, which is understood as a value system that emphasizes change, consumerism, and particularly secularism, retrieve "doctrines, beliefs, and practices from a sacred past."[16]

Although such a characterization may be appropriate for some movements in Iran, Pakistan, or Egypt as examined by Lawrence, it does not hold for most of the Islamist groups in Turkey, and certainly not for the Islamism of the Refah/Fazilet Party. There are Islamist groups in Turkey that could be described as fundamentalist, such as the Aczimendi order mentioned in chapter 2, but these are quite marginal and not particularly welcome or even recognized by other more popular orders, such as those surrounding the Nur movement or Islamist circles such as the Refah/Fazilet Party.[17]

Another popular form of association based on Islam is religious orders (*tarikat*) that do not have any legal basis, but are sustained via social networks and personal connections. These religious orders may have intricate relations with different political parties, but it is quite a stretch to qualify their organization and activity primarily as ideologically based and anti-secular. The political parties with which they have ties are not necessarily only the Islamist ones, and they have variably supported conservative or center-right secular parties as well.[18]

There are also Islamist intellectuals whose views may bear traces of fundamentalism, but it is difficult to qualify the totality of the work of any one of them as fundamentalist. For example, Abdurrahman Arslan, who leans toward mystical Islam, is anti-modern to the point of refusing to use computers or have a telephone in his home, and has been writing extensively against all aspects of modernity, including secularism, capitalism, consumerism, and nationalism.[19] However, Arslan is also against the politicization of Islam or any ideology that seeks state power, which disqualifies him as a fundamentalist. Another prolific Islamist writer, Ali Bulaç, whose views influenced the policies of Erdoğan while he was the mayor of Istanbul, is famous for the recovery of the "Madina Document," which was used as a legal-constitutional frame when Mohammed ruled Madina in 622–32. Bulaç claimed that the Madina Document, which allowed for an administrative order based on multiple legal systems of different religious communities, could be adapted and implemented in Turkey so that there would be an Islamic legal system alongside a secular, a Judaic, and a Christian one under the same state, where everyone could live in accordance with the legal system of their own choice.[20] Although this proposition certainly qualifies as a retrieval of a doctrine or practice from the golden age of Islam, and hence fundamentalist, Bulaç is also an enthusiastic advocate of very modern ideals such as economic liberalism, basic liberal rights and freedoms, and democracy.

It is also significant that both these writers and others among this circle of Islamist intellectuals are very well read in both Islamic and Western intellectual traditions and history. In most of their writings, their lists of bibliographical references often include scholars and philosophers ranging from Aristotle and Plato and from Ibn Haldun and Ibn Arabi to Kant and Hegel or from Cassirer, Foucault, and Habermas to Balibar, Giddens, Gellner, and Benedict Anderson.[21] What marks the writings of these authors is a thorough and well-informed interrogation of modernity, but as Roxanne Euben points out, such an interrogation need not imply a stark negation of modernity. Euben notes that "Islamist critiques of modernity . . . are best characterized as an attempt to simultaneously abolish, transcend, preserve and transform modernity . . . rather than an a priori negation of it," which fairly qualifies the works of Turkish Islamist intellectuals as well.[22] If "fundamentalism" is to be understood as anti-modernism and anti-Westernism, it does not justly describe the views of these intellectuals.

As for the Islamism of the Refah Party, as is illustrated in subsequent chapters, neither its discourse nor its policies have been consistently antisecular, and certainly they have not been anti-Western. They have been firmly against the Westernism of the state on the grounds that it is incompatible with Turkey's "true national culture" and that it has been implemented as a servile imitation of the West, but they have never expressed in word or deed any animosity against the West itself. They have refused to recognize the West as a superior power, especially in cultural terms, but they have consistently approached Western countries as allies. Operating on such a legacy, the Refah Party's descendant, the AK Party, has not only been fully supportive of Turkey's candidacy for the European Union, but actually declared it the party's top priority mission when it came to power in 2002.

The Refah Party's Islamism is also not fundamentalist in that retrieving "doctrines, beliefs, and practices from a sacred past" does not really qualify their ideology, their policies, or the ideals that they project to the future of Turkey. At every opportunity the Refah Party and its supporters have resorted to a liberal discourse of individual rights and liberties rather than citing postulates from the Koran. Particularly the moderate wing within the party, which was in power in Istanbul's city administration and later separated to form the AK Party, has long been promoting democratization, restoration of basic rights and freedoms, economic liberalism, and decentralization of state power. These policies later became the basis of the AK Party's program. What marked the Refah Party's Islamism was an antagonism against the Westernizing secular state, which was blamed for undermining Turkey's "true identity" and implementing policies to the detriment of the "true cultural values" of the Turkish people.

This ideology is not different from that of any other nationalism that places at its core not an ethnic or linguistic essence, but an identity based on vernacular religion. Indeed, as illustrated in detail in chapter 4, the Islamic identity promoted by the Refah Party is not forged for the larger transnational Islamic community (the *umma*), but is tailored exclusively for a Turkish-speaking audience living in Turkey. Furthermore, it takes Islam not as a religion but as a culture deeply rooted in the Ottoman past, and promotes the idea of an Ottoman-Islamic civilization as Turkey's "true national culture" and as an alternative to the country's official secular, West-oriented, and ethnic-based identity. This is not a return to the golden age of Islam, but rather is the restoration of what is believed to be Turkey's "true culture" and its potential as a "glorious civilization."

Even though the Refah Party had people with fundamentalist tendencies among its ranks and had occasionally made hostile statements against secularism (but not modernity) during the earlier years of its growing influence, it gradually veered toward a moderate center-right position as its support base increased. After the Refah Party ceased to exist in 1998 and was replaced by the Fazilet Party, the political discourse of the party changed substantially and its leaders started to openly endorse secularism. They started to promote the idea that while the Fazilet Party was the truly secular party in Turkey, it was the state that was actually anti-secular and undemocratic because it was not recognizing freedom of conscience and was directly meddling in religious affairs, whereas under true secularism the state and religion should remain separate. The certain break from any fundamentalist tendencies came with the formation of the AK Party, which separated from the Fazilet Party after it ceased to exist and after the ensuing split of its two factions in 2001. This split resulted in the formation of the Refah/Fazilet Party's direct descendent, the Saadet (Felicity) Party, and the AK Party, formed by the moderate wing. During the elections in November 2002, the AK Party drew a majority of the Islamic vote as well as the votes of secular conservatives, coming to power with an overwhelming majority.[23]

It should be noted that other Islamic or Islamist groups in Turkey that do not follow the Refah/Fazilet Party's line and approach to Islam have substantially different views on modernity, secularism, Islamism, and Westernism. In this respect, there is no monolithic Islamist movement in Turkey, and the arguments presented here apply only to the Islamism of the Refah/Fazilet Party. However, this is not a generalization based on the study of a single case, because the Refah/Fazilet Party represented an overwhelming majority of political Islam in Turkey. There is only one other political party, the Grand Unity Party (Büyük Birlik Partisi, or BBP), formed in 1992, that can be qualified as "Islamist," but this is quite a marginal party with a narrow support base (it captured 1 percent of the national vote in 2002) that did not have a significant impact on formal politics or on the Islamist movement.

It is also important to distinguish between *Islamic, Islamism,* and *Muslim.* As noted earlier, *Islamism* is used here as a political ideology, and *Islamist* is used to refer either to proponents of this ideology or to actions, interventions, and policies that are undertaken in the name of Islamism. *Islamic,* on the other hand, is an adjective used here to indicate a view, thought, style, or practice that makes reference to Islam as a religion, but is not part of an Islamist ideology, as in "Islamic art" or "Islamic intellectual traditions." This distinction allows us to differentiate between "Islamist intellectuals," who are mainly the ideologues of political Islam, and "Islamic intellectuals," whose activity involves Islamic thought, scholarship, or art that is not part of the production of an ideology. For example, the works of writer

Ali Bulaç and poet İsmet Özel are often chunked together and analyzed by studies on "Islamist intellectuals" in Turkey.[24] However, the work of Ali Bulaç, who has written extensively in Islamist newspapers and magazines and was a consultant to the city administration of Istanbul under Erdoğan's mayoralty, qualifies him not as an Islamic but as an Islamist intellectual who actively contributes to the development of party ideology, whereas the work of İsmet Özel, who is considered one of Turkey's most distinguished poets, is celebrated by Islamists and secularists alike, and has produced thoughtful essays on modernity and Islam in Turkey, does not involve the production of a particular ideology at all. In fact, Özel is sharply critical of any quest for power, which he believes will have only fatal consequences for Muslims.[25] Özel's work can best be described as one of the most sophisticated criticisms of modernity in Turkey, and the fact that he takes an Islamic point of view qualifies him as an Islamic intellectual at best.

On the other hand, the term *Muslim* is used here to refer to those who identify themselves as the followers of the Islamic faith, regardless of their political opinions. Hence, just as there can be Islamist Muslims, there are also secular Muslims. It is important to make this distinction, because the word *Muslim* was used strategically by Refah circles to refer exclusively to Islamists or supporters and proponents of political Islam. This is a rhetorical strategy that attempts to monopolize the definition of *Muslim* to the benefit of the Refah Party and divest Muslims who are not interested in Islamism or are even against it, as were most secularists, of their faith.

Modernity and Secularism à la Turca

Official Turkish modernity took shape basically through a negation of the Islamic Ottoman system and the adoption of a West-oriented mode of modernization, yet it represents neither a blind submission to Westernism nor a totally imitative and inorganic adaptation from Europe.[26] Rather, the founding elite conjured up quite an original modernity project that was made possible by establishing a critical distance from two extremes that were both seen as dangers for the future of Turkey. On the one hand, if Westernism were taken to its extreme, Turkey would run the risk of losing its national uniqueness and distinctiveness. On the other hand, if the Islamic legal frame of the former Ottoman system were maintained, Turkey would not be able to modernize and become part of the Western "civilized world" as it deeply aspired to do. Hence, the official modernization project took shape by maintaining a distance both from excessive

Westernism, on the one hand, and from stagnant Islamism, on the other, thereby creating a unique in-between, hybrid modernity à la *Turca*. In other words, what has often been seen as a "paradox" or "dilemma" of Turkish modernity in that it has failed to take root in society because of its top-down, imitative quality, is in fact a creative innovation that has indeed been institutionalized into the current constitutional system. Secularism as a founding principle that has been successfully institutionalized (in the sense that it has endured as the core constitutive principle) as the single most important constitutive element of the Turkish constitutional system is the outcome of this innovation. The fact that it has been successfully institutionalized does not mean that it is the outcome of a societal consensus or a democratic process. On the contrary, as in the case of any other experience of state building, the Turkish nation-state was built upon harsh authoritarian measures, oppression, and elimination of rivals through dictatorial means.

Studying modernity through the Turkish experience proves to be quite an informative undertaking, especially in revealing the ways in which modernization is linked with the building of a nation-state. The Turkish experience has been marked by an uninterrupted modernization process that spanned a period of two centuries starting at the end of the eighteenth century with the reform programs of the Ottoman rulers, culminating in the formation of a nation-state in the early twentieth century, and continuing to this day, as Turkish modernization is under negotiation more than ever with the country's pending membership in the European Union.[27] Also, the fact that Turkey never became a colony but did uphold European norms of modernity and civilization as the only valid reference allows for the study of modernity and its link to Westernization in the absence of an external colonial power.

A unique feature of the Turkish experience of modernization as a state- and nation-building practice is that it is quite easy to delineate and trace the modernization project and its effects through various interventions of the state in public and private life. Indeed, subsequent chapters illustrate how the state has been directly involved in shaping not only the public but also the private sphere through its modernizing interventions in daily affairs. Throughout the twentieth century, the state was involved in matters from the clothing of its citizens to the music they were to listen to, from the type of leisure activity they would be engaged in to the type of family relations they would have. These telling interventions allow for the analysis of modernity as a self-constitutive project of the nation-state in relation to society. In other words, it provides important insights into the various strategies and techniques used toward the constitution of the modern nation-state, where modernization has become the single most important device in the hands of the state in constituting not only a modern state apparatus but also a modern society. Therefore, twentieth-century Turkish politics offers an amazingly rich and diverse range of opportunities for studying different facets of modernity and modernization, as well as the sorts of strategies and techniques used to institutionalize such a major undertaking. The scope of this study allows for the analysis of only a small sample of these modernizing interventions in subsequent chapters.

Perhaps the most important contribution of studying the Turkish experience to the scholarship on modernity will be demonstrating the relationship of modernity to religion and Islam and the issue of secularism. Contrary to the classical assumption that modernity displaces religion, the Turkish case illustrates that the relation between modernity and religion is far more complicated and subtle.[28] First of all, since Turkish modernity was institutionalized in a society that had been governed by Islamic principles for six centuries, the outright rejection or suppression of religion was virtually impossible. Hence, the institutionalization of modernity involved not a direct exclusion of Islam, but rather an engineered *inclusion* of Islam within the modern political system. In other words, a specific understanding of modernity and secularism had to be carefully forged and implemented in a society that had lived by Islamic values, principles, and references and under an Islamic legal frame for centuries. It is exactly for this reason that Turkish modernity could not have been a purely imitative and cosmetic appropriation from the West. For it to take hold, it had to be an innovative, hybrid adaptation tailored to the particularities of local sociopolitical practices and Islamic frames of reference.

The Atatürkist innovation was to bring Islamic authority under the full and absolute control of the secular state. Rather than following the common pattern where all religious affairs are separated from formal political affairs, the institutionalization of secularism involved bringing all religious activity under the direct control and monopoly of the secular state. In 1924 a Directorate of Religious Affairs was formed to act as the ultimate authority on the knowledge and practice of Islam. The directorate would operate directly under the Office of the Prime Minister, and its chair and board would be appointed by the president. Simultaneously with the establishment of the directorate, all other practices and authorities of Islam were outlawed, including the caliphate, which had been the institutional ruler of Islam all over the world since the sixteenth century. Autonomous religious lodges (*tekke* and *zaviye*) and sufi orders (*tarikat*) were banned. A secular civil code was adopted from Switzerland to replace the previous codes based on Islamic law (Shariat), and this code outlawed all forms of polygamy, annulled religious marriages, and granted equal rights to men and women in matters of inheritance, marriage, and divorce. The religious court system and institutions of religious education were abolished. Under the new secular penal code, the "use of religion for political purposes" was banned, the Ottoman dynasty was expatriated, the article that defined the Turkish state as "Islamic" was removed from the constitution, and the alphabet was changed, replacing Arabic letters with Roman ones.

Autonomous Islamic authorities were dissolved one after the other, and the Directorate of Religious Affairs was authorized to oversee the knowledge and practice of Islam, which included the supervision of all mosques and the public sermons given there, the appointment of imams, and the production and dissemination of Islamic knowledge.

One of the most controversial attempts to bring Islam under the control of the secular state was changing the call for prayers (*ezan*) from Arabic, the sacral language of Islam, to Turkish. In this case, "control" was attempted by the nationalization of a prevailing Islamic ritual. The first call for prayers in Turkish, translated into "pure Turkish" by the Turkish Language Association founded by Atatürk, was chanted in 1932 in the Ayasofya Mosque in Istanbul, and then standardized throughout mosques around the country upon the orders of the Directorate of Religious Affairs. Since the *ezan* is chanted five times a day from atop minarets scattered around cities and is intended to be heard by everyone, it is a highly salient mark of the undeniable presence of Islam in the public sphere. By having the *ezan* chanted in Turkish, the secular state not only brought under control Islam, which had gained a unique public presence through sound, but also submitted it to nationalist discourse. This intervention, however, never became popular, could not be institutionalized, and was abolished by the populist Democrat Party regime in 1950.

Therefore, the institutionalization of secularism involved not exclusion, but a tightly controlled inclusion of Islam in the public sphere. This gesture of public inclusion was the means by which the authority of the secular state was realized and consolidated. In other words, the formation of the nation-state involved the creation of a secular-national public sphere where, contrary to the common understanding that secularism excludes religion, religious practices, knowledges, and activity were monitored and given a specific public presence. While official Islam was given a limited and closely supervised place in the public sphere, autonomous Islamic practices were disallowed.

However, this unique synthesis was by no means left unchallenged. The search for the specific path that Turkish modernity would take—a search that dominated nineteenth-century political writing, reform proposals, and all the successful or failed reform programs of the Ottomans—resulted in a parade of rival ideas and projects that combined to different degrees secular and legal-rational experiences inspired by Europe with Islamic customs, norms, and references. Throughout the twentieth century the official secular Turkish nationalism of the state was continually challenged by such rival projects, including Islamist, Kurdish, and Marxist movements that produced alternative projects of modernity and nationalism. Among these, the Islamist challenge was no doubt the most significant in unsettling the foundations of the secularism that had silenced opponent ideologies for a long time.

The Emerging Visibility of Islam in the Secular Public Sphere

Under the overbearing gaze of the modernizing state, the relationship between Islamic social formations and the modern sociopolitical order has been marked by strategies of inclusion and exclusion and authoritarian control mechanisms rather than by dialogue and debate. Even though Islamic formations remained in various forms throughout the twentieth century, most of these were gatherings around orders *(tarikat)* that were maintained due to their deeply entrenched traditions of secrecy and covertness. Islamist discourse and Islamic thought survived around such informal social gatherings, sustained mainly through literature, poetry, and music. While the national public sphere was thriving under the supervision of the state and secularist elite circles, Islamic formations maintained a rather low profile, surviving through personal networks and communal gatherings that avoided public visibility, and thereby the domineering gaze of the state.

It was not until the mid-1980s that autonomous Islamic practices started gaining visibility in the secular public sphere. Increasing numbers of men and women were assuming Islamic identities, which were gaining a salient public visibility mainly through women's headscarves. The Refah Party capitalized on this development and started increasing its support base rapidly. The Refah Party had been a part of the political scene since the late 1960s, but until the early 1990s it had remained a small party (gaining less than 10 percent of the national vote) and was identified as a right-wing, conservative party rather than as Islamist. Only after the late 1980s did the Refah Party start to assume a more explicitly articulated Islamist identity and become more outspoken in its endorsement of an Islamist discourse. This new trend carried the Refah Party to the top, bringing the party its first major electoral victory during the local elections of 1994, which placed an Islamist administration in the municipality of Istanbul, making Recep Tayyip Erdoğan Istanbul's first Islamist mayor. A year later, in December 1995, the Refah Party emerged as the top party in the general elections, placing its leader, Necmettin Erbakan, in the seat of the prime minister in 1996 as part of a coalition government. Apparently this placement went beyond the limits that the secular system could bear. The Refah Party's reign lasted only a year. After the famous February 28, 1997, decree of the National Security Council calling for the Refah-led coalition government to use stronger measures against the rising threat of Islamism, the coalition government fell, and Necmettin Erbakan's short but significant incumbency ended.

With the rising power of the Refah Party, secularism, which had enjoyed a relatively unchallenged authority in the public sphere, found itself facing a serious challenge from Islamism, which was thought to be permanently marginalized and pacified. The realization that Islam was no longer under the state's control and had become a serious political contender came as a shock during the local elections of March 1994.

The 1994 local elections have become one of the landmarks of contemporary Turkish political history. The emergence of the Refah Party as the victor in the city administrations of most of the major cities, including Istanbul and the capital, Ankara, was perceived as an astounding historical moment by both secularists and Islamists, but for opposite reasons. While the Refah Party's supporters were celebrating the Islamist victory with slogans such as "The Other Turkey Is Coming to Power,"[29] various secularist groups were reacting sharply and immediately in shock and panic. Turkey witnessed one of the most fervently embraced and rather unconventional political protests of its recent history. Within a matter of days, a "blacklist" of all the businesses and enterprises that had provided financial support for the Refah Party was anonymously prepared and circulated through faxes calling for consumers not to do business with these places. This form of protest became so popular and effective that certain businesses that had been "mistakenly" placed on the list had to place large ads in newspapers denying such allegations. Other forms of secularist protest ensued. Grassroots organizations and associations were established to act as centers of resistance against the "Islamic threat." New local newspapers and journals were founded, financed and published by secularist voluntary groups. The word *modern* (*çağdaş*) came to be used synonymously with *secular* and was evoked to indicate a political alliance against Islamism. Secular associations with names that included *modern*, such as the Support for Modern Life Association, the Modern Womens League, and the Modern Writers Association became popular, and similar new secular associations began to mushroom.

In sum, the electoral victory of the Refah Party in 1994 served to mobilize an autonomous secularist grassroots movement that resulted in the revitalization of official state ideology and the resurgence of the iconic figure of Mustafa Kemal Atatürk as a symbol of secularism. It was at this time that Atatürk pins suddenly became very popular; secularist men and women of all ages began to attach pins with Atatürk's portrait to their coats, sweaters, shirts, and blouses as a statement against Islamism. What is so significant about this renewed commitment to secularism is that it became an important indicator of how secularism had indeed taken root in civil society as the official state ideology and had become the norm by which many chose to live their lives and made their political commitments. Ironically, the growing influence of political Islam served to reveal the power of secularism not just as a state ideology backed up by the military, but also as an autonomous movement rooted in civil society.

In spite of its unintended consequence of revitalizing secularism, the electoral victory of the Refah Party in 1994 showed without a doubt that secularism could no longer enjoy the position of unrivaled authority in the public sphere. Political Islam could no longer be kept at bay at the periphery; it was now an undeniably prominent political contender fully equipped to challenge secularism on its own terms (i.e., modern parliamentary democracy), and on its own grounds (i.e., in a city like Istanbul, where secular modernity had been deeply entrenched culturally, socially, and economically).

The arguments developed here mainly apply to the Islamism of the Refah Party as it was developed and implemented around the city administration of Istanbul under Erdoğan's mayoralty between 1994 and 1998. Because the Refah Party ceased to exist and was then reborn as the Fazilet Party in 1998, the organizational structure, basic ideological tenets, and the cadre of the party remained intact without a change through 2001, when the Fazilet Party also shut down. There were some important shifts in policy, such as the open endorsement of secularism by the Fazilet Party mentioned earlier, but these were only strategic policy maneuvers that allowed the party to adapt to changing circumstances rather than significant shifts in party ideology. Hence, what is said about the Refah Party's main ideological line applies directly to the Fazilet Party as well. As for the AK Party that was formed by the moderate wing of the Refah/Fazilet Party after its split in 2001, there were some more important changes in order.

Even though the AK Party is a descendant of the Refah/Fazilet Party, it does not represent a direct continuation of either party, but rather is a modified version of the Islamist line of the latter. The founders of the AK Party under the leadership of Erdoğan left the Refah/Fazilet Party in order to pursue a more liberal, less confrontational political line by further endorsing secularist ideals, downplaying Islamism, and giving priority to economic liberalization and development. However, even though the party is trying to dissociate itself from political Islam, it still maintains the same Islamist discourse that was developed around the Istanbul city administration under Erdoğan. First of all, Erdoğan's think tank, composed of journalists, writers, and intellectuals who were operating as the party's ideologues during the years the Refah Party was in power remained almost totally intact. Most of the current leaders of the AK Party, who are cabinet members or parliamentarians, have also held leadership positions within the Refah/Fazilet Party and have been working closely with Erdoğan since he came to power in Istanbul's city administration in 1994. Also, the newspaper *Yeni Şafak*, which is the AK Party's unofficial newspaper, was home to several columnists and writers who were also working as consultants or aides to the Refah Party's Istanbul city administration under Erdoğan's mayoralty, some of whom later became AK Party parliamentarians. Representing the AK Party's ideological line, *Yeni Şafak* continues to endorse a liberal-Islamist perspective that combines economic and political liberalism with conservative social values and a sense of national identity and culture that takes Islam as its essential defining value. In other words, Islamism is still the intellectual foundation of the AK Party's ideology, as is especially evident in the understanding of national culture and identity projected in *Yeni Şafak*.

In this study I examine various sites where Islamist interventions accomplished in the public sphere through use of the resources of the city administration of Istanbul resulted in the formation and dissemination of an alternative Islamist modernization project and a new national identity. These interventions included the rearrangement of public squares, the alteration of concert halls or drama performance repertoires and regulations, the controversial celebration of commemoration days, and the insertion of images of women in public spaces, such as the new visibility of religious headscarves worn by female students in schools. This study analyzes a series of such interventions with regard to bodies, places, and history so as to discern the nature of the emerging Islamist discourse that is confronting secularism in everyday urban contexts.

Modernity as the Defamation of the Present

The debate on modernity and its meanings reflects two rather incompatible points of departure with different concerns at stake. Some of the most influential authors in the field, such as Marshall Berman and Jürgen Habermas, are primarily concerned with the normative value of modernity, and much less interested in the analytical use of the term. Both Berman and Habermas acknowledge the decay and suffering inflicted by processes related to modernity, and propose ways to sustain and realize its promise and creative potential for a better life. Others, who are less interested in redeeming modernity, such as Zygmunt Bauman, suggest that it is only the postmodern mode, which is a critical self-awareness of modernity and a "coming to terms with its own impossibility," that offers the possibility of overcoming the totalizing and coercive effects of modernity.[30] Yet this is still a normatively motivated approach that does not offer much in terms of the analytical use of the concept.

The other departure point is best articulated by Michel Foucault, whose concern is not so much the normative positioning of modernity, but rather a search for a conceptualization that would best qualify the modern moment. For Foucault, modernity is a critical attitude taken toward the present so as to overcome its limitations.[31] Understanding modernity as an attitude avoids problems arising from totalizing definitions that can be generalized across time, space, and culture. Modernity understood as an epoch imposes a sense of uniformity on everything that happens within a temporal frame; as a lifestyle creates a sense of a monolithic culture and as an exclusively European experience asserts a sense of spatial homogeneity, as if modernity was experienced the same way throughout Europe. Such totalizing conceptualizations, no matter how sophisticated, as in the works of Berman, Habermas, and Bauman, overlook diversions and particularities that, if acknowledged, can yield very different and contrary accounts. Since diversions and particularities are the rule in non-European experiences of modernity, Foucault's understanding of the term emerges as the most useful option in analyzing such alternative modernities.[32]

For purposes of analyzing modernity in Turkey, I find it necessary to further elaborate on the ways in which modernity can have such transformative power when it is understood as an attitude toward the present. I will take this definition a crucial step further and propose that modernity is an attitude in action that intervenes in the present so as to construct it as questionable and troublesome. In other words, the present is not a given set of circumstances upon which the modern subject merely reflects, but rather it is reimagined and reordered so as to be perceived and experienced as inadequate and defective.

The transformative power of modernity comes from the idea of progress, which reorients the subject toward an ideal future, where movement itself becomes a virtue. Built upon the ideals of the Enlightenment, modernity entails a constant movement, a drive to forsake the present for a better future. Therefore, to be modern is to have broken ties with the past and the present, to be on the move. This movement involves not only the projection into the future of the new and the advanced, but also the projection into the past and the present of the old, the backward, and the traditional.

Therefore, modernity is not only about the contemplation of an ideal future, but also about the construction of the present as deficient and flawed. Modernizing forces are concerned not only with paving the way toward a better future, but also with finding fault in the present. If modernity is to be a movement forward, it also has to be a movement away from the present, which is experienced as a malady. The present circumstances have to be deprecated so as to provide just cause for remedial intervention. Hence, modernity is made possible by the defamation of the present. Suddenly diverse practices, customs, values, styles, and forms that have been in practice at their own pace are framed, labeled, and defamed as backward, traditional, inefficient, irrational, primitive, or corrupt and decomposed, against which the ideals of modernity can be articulated and the modern-subject can be oriented.

Even though there is a great deal of disagreement about what modernity is, most accounts acknowledge that one of the most salient qualifying features is the state of constant change, the ephemeral quality of the present. Bauman notes that "modernity is an obsessive march forward," a march that has to go on, "because any place of arrival is but a temporary station."[33] For Marshall Berman, to be modern is "a struggle to make ourselves at home in a constantly changing world."[34] It is about "longing to create and to hold on to something real even as everything melts."[35] What is not directly acknowledged in these accounts is that the transience of the present is not a given condition or an outcome of modernity, but is how it has to be experienced so that modernity can come into being. In other words, the present is not an objective condition in which modern subjects find themselves, but an uninviting projection that serves to constitute the modern subject as longing for something in the future. To be modern is to see and experience the present as that which is decaying and melting away, is flawed, and has nothing to offer, so that a longing gaze is turned toward the future. In this sense, it is possible to see Berman's account not as an observation of modernity, but as constitutive of it. Berman's description of the present condition as a "constantly changing world" where "all that is solid melts into air" is itself a modernizing moment that induces an alienation from the present and orients the reader toward the future.

If modernity is an intervention that incites such a movement, its promise of a better future can never be attained. For the instant that the ideal projected into the future starts to take shape in the present, modernist criticism starts to frame it as imperfect and faulty. In modernity, the future is never to be achieved but always to be sought. As Connolly notes, "In modernity, modernization is always under way." Hence, modernity is never complete; its agencies continually "form and reform, produce and reproduce, incorporate and reincorporate, industrialize and reindustrialize."[36]

Modernity can range from an attitude toward some local or personal matter to a full-fledged political project based on an ideology. This study is concerned only with the latter. In the hands of the state, modernizing interventions turn into a large-scale modernization program with a particular national ideology that is institutionalized to become the norm toward the formation of a modern order. In the hands of political parties, contending notions of modernity are turned into alternative projects that are implemented to the extent that the political forces upholding them have the means to intervene in daily life.

Another aspect of the modernizing intervention is that it is a means through which political agency is created. The intervening subject, by defaming and deprecating the present and projecting an ideal future, establishes itself as the agent of modernity who will lead the transformation toward that future. Whether it is the state or contending political forces, the intervening subject seeks to save the nation from its present malaise and lead it toward the future that can be reached only via the path that is paved by this particular subject. Hence, modernizing interventions always involve the construction of some form of a victim-hero binary. The hero, usually the state or the political force that seeks state power, is to step in and rescue the victim, the nation, from the present malady that it suffers and take it toward a prosperous future.

I study modernity as a series of interventions in the public sphere, namely those related to bodies, places, and time. Modernity is an intervention on bodies when it attempts to regulate and control the public visibility of bodies, their shapes, and their clothing. It also involves a reordering of space, as in the development of contending uses of urban spaces and the restructuring of cities and public places. Likewise, it is an ordering and reordering of time, as in official and alternative constructions of national history. Whether perpetrated by the state or by other political forces, these interventions seek to transform and change an existing set of practices, patterns, and forms into something else. It is in this act of transformative intervention that I locate modernity. This is a transformation that is made desirable by projecting it as "advancement and progress" rather than as aimless change. It is in this defamatory and transformative intervention that political agency is created and the modern subject emerges.

Turkish modernity has been built upon such narratives of self-defamation, be it produced by the Westernist urban elite of the late nineteenth century or the Islamist writers of the late twentieth century. Deniz Kandiyoti draws attention to the ways in which critical accounts of current daily practices in the nineteenth-century press in Istanbul involved the production of highly distorted images that were far from reality. According to Kandiyoti, while accounts of family and marriage practices in Istanbul published at the time were highly critical of the prevalence of "primitive" and "non-rational" practices such as teenage marriage, extended families, and polygyny, more recent studies clearly indicate that such practices were in fact quite rare in Istanbul at the time. As Kandiyoti explains, "The 'modernists' could formulate their vision of the modern family only with reference to an assumed prior state that was defective and in need of reform, regardless of whether the patterns in question actually obtained in their society."[37] As illustrated in subsequent chapters, it was through such strategies, which projected a backward, deprived, and uncivilized vision of the present, that the impetus for change and modernization was created. Likewise, Islamist writers of the 1990s and the present generate similar narratives of urban life in Istanbul as desperately degenerate and impaired and in urgent need of remedial intervention of the kind that only Islam-based movements can undertake. Even though the system of meaning that frames this discourse is quite different from the Westernizing, secularist interventions of the late nineteenth century, it resorts to similar techniques and strategies in mobilizing a movement toward an equally modernist national project.

As observed both in the secularist interventions during the founding years of the republic and in the Islamist interventions of the 1990s, modernity is an intervention that institutes such binaries as backward-advanced, degenerate-salubrious, traditional-modern, primitive-refined, barbarian-civilized, and rural-urbane so as to secure a constant impetus for movement from the lower end of each of these binaries to the higher. In the hands of the state, modernity becomes a national project conjured up to transform society away from the present toward advancement and civilization that lie in the future. Such modernizing projects find their driving force and legitimacy not only in glorifying a civilized future, but also in defaming the present as a deficient malignancy brought about by the pre-modern, traditional, backward, irrational, despotic styles of governance that have plagued society for so long.

If modernity involves the projection of an ideal future and a defamed present, there can be as many modernist interventions as there are such projects, or utopias, that are conjured in any given circumstance. This work starts with the premise that there are as many modernities as there are instances that evoke the idea of modernity or progress in order to frame a particular political ideal or project. In other words, modernity is a spatial, temporal, and corporeal field wherein many contending projects take shape, intervene, and compete. Hence, this study seeks to locate and examine modernity in interventions related to bodies, places, and time. It examines how the construction of the gendered national subject, the making of national public space, and the writing of national history become the sites from which the state and its contenders constitute themselves as political agents in the creation of the national subject and its transformation toward the projected ideal.

Performative Politics: Negotiating the Constitution and the Nation in Everyday Life

It is important to highlight the broader understanding of politics endorsed in this study, which takes the media of everyday life and the public sphere as the sites of the political. Everyday life is not only about routinized patterns of production and consumption, but also about a complex field of performances, visibilities, political negotiations, and contestations. Indeed, everyday life is the field of politics and power. Often issues that are thought to belong to the realm of "high politics," such as the building of a nation-state or the negotiation of a constitutional system, are addressed in fields of formal politics constituted by the state apparatus and bureaucracy, key institutions of the political system and political parties. This way of understanding politics is based on a conceptual separation of state from society, where the state is construed as the agent of authority and power, whereas society is conceived as the peripheral domain subject to the authoritative and controlling interventions of the state. In this framework, society is conceived as being outside the realm of the political such that "political participation" implies that society is something external that needs to be introduced into the realm of politics. As such, society is understood to take part in the political realm only via certain institutionalized channels, such as elections, or via political activism realized through the institutions of civil society.

It is only when such a conceptual bifurcation of state and society is suspended that the realm of everyday life can be recovered as a field that is a central location of politics and power, where the key pillars of the sociopolitical system are constructed, negotiated, and contested. I maintain that it is through various interventions in everyday life that the state and other subjects are able to constitute themselves as political agents and establish identity categories in the public sphere that give rise to the privileged positions of authority assumed by the state, the media, and others in elite positions. In other words, relations of power that operate to constitute the state and other political actors as privileged subjects work through and from various fields that constitute everyday life.

In sum, politics is located not only around formal political institutions but also in mundane daily practices, such as shopping, eating, listening to music, and getting dressed. More often than not, such daily activities become the media through which sociopolitical systems and constitutional orders are built, institutionalized, contested, negotiated, and changed. In this study I look at various sites of daily public activity ranging from restaurants and public squares to clothing habits and commemorative practices in order to demonstrate the ways in which in Turkey modernity is being negotiated around the constitutional norm of secularism and its main contender, political Islam.

This study is as much about the political dimensions of daily public life as it is about the making of the constitution, as these dimensions are fundamentally connected to the public sphere and the making of the national subject.[38] The latter two notions, those of the public and the nation, are two important loci around which the analysis of this study is built.

The secular constitutional system in Turkey and the Islamist challenges brought to it accentuate the importance of daily activity and public life in the making and negotiation of the national subject. For example, the dispute over wearing the Islamic headscarf, dealt with in chapter 2, is an excellent illustration of the way in which a seemingly trivial daily activity, getting dressed for school, is indeed directly related to the negotiation of the norms of the constitutional order, namely secularism, modernity, democracy, and nationalism. A constitution not only provides the legal base for the foundation of a modern state, but also defines the nation over which the state will rule, and the national subjects that will become its citizens. It is this concern with forging a national subject that impels the state to monitor and intervene in daily social activity.

Furthermore, a constitution is not a closed text that is held as a set of nonnegotiable hegemonic principles once finalized and sanctioned. Constitutional principles and norms become what they are (i.e., constitutive of a social and political order) by entering the realm of the everyday and providing the principles around which daily life is organized. Anne Norton draws attention to the importance of the realm of everyday life where the power of a constitutional political idea to transform ideology to common sense is tested.[39] Various cases studied in subsequent chapters are all instances of daily activity, ranging from dressing and dining to various acts of consumption, entertainment, and celebration, which have gained highly charged political meanings far beyond their immediate functions, all relating to the negotiation of modernity and the constitutional norms of secularism and nationalism.

Negotiation is a key word here, as it draws attention to the constitution as a never-finalized set of principles that are under constant debate and contestation, thereby becoming the locus of analysis of this study. The cases reviewed in subsequent chapters have all been selected exactly because each of them is a site of negotiation where a particular understanding of a national subject in relation to a project related to modernity is formulated, displayed, debated, or contested. This book is structured around this analytical frame that delineates three main sites of negotiation: the body (clothing and appearance), place (the use and restructuring of urban space), and time (the making and performance of national history). Chapters 2, 3, and 4 look, respectively, at the body, place, and time, as they emerge as the three main sites of the public sphere from which negotiations of constitutional principles are carried out. In other words, these consecutive chapters illustrate the ways in which bodies, places, and times serve as different media through which official and contending national identities are articulated, institutionalized, and contested.

I argue that through such daily negotiations of the national subject various parties emerge as the actors or agents of negotiation. Hence, acts of negotiation not only serve to open up constitutive norms and principles and the identity of the national subject to contestation and scrutiny, but also serve to constitute political subjects who acquire agency through the positions they take in these acts they perform. In other words, the act of negotiation is not only a deliberative act but also a performative act,[40] in the sense that negotiation not only opens up constitutional principles to contestation and discussion but also serves to constitute the negotiating parties with particular subjectivities vested with political agency. In the act of negotiating the constitutional principle of secularism, an Islamist political identity is created and various strategies are employed that vest this Islamist subject with political agency. Likewise, in coming to the protection of this constitutional principle the state and other intervening subjects take on a secularist subjectivity and reestablish their political agency in their confrontations with contending parties.

I prefer to refer to the ongoing interventions and negotiations in the public sphere not as identity politics but as performative politics, because *identity* is more readily understood as a label of a subject position that exists prior to the identity that is ascribed to it. Hence the term *identity politics*, which is widely used in scholarly literature, invokes the idea that contestations and negotiations involve the symbolic representations of subject positions, and not the subjectivities themselves. *Performativity*, on the other hand, suggests that the naming or labeling of an action, a presence, or a subjectivity is the very act by which that action, presence, or subjectivity comes into being.[41] Understood as such, *performative politics* better captures the performative nature of the formation and contestations of subjectivities, as it refers not only to the labels and symbols of subject positions, but also to their construction and contestation.

The cases studied here illustrate how both secularist and Islamist interventions related to bodies, places, and times are performative acts through which political agency is created. Both parties use various techniques and strategies in mobilizing existing binaries such as class, gender, ethnicity, and other hierarchical categorizations in order to vest themselves with political agency to uphold their own political projects. Just as in the early years of the republic the new Turkish state intervened in urban life in order to gain political agency and establish its own national project as the constitutive norm of the new social-political order, in the 1990s the Islamist groups emerging around the Refah Party resorted to similar strategies to constitute themselves as the agents of the Islamist alternative of a project of modernization.

Throughout the analysis of the subsequent cases, I argue that Islamists who have been seemingly opposing the secular West-oriented national project of the republic have been using almost identical strategies and techniques to develop and promote their own political project, which is equally modernizing, nationalist, and totalizing. The Islamist movement of the 1990s developed and promoted an alternative national identity that defines the nation as an essentially "Ottoman-Islamic" civilization, in contrast to the official West-oriented secular identity of the nation.

Bodies, Places, and Times

The argument developed in subsequent chapters is that, through various interventions related to bodies, public spaces, and national history, Islam is confronting, negotiating, and challenging secularist constructions of the national, modern, Western Turkish subject, as defined and interpellated by the constitution and monitored by the state.[42] Such Islamist confrontations challenge and subvert official constructions of the national subject as secular and Western by producing and displaying the self as Eastern, Ottoman, authentically local, and Islamic.

The main thesis of this work is that Islamic interventions in the public sphere have subversive effects on secularist modes of power and control, but once these subversive acts are incorporated into an Islamist political project that is questing for power, they become parts of a contending Islamist ideology that is equally totalizing and nationalist, and therefore constitutes an alternative modernization project that seeks to transform the nation toward an alternative future. Although new Islamic visibilities and performances contest and subvert the authority and privilege of secularism in public fields and open it up for negotiation and contestation, they quickly become subsumed within the larger frame of the metanarrative of the modern nation-state in the hands of the Islamist political party and end up reproducing a similarly totalizing discourse of modernization. Various Islamist interventions related to bodies, places, and times examined in subsequent chapters illustrate how Islamism is transformed from a subversive critical discourse into a political ideology that reproduces the same binary oppositions around gender, class, nationhood, and orientalist categorizations of self-identification that serve to maintain and reproduce the basic postulates of modernity as a metanarrative, the modern nation-state and the public sphere as a field of power relations and totalizing influences.

Chapter 1 critically engages the literature on the public sphere and develops the argument that as an analytical category, the public sphere needs to be thought of as a field of appearances, visibilities, and performances through which subjectivities are formed and national identity is negotiated. Questioning the Habermasian notion of the public sphere as a site of debate and dialogue, chapter 1 develops the notion of the public gaze that emerges as an organizing force in the constitution of the perimeters of the public sphere.

Chapter 2 analyzes modernizing interventions related to bodies, first by the secular state in its founding years, then by the Islamists in the 1990s. In both cases, these interventions took the form of denigrating a common daily practice such as the use of particular clothing in order to "rescue" the body from the denigrating effects of its immediate circumstances and to project upon it the ideal future. In the founding years, the body was "liberated" from the oppressive confines of Islam, as symbolized by the veil, and dressed to give it a modern, Western appearance. The Islamist interventions, on the other hand, have reveiled the body and used the religious headscarf as the symbol of their political struggle toward rescuing the nation from the ill effects of the secular state and reinstituting its true culture and identity founded upon the notion of an Ottoman-Islamic civilization.

Chapter 3 examines the making and reorganization of social space, as illustrated by the restructuring of various city spaces in the construction of both secularist and Islamist identities. The structuring of social space, ranging from the making of city squares and arrangement of public places to the design and decoration of restaurants or concert halls, most evidently involves the materialization of a political ideology and a national identity that it projects. Interventions related to places take the form of restructuring social space so as to create spatial binaries such as urban-rural, metropolitan-provincial, suburbia-slum, city center–ghetto. Therefore, modernizing interventions related to places are not only about the making of the center, the metropolitan area, or the urban area but also about the designation of places as peripheral or provincial. This chapter particularly addresses the idea of making the center, both the city center and also the spatial center of the nation, through a dislocation of the old or rival centers and associated alternative national projects. In other words, the rivalry among projects of modernity and nationalism finds articulation in a struggle for the designation of cities and city spaces with differential national meanings and significances. Although secularist interventions create a new center by, say, building the capital city Ankara virtually from scratch, Islamist interventions mainly seek to challenge and displace secularist constructions by inserting symbols of their alternative national identity constructed around the notion of an "Ottoman-Islamic civilization" in city centers and places of national significance.

Chapter 4 discusses the notion of "national time" as it is constructed around a "founding moment." It analyzes the unofficial commemoration of the conquest of Istanbul on May 29 by Islamic circles and the effects of these celebrations on official national history and the established sense of nationhood. Both the secularist construction of national history and its Islamist alternative illustrate how modernizing interventions in time, just as in bodies and places, also involve a rupture between the immediate past, which is projected as catastrophic, and the idealized future toward which the intervening subject is to guide the nation. For the state, this intervention is the restructuring of time around a founding moment when it emerged as the author and creator of a new national history. Islamist interventions related to time take the form of the public performance of an alternative national history through commemorative practices, particularly the unofficial celebration of the "Conquest of Istanbul Day," which seeks to incorporate the Ottoman experience into the national memory and locates a different founding moment that serves to establish a new sense of national time.

1

Performative Politics and the Public Gaze

This study embraces a broader approach to the study of politics by taking the context of daily life in the public sphere as the main locus of political activity. Politics is understood not as confined to an analysis of political structures or formal institutions, but as an ongoing activity of negotiations and confrontations in daily life through which hierarchies of power, political agency, and subjectivity are constructed. If politics involves the generation of power relations through various interventions in different fields of daily life, politics needs to be conceptualized as inseparably associated with a fluid understanding of culture that can be studied only from multiple perspectives beyond the confines of a particular discipline. The notion of politics embraced in this study requires the employment of a wide range of different methodologies. This study, therefore, makes combined use of methodological techniques conventionally associated with anthropology (e.g., thick description and participant observation), history (historiography and archival research), literary criticism (textual analysis and semiology), communication (content analysis), and political science (interviewing), among others. In addition, diverse disciplinary debates are brought into dialogue around interdisciplinary themes such as urban space, gender, nationalism, subjectivity, performativity, modernity, Islam, and secularism.

However, I also acknowledge that such interdisciplinary undertakings run the risk of spreading themselves too thin and lacking a theoretical focus that would provide the cohesion and consistency that sound scholarship necessitates. In order to avoid this problem, I found that employing the notion of the public sphere as the theoretical and conceptual basis for this study provides a helpful solution. Because the "public sphere" is a site wherein a wide range of issues relating to politics and culture, ranging from the formation of subjectivities around gender roles, class, ethnicity, religion, or urbanity to issues of modernity, nationalism, and citizenship, are all closely interrelated.

Taking nationalism and nation-building projects as a central concern, this study also builds upon the main premise that the building of a nation is intrinsically tied to the making of the public sphere, so much so that they are in fact one and the same process. Building of a nation-state involves the drawing of both material and metaphorical boundaries, including territorial, national, ethnic, racial, cultural, and religious boundaries. Drawing the boundaries of the nation involves setting the terms of inclusion more than does determining its externality. In other words, the founding of a nation-state is predicated upon determining who will constitute the nation—who will be the members of the national community, what language they will speak, what their history will be, what sort of a lifestyle they will have, what their identity will be. As this study demonstrates, in the making of the nation-state in Turkey, the state is heavily involved not only in creating the identity of its citizens but in shaping and monitoring their lifestyles and their private affairs as well. The state carries out these self-constitutive tasks by tightly monitoring and controlling the formation of the national public sphere. It is also in this public sphere that the contestations of official national ideology are carried out and alternative national identities emerge. It is in this field of contending national ideologies and projects that the national subject comes into being in the public sphere.

This chapter seeks to critically expand the notion of the public sphere and introduces the idea of the "public gaze," which is a theoretical innovation that opens up new ways of thinking about citizenship, national belonging, and political participation. The notion of the public gaze is a critical intrusion into the debate on the public sphere, for it reveals that the "public" is not a neutral space of debate and dialogue, but is a subjectivity, often represented by the media, with a particular, privileged, yet unmarked identity.

The Public Sphere and Sites of Negotiation

The main analytical concept of this study, "site of negotiation," is an elaboration on the notion of the public sphere, which is based on the idea of debate and dialogue on issues that are of public concern. The notion of the public sphere has become a key element of discussions of political participation, civil society, and democracy since Jürgen Habermas introduced his account of the public sphere as a nonexclusive realm of private individuals debating issues of "common concern."[1] Habermas conceptualizes the public sphere as an ideal realm of debate and deliberation through which the emancipatory power of reason can overcome domination.[2] In his account, the ideal public sphere is based on three principles. First, it is constituted by rational-critical debate on common issues that, subjected to reason, are expected to yield policies that serve the common good. Hence, in ideal circumstances the act of deliberation becomes an act of emancipation. Second, particular interests and status differences belong to the realm of the private, and therefore should be bracketed out of public debates, because they will work only to distort and obscure the attainment of rational solutions and "common" ideals.[3] Third, the ideal public sphere is inclusive; "access is guaranteed to all citizens."[4]

It follows from these principles that emancipatory democratic ideals may be attained only when the particularistic demands and interests of the debating individuals are bracketed out as matters of private concern. Hence, debate and dialogue, or what Habermas refers to as "rational communication," is seen as a key element in the formation of the public sphere, where individuals are expected to debate issues of common concern. For Habermas, issues of "common concern" involve the good of society in general and not the particularistic interests of social groups held together under "constitutional patriotism."[5]

This conceptualization takes for granted that at least ideally the public sphere is a field wherein emancipation and democratic liberties are possible. It overlooks the ways in which the public sphere can function as a field where power relations and hierarchies are produced and sustained to the detriment of most participants.

Rather than engaging the normative dimension of the debate on the public sphere, which keeps revolving around how the public sphere should and should not function, I want to draw attention to the analytical use of the terms of the debate. I focus mainly on the notion of dialogue, since it emerges as the constitutive element of the public sphere. I expand this category and use *negotiation* instead, because it is broader in that it includes not only verbal exchanges but also performative acts. Because *dialogue* suggests a verbal exchange between two parties, it excludes public moments constituted around nonverbal performative acts that address no one in particular, but the public in general. *Negotiation* is a broader term that includes not only verbal exchanges, but also all forms of questioning, subversion, or contestation.

If the public sphere forms around moments of negotiation, it is necessary to have a clearer understanding of what an "act of negotiation" is. An act of negotiation involves who negotiates, what is being negotiated, how it is negotiated, and where.

First and foremost, negotiation involves parties, that is, subject positions from which it is carried out. Such subject positions do not exist prior to the act of negotiation, but are products of it. In other words, the act of negotiation itself is a constitutive moment whereby subject positions emerge in the public sphere. The American national subject emerges through various public negotiations in daily life as it situates itself as the unmarked "American" by marking its various internal others, such as the African American, the Asian American, the Native American, and so on. Similarly, the Turkish national subject is continually shaped and reconstructed as secular and ethnically Turkish through daily public negotiations that mark the internal others as Islamic, Ottoman, or Kurdish.

Second, negotiation involves the sort of issue that is being negotiated. Habermas clearly states that public debates are about the "common good." Here, "common" refers to a community bound together by some sort of common interest constituted by citizens. This unmarked referral makes tacit reference to a national subject and assigns that subject an a priori status. What is being debated is not the "good" of the presumed national subject, but in fact the *constitution* of the national subject. In other words, what is at stake in public negotiations are always the constitutive norms and principles that define the national subject.

Third, the means or the medium of negotiation is also crucial. Negotiation does not take place only when contending parties sit down, exchange views, and try to reach some sort of a consensus. The burning of the American flag, a highly controversial act in the United States, is rather difficult to pass as a moment of public dialogue, but it is certainly a moment of public display whereby a constitutional norm (the flag's symbolizing the unity of the nation) is called into question. Likewise, in Turkey, secularism as a constitutional norm was effectively contested and opened up to negotiation by the appearance of students wearing the Islamic headscarf on university campuses. Therefore, public negotiations take place not only in verbal dialogue and debate, but also and widely in various public performances, visual displays, or even common daily activities, such as wearing a particular type of attire to school.

Finally, the place where negotiation takes place is also important. It is this element that draws attention to the significance of space and place in the formation of the public sphere. Habermas locates the original site of public dialogue in eighteenth-century West European salons, cafes, and other gathering places.[6] Later, as the public sphere went through a structural transformation, the space of public deliberation was overtaken in importance by the media. In this account, the act of debating constitutes a place as public. But when public negotiation is understood in the larger sense as any sort of verbal, bodily or spatial articulation, performance, or display, any location can become a place where the public comes into being. Streets, parks, restaurants, shopping malls, classrooms, certainly the media, and any other place or object that is open to the public gaze can be a site of public negotiation. Even the body itself can become a site of negotiation, as in the case of the Islamic headscarf.

In sum, the public sphere is constituted by moments of negotiation where subject positions are formed as the norms, and constitutive boundaries of the national subject are asserted, endorsed, contested, challenged, or subverted through various performative acts in daily life.

The Public Sphere: Emancipation or Subjugation

The critical debate triggered by Habermas's idealization of the public sphere as a potential field of emancipation focuses mainly on the problematic way in which particular identities and differences are bracketed out. Whether the identities are those of women,[7] the working class,[8] or other marked identities defined around race, nationality, or religion,[9] the exclusion of identities is seen not only as discriminatory but also as an important impediment to the attainment of the common good. Most of these criticisms are concerned with developing justifications for the inclusion of such underprivileged groups in the democratic process, but they share with Habermas the ideal that the public sphere is indeed a field of liberation and emancipation.

Taking a more radical position in this debate, other writers question the emancipatory power of public discourse itself and challenge the normative basis on which the ideal public sphere is grounded.[10] For these critics, the bracketing out of particular interests and identities is not just an attempt to remove the obstacles toward the achievement of the common good, as Habermas claims, but is actually constitutive of the public sphere. In other words, they argue that the public sphere is sustained precisely as a result of the exclusion or abasement of particularities, and that power and domination are inherent in its founding logic. Joan Landes, for example, argues that the exclusion of women is not just a historical coincidence but is actually constitutive of the public sphere, which finds legitimacy in the exclusion of particularities.[11] The search for universal goals and appeals to the common good are mechanisms that work to conceal the subjugation of abased subjectivities.

Likewise, in their accounts of the American public sphere, Lauren Berlant and Michael Warner both incriminate the founding logic of the public sphere.[12] They show that not only the exclusion but especially the *inclusion* of particularities and identities is the most powerful way in which the public sphere becomes a site of subjugation. It is in the naming and marking of bodies into racialized, gendered, or classed categories that the privileged position of the public is sustained and reproduced. In this account, gaining public visibility through bearing the marks of publicly established identity categories such as "poor" or "black" can become an ultimate form of subjugation to the authority and the overbearing gaze of the public subject. In contrast to the view that attributes emancipatory ideals to the expansion of the public sphere, Warner and Berlant suggest that the public sphere itself is the source of subjugation and control, where inclusion and exclusion have almost the opposite effects. Contrary to the Habermasian celebration of inclusion, gaining public visibility, that is, being included in the public sphere, is the very act by which the body is subjected to power and control.

The Gaze of the Public Subject

The account of the public sphere as a field wherein bodies are marked and identified in ways that subjugate them into hierarchically established identity categories is a radical shift away from the Habermasian conceptualization of the public sphere, primarily in relation to how and where the public is constituted. For Habermas and others who define the public sphere in relation to speech and debate, the public sphere is constituted in every instance when people engage in dialogue on political issues, thereby resulting in the formation of a "public opinion."[13] In contrast, for Warner, the public is a subjectivity. It is constituted through the emergence of a disembodied, impersonal, authoritative voice that finds its place in the print media.[14] Warner notes that "the moment of apprehending something as public is one in which we imagine, if imperfectly, indifference to those particularities, to ourselves, we adopt the attitude of the public subject, marking to ourselves its nonidentity with ourselves."[15] As Warner suggests, this public subject is not marked, because its privileged existence depends upon its remaining invisible and inaccessible.

The voice of the disembodied public subject is quite explicitly illustrated in Turkish newspapers. One frequently comes across headlines such as "We Showed Europe How We Play" (referring to a soccer game), "We Cannot Let Greeks Get Away with This" (referring to diplomatic tension with Greece), "We Are Being Counted Today"[16] (referring to the census), or "This Is Our 'Braveheart'"[17] (referring to a woman who went up to Islamist demonstrators and shouted, "Long live secularism!"). Turkish newspapers and magazines are full of such examples, where a public subject is evoked through referrals to various others—the European, the Greek, the Islamist—that serve to construct an abstract space where the unmarked Turkish public subject can be situated. Even when there is direct referral to the public subject (as in "We Are Being Counted Today"), it is still unmarked and abstract and is evoked only through an interpellative act of counting. As these examples suggest, the public subject itself remains unmarked, yet gains presence by marking its others. The others of the public subject can be national-external others, such as Greeks or Europeans, or they can be internal others, such as Islamists. In the example of the "Braveheart" woman who stood up against Islamists, the marking of the internal other as the Islamist is evoked as a national moment, thereby establishing the national subject as unmarked but clearly and naturally secular. By marking its periphery, the national subject situates itself at the center through such interpellative acts without having to name and mark itself as Turkish and secular.

It is in such political discourse that a subject position emerges, imagined as the public. This is not a specific group of actual people, but an imagined public body with a particular yet unmarked identity. In his discussion of the American public sphere, Warner points out that what is presented as a neutral space from which the public subject speaks is in fact a bracketing of an unmarked subjectivity: male, white, middle class, normal.[18] Likewise, Berlant notes that the "specifically white male privilege has been veiled by the rhetoric of the bodiless citizen, the generic 'person' whose political identity is a priori precisely because it is, in theory, noncorporeal."[19] This public subject is disembodied and abstract, and it draws its privilege and authority from remaining unmarked yet recognized. In order to sustain its privilege without becoming visible, it gains presence only by marking its others.

The authoritative presence of the public subject is established not only through a voice, but also, and more so, through a disembodied *gaze*. The media do not only speak the public subject into presence by assuming its voice, but constitute it by becoming its gaze. The media—with their cameras, videos, satellites, monitors, and studios—invest the public subject with the privilege and authority of gazing at almost anything and everything it wants. By categorizing bodies in accordance with the marks of recognition that they bear, the public gaze enjoys the authority and privilege of naming and hierarchically positioning various identity categories in the public sphere while maintaining its own invisibility and inaccessibility. While marked identities are evoked as particulars and minorities, the public gaze assumes the position of an unmarked, generic subject. The particular identities are expected to wage a struggle to gain visibility and a voice in the public sphere, while the public subject assumes an unidentifiable voice and presence. It is in this unmarked, invisible center that the national subject finds its privileged presence.

The public gaze looks at and opens up places so as to make them public, but it also turns away from other places so as to make them private. Simply put, gaining public visibility means opening up and becoming visible under the public gaze. In the terminology of the 1990s, while *coming out* means placing oneself under the public gaze by bearing a mark of public recognition, the term *closet* is used for abstract spaces where one's sexual, political, or religious orientation remains undetectable and unrecognized by the public gaze, because such marks of recognition are concealed. Both these metaphors illustrate the visual nature of the public sphere.

In sum, public spheres of the late twentieth century are constituted more visually through displays and performative acts rather than through debate and dialogue alone. They are fields of performances, appearances, images, and displays. Instead of taking this fact as an indication of the degeneration and disintegration of the public sphere, as Habermas does,[20] I take it as an expansion and complication of the ways in which the public and its externalities are constructed around visually constituted fields. The term *public* needs to be understood not only in terms of who says what to whom, but primarily in terms of who appears how, where, and doing what. It is analytically more useful to understand the notion of the public sphere as a real effect of everyday relations of power, of exclusion and inclusion, of an ongoing production of hierarchies of difference as they are constituted not only through speech, but also visually through images, displays, and performances.

Everyday Life: The Proliferation of Identity Marks

The public subject gains presence through marking its various others as constructed through the marking of bodies and places, thereby bestowing them with public recognition. The marking of bodies and places as the particular and the different involves the construction of identities by inscribing various meanings to certain bodily features, the color of one's skin, the shape of one's body, articles of clothing, accessories, body movements, and gestures. Therefore, bodies come to bear various marks of public recognition, thereby becoming gendered, racialized, classed, nationalized, made profane or sacred. Furthermore, a body comes to be vested with such marks of identity not only through how it appears in public, but also through where it appears and what it does there. Bodies are classed and hierarchically positioned through the places in which they appear and the activities in which they engage. The type of neighborhood where one lives; the means of transportation one uses; the school one went to; the part of the country one is from; the places where one shops, eats, or gets a haircut; what one eats; and the type of music one listens to—all serve a purpose beyond their immediate and apparent functions. They situate that person within the hierarchically constituted categories of status and class, which are juxtaposed with other hierarchically established categories such as race, gender, religion, age, and so on.[21]

Turkey provides an abundance of examples of the ways in which various articles of clothing and accessories as well as social spaces become heavily imbued with political meaning, transforming them into markers of identity. For example, in the 1970s when all political alignments were polarized into the left and the right under the impact of the Cold War, a highly detailed repertoire of daily activities had developed, concertedly serving to situate a person as belonging to the left or the right of the political spectrum. A person's political position could be inferred from what he wore, where she dined and what she ate, what kind of music he listened to, which movies she watched, what kind of vocabulary he used in daily conversations, the type of mustache a man had, the kind of hairstyle a woman wore, and so on. A leftist would be unmistakably recognized by his or her green "parka" coat. A leftist man would wear a thick mustache that did not go below the lip line (otherwise, he would be seen as an ultra-nationalist), and a leftist woman would wear baggy clothes and no makeup. Both would be hanging around particular locales, listening to urbanized versions of folk music, speaking with a so-called pure-Turkish (öz-Türkçe) vocabulary that had been cleansed of the Arabic remnants of Ottoman-Turkish, and so on.

With the end of the Cold War, political alignments in Turkey came to be articulated mainly along the Islamist-secularist divide, giving rise to new identities and new visibilities in the public sphere. But the pageantry of political alignments through visual displays and public performances continues. New veiling, the Islamic headscarf, or the "hoop-beard" (çember sakal: a particular style of close-cut beard that is associated with Islamic piety) are similar symbols of Islamism that are used to mark bodies. Again, the places where people shop, dine, and live, as well as particular types of greeting and vocabulary, have all taken on symbolic meanings as they have become markers of political alignments. One is identified as an Islamist if one speaks with a particular vocabulary heavily laden with Ottoman-Turkish/Arabic words, has attended Imam Hatip high schools (vocational schools for imams), lives or hangs out in certain neighborhoods, such as the Fatih district in Istanbul (because this district contains the headquarters of a famous religious order), and so on. In sum, participation in the public sphere and the articulation of political positions involves not only who says what to whom, but, more important, who appears where, how, and doing what.

Hence, the public sphere should be understood as a field of displays of bodies and places reproduced on an everyday basis whereby various particular identity categories are constructed. Since the production of these categories is an ongoing process of everyday activity, they are never settled once and for all. They are sustained to the extent that they enter the realm of the everyday, where wide ranges of practices of daily activity are institutionalized in the form of habits and routines.[22] In everyday life, the stability and endurance of identity categories depend on the extent to which they become inseparably linked with daily activities, habits, and unspoken conventions of daily conduct. Any practice or style, such as those related to clothing, eating habits, types of vocabulary, or shopping patterns, that manages to enter the realm of everyday life is repeated both spatially (i.e., in many places by many people simultaneously) and temporally (i.e., every day, or the same time every week, month, or year). The source of power is in the indiscernible, miniscule, but both spatially and temporally proliferating nature of everyday practice, which repeatedly constitutes particular identity categories on a daily basis.

Just as the production of identity categories is sustained by everyday practice, so are their contestations. Michel de Certeau explores various ways in which daily activities serve as tactical sites from which the totalizing disciplines of power can be resisted. In situating these subversive acts, de Certeau draws attention to activities such as reading, shopping, or cooking, which are vested with tactical power due to their anonymity.[23] Because they are anonymous, such acts of consumption may act in ways that transcend and transform the publicized ways of consuming and may, in fact, work to subvert and undermine the power of such mechanisms. According to de Certeau, such subversive acts are possible only in the absence of place and visibility; that is, an act of consumption can be used as a subversive tactic by taking advantage of its anonymity and lack of place. Michael Warner makes a similar observation when he sees the possibility of evading public control, or what he refers to as "counterpublicity," in the anonymous interventions in public spaces, such as graffiti. In Warner's view, graffiti is an effective intervention precisely because it marks the presence of those who create it in the public sphere without making them visible, making them "difficult to criminalize or minoritize" because they are "impossible to locate."[24] Hence, Warner notes, "Although emancipation is not around the corner, its possibility is visible everywhere."[25]

However, remaining invisible does not necessarily work to the advantage of underprivileged identities. Rather, it allows the public gaze to inscribe its own meaning on such anonymous interventions in the public sphere. Therefore, to continue with Warner's analogy, even if the graffiti could have been done by, say, rich white teenagers, it is more readily attributed to poor black men, thereby serving to further incriminate black and lower-class subjectivities. Since the public subject maintains the privilege to categorize and hierarchically establish particular identity categories, public anonymity may actually serve to enhance the privilege of the public subject by allowing it to inscribe its own meanings on such situations of anonymity.

Therefore, public invisibility does not necessarily avoid the subjugation of bodies to the power and control of the public subject. But are there no other means to avoid or escape the overbearing and dominating gaze of the public? In the subsequent pages I will explore ways in which gaining public visibility in certain ways may in fact serve to subvert, challenge, or undermine the privilege and authority of the public gaze.

The Returned Gaze of the Public Spectacle

The idea that the public gaze functions as a mechanism of control and supervision is developed by Michel Foucault in his writings on the Panopticon, an architectural invention serving as "a technology of power designed to solve the problems of surveillance."[26] Here the architectural design of a prison subjects the inmates to a constant sense of being watched and supervised, which eventually leads to the interiorization of this invisible gaze, allowing the exercise of power without an agent. As Foucault notes, the Panopticon induces "in the inmate a state of conscious and permanent visibility that assures the automatic functioning of power."[27]

However, Foucault uses the notion of the gaze in quite a different manner in another context. In the *Order of Things* Foucault discusses multiple functions of the gaze in his examination of Velázquez's painting *Las Meninas*. The painting depicts the court of King Philip IV, where the princess, her entourage, a painter, and a bystander constitute a spectacle, most of them gazing toward the position of the observer. From the gaze and gestures of the painter, we understand that his painting—which is not visible to the observer—is of a subject situated outside the painting, exactly where the spectator is. A clue as to the identity of the subject is provided by a mirror that reflects the image of the subject/observer; it is the king and his wife. The spectacle of gestures and gazes, with the addition of the image in the mirror, juxtaposes the functions of three different connoted observers: the subject, the observer, and the artist.[28] Foucault notes that "these three 'observing' functions come together in a point exterior to the picture: that is, an ideal point in relation to what is represented, but a perfectly real one too, since it is also the starting-point that makes the representation possible."[29]

In this account of the relationship between the spectacle and the observer, there are two different ways in which the gaze functions. The first is as the visible gaze of those who are a part of the spectacle. The second is as the invisible gaze of the observer, as it is evoked by the specific way in which the spectacle is arranged and presented. Although Foucault's work is often cited for the latter—that is, the invisible gaze of the observer, vested with the power to organize, define, and control by virtue of its invisibility and inaccessibility—I focus on the former gaze, the visible gaze of the spectacle. This gaze, in combination with the arrangement of space and objects and the positioning and clothing of bodies, functions so as to call into being an observer. Drawing on Louis Althusser's notion of interpellation, where the act of calling upon or hailing constitutes a subject, I refer to this as the interpellative function of the gaze.[30] Althusser cites the example of a police officer hailing a passerby. This specific act of hailing, argues Althusser, constitutes the anonymous passerby as a citizen of the state who is now subjected to its laws. Hence, the act of calling upon or hailing someone is an act of recognition whereby a subject is called into existence by being recognized and acknowledged as a particular type of subject, such as a citizen, an individual, a unique person with a unique name, a man, a woman, a child, a worker, a Christian, or a Muslim.

In this respect, it can be argued that any type of display or spectacle, by virtue of presenting itself to an audience, evokes an observing subject, regardless of whether there is an actual audience present or not. Furthermore, as suggested by Foucault's reading of Las Meninas, a spectacle can interpellate not only a generic observer, but a particular subject with a particular identity. Indeed, the spectacle in Las Meninas evokes not only a generic observer, but also the artist as well as the subject. The specific ways in which the gazes are arranged—the canvas in front of the painter depicted in the painting, the mirror, the clothing and the positioning of the bodies—concertedly evoke, through recognition, a particular subject with a particular identity: the king and queen. As Foucault notes, the mirror in the painting draws "into the interior of the picture what is intimately foreign to it: the gaze which has organized it and the gaze for which it is displayed."[31]

In sum, the visual display of bodies, gestures, gazes, and space can be seen as an interpellative act whereby a particular observing subject is constituted. This gaze is interpellative, because through recognition it calls into being a subject in the position of the observer, thereby constituting it with a particular identity. Just as the spectacle in Las Meninas interpellates into being a particular observing subject with an identity, the spectacle in the public sphere interpellates the public subject with a particular identity. If the medium of the public sphere is everyday life as a continually reproduced spectacle of bodies and places, this spectacle evokes the public subject as the invisible observer on a daily basis. Furthermore, just as the way in which a particular observing subject is evoked through the spectacle in Las Meninas, the specific ways in which spectacles are arranged and displayed for the public gaze evoke not only a generic public subject but one that is gendered, racialized, classed, nationalized, secularized, and so on.

The Public Subject and Its Others: Possibilities for Subversion

If public spectacle interpellates a particular public subject in the place of the observer, and since spectacles in national public spheres interpellate the national subject, manipulating the spectacle is an effective means through which national identities are constructed or contested. The media provide various sites of public spectacles through which a variety of different subjectivities are produced. A particular magazine, with its cover photograph, its headlines, the display of its pages, its choice of topics and photographs, and the way in which it addresses its audience, constitutes a spectacle that interpellates a particular public subject. However, the public subject should not be confused with the immediate audience that the magazine addresses. For example, *Cosmopolitan* is a magazine that may be widely read by women, but the way in which images of women are portrayed and constructed on each page and in each story evokes a male public gaze. Women readers are meticulously instructed in effective ways to display their bodies by making themselves visible as "desirable women" in the male gaze. They are instructed as to the specific marks that they need to be wearing, carrying, or instilling onto their bodies—such as a certain type of figure—so that their bodies will be recognized as attractive and desirable.

A similar example of a public spectacle provided by the media in Turkey is the widely popular weekly magazine *Aktüel*, which is a predominantly visual conglomeration of political, social, and entertainment news reports, research articles, and gossip columns. Although *Aktüel* always includes investigative reporting on prominent political issues, it also frequently uses on its cover the photographs of women, either pictures of female public figures with enhanced sexuality or half-nude models loosely representing some aspect of the cover story. Although *Aktüel* is probably read equally by men and women as the immediate audience, the overall presentation of articles, photographs, cover pictures, and reports constitutes a public spectacle that interpellates a public subject that is male, upper-middle-class, urban, Turkish-national/patriotic, and secular. The current events and political issues covered interpellate a secular, national subject; the types of stories and places usually reported in the arts and entertainment sections evoke an urban, upper-middle-class gaze; and the abundance of images of women, almost always in sexually enhanced presentations, evoke the male gaze.

These illustrations are examples of the ways in which the media functions as a site of public spectacle that interpellates a gendered, racialized, or classed public subject that is indeed constructed in the abstract and invisible position of the observing gaze. It should be noted that the media are only one of the sites of everyday life that produce such public spectacles. Even though the media are instrumental in the constitution of the public gaze, their immediate presence is not necessary for the constitution of a site as "public." As I have discussed earlier, the act of opening up the body or a place, thereby making it visible and accessible to the public gaze, is what constitutes a spectacle as "public."

The daily temporal and spatial proliferation of public displays is crucial in constituting the basis for the possibility of change and subversion, because it makes possible uncontrolled and unanticipated interventions into the public sphere. These interventions can be effective in undermining the authority of the public gaze if they do not readily lend themselves to the existing identity categories, which operate to reproduce the privilege of the center. In her discussion on the discursive construction of gender identities, Judith Butler notes, "If the rules governing signification not only restrict, but enable the assertion of alternative domains of cultural intelligibility, i.e., new possibilities for gender that contest the rigid codes of hierarchical binarisms, then it is only *within* the practices of repetitive signifying that a subversion of identity becomes possible."[32] As Butler suggests, it is possible to contest identity categories that are imposed upon bodies and places by the public gaze not by avoiding the gaze and remaining invisible, but by gaining public visibility in ways that escape and undermine existing categorizations. Such new visibilities often elicit bafflement, outrage, or scandal precisely because they are unanticipated and uncategorizable. These interventions threaten the privilege of the public gaze, because they challenge its authority and ability to classify, categorize, and hierarchically position its others, thereby undermining the reproduction of its constitutive boundaries.

This is exactly how the appearance of female students wearing the Islamic headscarf in urban public spaces in Turkey is subverting the authority and control of the secular public gaze. The subversive effects of Islamic visibilities, such as the headscarf, come from their power to disrupt the binary oppositions established within secularist discourse. Under the modernizing interventions of the state, the institutionalization of modernity in the public sphere was predicated upon the preservation of binary oppositions that sustained secularism as the center and Islam as the periphery. The secular gaze has marked Islam as the traditional, the uneducated, the backward, the lower class. Therefore, within secularist discourse, Islam and secularism, Islam and modernity, Islam and Westernism cannot go together. The presence of one is predicated on the absence of the other. Secularism is public, Islam private; secularism is knowledge, Islam is belief; secularism is modern, Islam is traditional; secularism is urban, Islam is rural; secularism is progress, Islam is reactionary *(irtica)*; secularism is universal, Islam is particular. It was with the appearance of university students wearing the Islamic headscarf on campuses that Islamic identities emerged in social spaces that were under the strict control of secularist discourse, thereby undermining the authority of secularism. By gaining an undeniable presence in a very public, modern, and urban place of knowledge and progress, the university, the headscarf disrupted all the binaries that were serving to sustain the privilege of secularism. When the headscarf attained such public visibility, the secular gaze was outraged and scandalized, because within the secularist worldview, Islamic identities could not have any sort of presence in modern, secular spaces such as the university. The secularist outrage eventually contributed to the National Security Council decree issued in February 1997, which called for strict measures to be taken against political Islam, including the enforcement of the ban on the headscarf. Soon after the intervention, a high-ranking military officer was asked, "Is it really the end of the world if civil servants begin wearing head scarves?" and answered, "Yes. It is the end of the world."[33] This is an explicit articulation of the unsettling effects of the Islamic headscarf, which represents a disruption of a public world constructed by secularism.

Surveillance: The Gaze of the State

I have discussed the notion of the public sphere in relation to the particularities it excludes or includes, but this discussion has so far neglected another important component of the public sphere: its relation to the state. The notion of the public sphere was developed by Habermas as an ideal mechanism through which the authoritative power of the state would be counteracted. Habermas notes that the ideal public sphere serves to "transmit the needs of bourgeois society to the state, in order, ideally, to transform political into 'rational' authority."[34] According to Habermas, the authoritative and potentially dominating power of the state can be overcome only through the development of rational discourse emanating from an autonomous public sphere. It is particularly because of this function of the public sphere that several authors have been concerned with the exclusion of particular groups from the emancipatory powers vested in the public sphere.

Writers such as Warner and Berlant, who have rigorously incriminated the emancipatory functions of public deliberation and have shown how such ideals work to conceal other forms of domination, tend to downplay the demands of various social movements to be included in the public sphere. If public visibility was only about subjecting oneself to the dominating and overpowering gaze of the public, why would there be widespread demands to be included in the public sphere, raised by various social movements as well as scholars, some of which have been mentioned earlier. I would argue that the mechanisms of power operating through the public sphere generate incentives not only for the evasion or contestation of the public gaze, but also for being recognized by it, especially in the form of citizenship. This ambivalence of inclusion-exclusion, or rather recognition-invisibility, results from the existence of not one but two dominant gazes in the public sphere: that of the public and that of the state.

The gazes of the state and the pubic often overlap, but they operate through quite different mechanisms and with different, sometimes conflicting effects. In order to highlight the difference between the public and the state, I will make use of the notion of "surveillance" as a mechanism that operates in slightly different ways than the public gaze discussed earlier.

As developed in Foucault's analysis of the Panopticon, surveillance is a mechanism of power that is effectively produced through the architectural design of the prison in the absence of supervising agents or the use of force. According to Foucault, the Panopticon mechanically produces a type of power that is both visible and unverifiable:

> Visible: the inmate will constantly have before his eyes a tall outline of the central tower from which he is spied upon. Unverifiable: the inmate must never know whether he is being looked at any one moment; but he must be sure that he always may be so.[35]

Therefore, it is not the presence of an actual supervisor, but the mere possibility of it, that results in the operation of power as an effective means of order and control. Foucault draws upon the example of the Panopticon to illustrate how modern societies function in much the same way, with similar mechanisms and techniques of power proliferated in order to create the effect of constant surveillance. In a world of digital information processing, mechanisms of surveillance are abundant. Our daily lives are increasingly subjected to surveillance mechanisms such as credit reports, income tax filing, voter registration, job applications, and so on. These procedures open up our daily lives to the possibility of constant inspection, of the kind of panoptic surveillance where there are no supervisors or inspecting agents, but a constant possibility of being inspected. Even the police force itself, which is usually thought of as made up of agents of supervision at work, may be perceived as a similar panoptic machine where an effect of constant surveillance is created not usually by the direct use of force, but more often by the visible yet unverifiable nature of police presence. Just as in the case of the Panopticon, the visibility of police patrol, the sound of sirens, the passing of a police car function to create the effect that a citizen will "never know whether he is being looked at any one moment, but he [will] be sure that he always may be so."

Surveillance mechanisms function differently than the public gaze. Foucault draws attention to this difference when he states, "Our society is one not of spectacle, but of surveillance. . . . We are neither in the amphitheater, nor on the stage, but in the panoptic machine, invested by its effects of power, which we bring to ourselves since we are a part of its mechanism."[36] I argue here that modern societies are in fact ones *both* of spectacle and of surveillance, insofar as the gazes of the state and the public constitute "society" in different ways. The constitution of the public subject, as discussed earlier, and the ways in which the public gaze is constituted involve spectacles that are slightly different than those of the surveillance techniques described by Foucault. Surveillance operates to bring about rule-governed behavior. It is a mechanism that enables the internalization of authority and control in order to bring about lawful conduct regulated by written codes. Whereas the public gaze operates to constitute the difference between public and private, the surveillance of the state operates to constitute the difference between the legal and the illegal. The former operates in a field of spectacles and establishes its authority through the marking and hierarchical categorization of bodies and places, whereas surveillance mechanisms function as the institutionalization and internalization of norms of legality and illegality. The public gaze draws its power from an ability to name and categorize, whereas surveillance mechanisms administered by the state always involve punishment and penalization, which are most effective when this threat is internalized and functions as a mechanism of auto-control. Surveillance techniques bring about the proliferation of legally admissible, "right" behavior, because they have already been written into legislation, rules, and regulations. The public gaze marks bodies and places in order to situate them in hierarchically established categories of difference, whereas the surveillance of the state interpellates the "citizen" as defined by the code. Bodies that are subjected to the public gaze are always particular and marked, whereas bodies that are subjected to the gaze of the state are legally constituted as citizens. The marking of bodies and places by the public gaze need not be, and usually is not, legally justified and codified.

Furthermore, when the public gaze is forced to see something it does not recognize, it is either baffled or scandalized and often responds by generating new categories, labels, and frames to domesticate the new visibility. But when the state is confronted with unrecognizable interventions—that is, conduct that is not legally defined—it may either create new legislation or resort to the use of force to constitute these as legally defined actions. When confronted with publicly unrecognizable interventions, the public gaze may deem them invisible, confining them to the private, whereas the state may declare such acts criminal and confine them to the realm of the illegal. The public gaze will close certain spaces to itself so as to constitute the private, whereas the gaze of the state will not hesitate to look into the private if it suspects illegality. For example, the American television series *Cops* depicts a succession of constant interventions into the private by the police so as to reestablish the boundaries between the legal and the illegal.

In the constitution of the public gaze, neither the public subject nor the identities that it marks are legally grounded, whereas the gaze of the state functions to interpellate individual citizens as defined legally. Surveillance functions and is effective only as a part of a legal system. Foucault acknowledges this when he notes, "The bourgeoisie is perfectly well aware that a new constitution or legislature will not suffice to assure its hegemony; it realizes that it has to invent a new technology ensuring the irrigation by effects of power of the whole social body down to its smallest particles."[37] In other words, surveillance is an efficient means of law enforcement, where legally grounded and codified order can be "irrigated" without resorting to the constant use of force.

Even though the public gaze and state surveillance mechanisms may overlap and be congruent at times, it is important to acknowledge the source of tension between them. This tension often becomes articulated as an implicit and sometimes as an explicit clash of power and interests between state authorities and the media. In Turkey this tension became explicit with the 28 February 1997 decree of the National Security Council (NSC). After announcing that Islamic reactionism (*irtica*) had become the top national security concern in Turkey, the NSC issued a decree warning the government to take more radical measures against the rising threat of Islamic reactionism. In succeeding months the military held meetings with various governmental, judicial, and nongovernmental organizations to brief them on the "Islamic threat" in Turkey. The military did not take control of the government, but it certainly reestablished itself as the ultimate overseer whose gaze would be the determining one in reorganizing the public sphere. The intervention of the military dictated to the media and the government how the new visibility of Islam in the public sphere was to be understood, categorized, and incriminated.

The variety of surveillance techniques, the ways they operate in the institutionalization of codified behavior and the interpellation of the "citizen" are complex issues that raise a series of questions about the constitution of the state, citizenship, and the legal system. Although these questions are relevant to my exploration of the public sphere, they require a different type of investigation, which I will not be able to undertake within the scope of this study. Here I am concerned with surveillance mechanisms employed by the state insofar as it has an undeniable presence in the public sphere, subjecting bodies to its gaze and thereby constituting them as citizens. Because citizenship comes with a bundle of rights, being recognized as a citizen entails the financial, legal, and constitutional opportunities and constraints that come with these rights. Therefore, although there may be incentives for the bearers of underprivileged identities to avoid the public gaze, there are also incentives for them to be seen and recognized by the gaze of the state as "citizens" in order to enjoy the rights granted to them by this status.

2

Clothing the National Body:

Islamic Veiling and Secular Unveiling

The body is one of the most important sites where modernizing interventions take place and the parameters of the public sphere are established. The body emerges as a significant site of interventions and negotiations for two reasons. First, it stands out as one of the most potent symbols of the nation and the state. State authority and power are often represented in the body of the ruler, the head of the state. Nationalist movements across the world employ the female body as a symbol of the nation.[1] Hence, the building of a state and the creation of a nation involve different interventions and inscriptions upon the body, whether through the regulation of clothing, the creation of an order of bodily aesthetics, or the assignment of carefully forged roles, such as mother or soldier, all serving one way or another the formation of a sense of nationhood and the establishment of state power.

Second, the physical space of the body itself is one of the spaces where public-private distinctions are established. In other words, the body is metaphorically employed not only as a symbol of the nation and its boundaries, but also as a material space where the boundaries of the public and the private are drawn toward the construction of the national public subject. Determination of the parts of the body that are to be open to the public gaze, parts that are to remain hidden, and the manner in which this display is to be carried out is one of the most effective means through which boundaries that mark the public and the private are drawn. Hence, intervention with regard to the body, especially the strategic covering of certain body parts in certain public places and not in others, can become an important tool by which boundaries that constitute the public sphere are established or contested. This chapter investigates both the metaphorical and the material functions of the body in the building of the new Turkish state and the Islamist contestations that developed in the 1990s.

Targeting the body as the symbol of the nation, modernizing interventions involve the incrimination of the present condition of the body as that which is corrupt and impaired, thereby framing it as in need of liberation and transformation. The intervening subject, whether the state or some other political actor with a modernizing agenda, can then project itself as the savior who will liberate the body from its present confines and take it toward its deserved future.

Even though this body that is assigned the role of the victim is invariably the female body, modernizing interventions also target the male body so as to constitute it as the "modern" subject that is capable of undertaking this transformation. In other words, while interventions constitute the female body as the victim-body that is portrayed as vulnerable to the deprecating conditions that surround it, the male body is simultaneously constituted as the hero-body that has the power and will to liberate and take under its protection the female body. This strategic gendering of bodies plays an essential function in the constitution of the nation and the state. As is illustrated in the following pages, while the female body comes to represent the nation, the male body emerges as the symbol of state power. Hence, by rescuing the female/nation, the male/state gains agency and legitimates its transformative interventions. It is this agency that allows the exertion of power toward the building of a new state and the transformation of society into a nation along the lines of a particular nationalist ideology.

The cases examined in this chapter illustrate that the body has been a site of intense interventions in Turkey both by the founding state in the 1920s and by the Islamists of the 1990s. In both cases, interventions ascribed to the female body a particular precariousness that construed it as vulnerable to the threats posed by its immediate circumstances, establishing the male body as the agent of transformation that would bring liberation to the female body and carry her toward a better future. In both cases the female body was taken as the symbol of the nation, and the male as the symbol and source of political power and agency. In both cases the body emerged as the medium for the advancement of contending national ideologies and political projects. The cases examined include the Hat Law and the promotion of women's images in the public sphere by the state, as well as a state-sponsored beauty pageant and the significance of the Islamic headscarf that emerged as the symbol of political Islam in the 1990s. These cases also illustrate the ways in which the public sphere is formed not so much around debate and discussion but through visual displays, bodily inscriptions, and performances.

The main argument of this section is that the body has emerged as a site of intervention for both secularist and Islamist modernizing projects that have sought to institutionalize their political ideologies by defaming the current condition of the body and establishing themselves as its emancipator and protector. Seeing this power of the body as a political field, the state used it in the 1920s in order to institute the norms of the public sphere and to transform official national ideology into the norm. The Islamists used the medium of the body in similar ways in the 1990s in order to contest and subvert established norms of the public and to promote their own national ideologies. This comparison suggests that just as the secular state used the body in realizing its modernization project, the Islamists employed the body as a site for interventions in implementing their own project of modernization.

The Constitutive Power of Clothing

Clothing is perhaps the most effective tool by which bodies are marked, categorized, displayed, and opened up to the public, or covered up and concealed as private. Studies on clothing tend to highlight its function as a symbol of social status, ethnicity, and individual values and life styles.[2] However, clothing is not an indicator just of status or class, and it is not a sign of an a priori identity. Rather, clothing is constitutive of subjectivities. Clothing inscribes bodies with gender, class, status, ethnicity, race, religion, and age. Clothing marks bodies so as to allow for public recognition and differentiation into these identity categories, determining whether a body is to be recognized as male or female, upper class or lower class, young or old, secular or religious. It gives a particular visibility to bodies, subjecting them to the public gaze, but it also covers up certain body parts so as to deny access to the public gaze, thereby constituting them as private.

The function and effects of clothing tend to be overlooked in the study of politics, seemingly dismissed as trivial, or at least as secondary to issues of "higher" political importance, such as prohibitive military or other authoritative measures used by states to control and monitor the public sphere. However, regulations and codes related to clothing and attire have been crucial tools by which states have constituted their power and authority not only within national public spheres, but also across national borders, as in colonial settlements. Helen Callaway shows how British colonial presence and authority in the colonies were maintained by "patterns of order and discipline regulating minute details of everyday existence for the rulers" and demonstrates how, "in this choreography of empire, the display of dress in all its forms carried a heavy weight of symbolic meanings."[3] The dictation of dress codes for the colonials regulating dresses, suits, hats, shoes, and accessories, as well as the places and the time of the day these could be worn, served to establish the privilege and authority of the British colonizers. Callaway shows how in India these interventions served to mark and differentiate the colonizer from the colonized, British space from Indian space, masculinity from feminine modes, and to maintain class distinctions and social exclusiveness.[4]

The constitutive effects of clothing operate not only through the marking of bodies for differentiation into identity categories, but also through imposing certain forms, figures, and modes onto bodies. In other words, it is not only the symbolic meaning of clothes that imbues them with constitutive power, but also their physical form, which has a constitutive effect in giving shape to the body or to behavior or in concealing certain body parts and opening up others. The corset is a good example of how the body is coerced into a particular figure that is set by the prevalent standards for beauty, aesthetics, and social class. The corset, which is meant to be undetectable and invisible to the public gaze, works not as a conveyor of symbolic meaning, but as a physical effect that imposes upon the body the dictates of standards related to fashion and aesthetics, which in turn serve the gendering and classing of bodies.

In a similar vein, Islamist writer Abdurrahman Arslan illustrates how clothing is one of the means through which modernity has had transformative effects on Islam. According to Arslan, one of the articles of clothing brought to Turkey by modernity and Westernization was blue jeans, now worn extensively as casual daily wear for all sorts of occasions, including regular prayers.[5] Arslan argues that when jeans are worn during prayer, their tightness forces the body to be involuntarily hasty in its movements, thereby creating tension and disrupting the tranquility of prayer.[6] Arslan provides other examples to argue that such modern articles of clothing as well as furniture, architectural styles, and spatial arrangements have had disruptive effects on Islamic styles and traditions, altering their holism and undermining their integrity.

Whether through the meanings it acquires in particular discursive contexts or through the confining, concealing, revealing, or structuring effects it induces upon bodies, clothing certainly plays a crucial role in the construction and contestation of subjectivities. It is perhaps one of the most powerful tools for the display of identities in daily life, due to its temporally and spatially proliferative quality. Once it enters the realm of the everyday, a type of clothing proliferates exponentially, rendering its source non-locatable. For this reason, the power of an article of clothing is vested in its capacity to work through the minute details of everyday life, making both control and contestation more effective.

Clothing plays a crucial role in the construction and contestation of subjectivities in the public sphere and in the creation of political agency in Turkey. First, regulations and interventions related to the clothing of bodies have been vital in the constitution and transformation of the public and private spheres. During the founding years of the Turkish state, such interventions served the establishment of a modern, West-oriented public sphere where a modern national subject was created. During the 1990s, with the emergence of the new Islamic veiling[7] in the public sphere, the religious headscarf as a particular type of clothing served to destabilize the public-private distinctions maintained and monitored by the secularist gaze, forcing the negotiation of alternative conceptualizations of the public and the private. These contested public-private distinctions involve bodies and body parts, as well as social spaces and places. Bodies and body parts emerge as spaces upon which the public and private are established, where clothing serves to conceal or to reveal body parts, thereby marking the distinctions between public and private upon the body. Islamic veiling operates very much the same way, by concealing certain body parts and revealing others (namely the face and the hands), thereby marking upon the body the boundaries of the public and the private defined by Islam.

This particular and potent function of clothing reveals a key feature of the private sphere, that it is always constituted in relation to the public. By definition, the private is that which is closed to the public gaze, so its existence is always in relation to and dependent upon the public. In other words, the boundaries of the "public" are formed exactly by delineating and marking that which is private. Marking the private is a mechanism through which the public is constituted. As such, manipulating, shifting, or displacing the boundaries of the private on one's body through clothing becomes an effective tool by which the established boundaries of the public are challenged and unsettled.

Clothes also serve to distinguish between public and private places through the differentiation of clothes worn publicly as opposed to privately. For example, bathrobes, pajamas, underwear, and lingerie are items of clothing that serve to mark private space. It can be argued that the main difference between a bathing suit and a similar piece of underwear is that the former is constitutive of a particular public space (i.e., a beach), the latter of a private space. The headscarf and new veiling are styles of clothing that are to be worn specifically in public spaces. In other words, while they serve to constitute a different (Islamic) understanding of privacy marked upon the body, they also serve to interpellate a public gaze for which the body is displayed in its concealed form, thereby constituting the space in which they appear as public.

Second, clothing serves to map other identity categories onto the public-private spheres so as to constitute the public and private realms as gendered, classed, racialized, nationalized, and secularized domains. In Turkey, clothing has played a crucial part in the constitution of the public realm as a secular domain and the private realm as Islamic. On the other hand, this secularist distinction was challenged by the increased and highlighted public visibility of Islamic attire. Indeed, the headscarf almost single-handedly served to contest and subvert the privileged status of secularism in the public sphere.

Third, interventions related to bodies through dress codes and regulations always operate through categories of gender, which turn the body into a political field upon which subjectivities are created, political agency is generated, and hierarchies of power are institutionalized. There is no doubt that interventions on the clothing of bodies serve to impose upon them gender identities. In turn, this gendering of bodies functions to generate a new system of power and hierarchy, in the creation either of state power or of a new order of power relations that seeks to challenge and replace the existing order. Such gendering interventions identify the female body with the nation and portray it as in need of protection, emancipation, and tutelage by effective leadership and management. Hence, the incarnation of the nation in the female body involves the simultaneous construction of the intervening subject as the savior, the political agent (e.g., the state) incarnated in the male body of the ruling elite. Such gendering interventions related to bodies implicate both male and female bodies, but the female is more readily and directly the target of interventions, whereas the male body is usually involved indirectly. By manipulating and controlling the public visibility of women's bodies, the intervening subject (the media, the state, or the leadership of other political forces) gains political agency of the masculine kind. While the formation and display of identities in relation to the advancement of political projects in the public sphere are achieved through the manipulation of women's public visibility, interventions related to male bodies serve to masculinize state power.

Finally, the power of clothing to constitute the public by marking the private upon the body vests the intervening subject with political agency. Regulating and manipulating the clothing of bodies become crucial tools by which subjects acquire the power and authority to shape and contest public-private distinctions. Interventions related to the female body are usually justified by a rhetoric of protection of the honor and well-being of the nation or its liberation from degrading and oppressive circumstances. By assuming such guardianship, the intervening subject legitimizes its power and authority to intervene with regard to bodies, construct the national subject, and dictate the boundaries of the public and the private spheres. It is through regulating and monitoring the public realm that the state acquires political agency and dictates its own norms and standards of nationhood. This is how the new Turkish state in the early years of the republic acquired political agency in creating and dictating a new national identity defined around the norms of secularism and a West-oriented modernity. It is also how in the 1990s the Islamists legitimized their nationalist project and acquired agency to speak and act on behalf of the nation.

Regulating Dress: Unveiling and the Creation of a New National Subject

During the 1920s and 1930s, the new Turkish state was heavily engaged in building a new state which involved the institutionalization of a new secular nationalist project constituted against the Islamic/Ottoman past. The body has been one of the most important media through which this project has been conjured and implemented. The Hat Law of 1925 is only one of the instances through which the state intervened with regard to bodies toward instituting secularism, nationalism, and Westernism in the public sphere. Even though this law involved men's clothing, discussions and public debate on the visibility of bodies increasingly revolved around women's attire. The state did not pass a similar law to regulate women's clothing and to ban the Islamic veil, but the issue was discussed extensively and was left up to local governments, some of which banned the veil through local regulations.[8]

Therefore, during the founding years the secular state used the medium of the female body and women's public visibility as a strategic means through which Turkey's new secular project of modernization would be institutionalized and its new national identity would be displayed for global audiences. There were several reasons why the female body became such a target for interventions toward the building of a new nation-state. First, Turkey is not different from other countries where the female body has come to symbolize the nation and its borders, both because of its reproductive capabilities and because femininity is a powerful trope of vulnerability, openness, and submission. Within the discursive context of nationalism that divides the world into the national self and its others, women's bodies function as "symbolic border guards" toward the drawing of these boundaries of difference, and their protection by the state.[9]

Second, the designation of the female body as the symbol of the nation in need of protection serves to construct the state as the political agent who intervenes with regard to bodies, rescues or liberates the female/nation from adverse conditions, and brings it under its own guardianship, thereby acquiring a masculine mode of agency and power. Under such discursive conditions, women's bodies gain enhanced public visibility where regulations and control of women's appearances are employed as an effective means through which new nationalist projects are implemented, serving to preserve the invisibility and masculinity of political agency. Hence, by regulating and controlling women's public appearances and thereby dictating the norms and boundaries of the national public sphere, the state is able to constitute itself as the agent of modernization and the guardian of the nation.

Third, and most important, because European perceptions of the Ottoman were heavily conditioned by Orientalist conceptualizations of Islam represented by images of veiled women and women behind harem walls,[10] what better means could the new secularist Turkish state find to distance itself from the Ottoman than by projecting images of women "emancipated" from the confines of the harem having a vivid presence in the public sphere wearing Western clothing? Indeed, women's emancipated and modernized visibility in the public sphere proved to be an excellent means through which the new state displayed its difference from and triumph against its Ottoman-Islamic predecessor.

Even though the founders used interventions with regard to bodies through the regulation of dress and attire quite effectively as an important component of their modernization project, this is not a strategy specific to the new Turkish state. Nora Şeni notes that the Ottoman state issued several decrees attempting to control and regulate the color and thickness of women's overcoats and the length of the veil and of scarves, starting as early as the sixteenth century.[11] Donald Quataert argues that these clothing regulations were not simply instruments of social control and discipline employed by the state. Rather, "the laws were instruments of negotiation, used by both the state and its elites, as well as by the various (occupational and religious) communal groups. . . . Clothing and head-gear helped give status and a sense of identity to members of the specific religious, ethnic and occupational communities in Ottoman society."[12] For example, in the 1720s several decrees were passed by the state that at-tempted to impose restrictions on women's clothing. One of these decrees justified the decision by noting that "some 'good for nothing' women had adopted various innovations in their clothing, imitating Christians in the deliberate effort to lead the public astray on Istanbul's streets."[13] In order to bring such transgressions under control, the state specified the precise measurements of the headscarves and the overcoats that women belonging to the Muslim community were allowed to wear. In a similar at-tempt to reestablish class differences, a regulation passed in 1727 prohib-ited lower-status men and women from wearing ermine fur. According to Quataert, although these earlier regulations served to create and maintain differences among various religious communities and social ranks, it was not until the mid–nineteenth century that clothing laws were enacted to promote homogeneity and uniformity within public offices. This change was brought about in 1829, when the Ottoman ruler Mahmut II passed a law requiring all civil officials to wear the same headgear, the fez.[14]

What seems to have occurred toward the mid–nineteenth century was not so much a switch from the creation of difference to a constitution of homogeneity, as Quataert claims (because all regulations involve the ho-mogenization of appearance within a category so as to create differences among categories), but rather the emergence of nationalism as demon-strated through the bodies of civil servants representing the state. The concern with the clothing of civil servants and the attempt to create a standard form of headgear suggests an increasing involvement with the idea of nationalism and the initial concerns with the construction of a na-tional subject. According to Nora Şeni, it was early in the nineteenth cen-tury, with the onset of Westernization, which included the idea of nation-alism, that clothing and attire became issues of central concern and public debate.[15] Şeni notes that during the nineteenth century "the pro-Western elites who contemplated Turkey through the gaze of the Europeans" were adopting and presenting European styles of clothing, garments, and accessories as "tools of civilization," in contrast to the Islamic/Ottoman traditional garments, which were seen as "signs of barbarity."[16]

Therefore, clothing has always been an important instrument used toward the construction of subjectivities, and with the advent of nationalism in the nineteenth century it became an important means through which a new sense of nationhood was created. What made the interventions of the political elite during the 1920s and 1930s different from previous interventions was that they were part of a more radical and revolutionary transformation toward the building of a new, modern nation-state. The political elite under the leadership of Mustafa Kemal Atatürk was much more rigorously involved in creating a brand-new nation governed by a new state and forging a new public sphere where the new national subject could be constructed. This revolutionary change involved a sharp break from the Ottoman past, an inscription of a historical rupture, an insistence on disjunctive change, on a revolutionary diversion from Ottoman ways. This revolutionary incision constituted the Ottoman/Islamic as the traditional, the backward, the obsolete, against which the national self could be constituted as new and modern. This major undertaking involved concerted interventions with regard to bodies, among other things, so as to create a new sense of nationhood and a new national subject.

It was under these conditions that the clothing and appearance of women's bodies in general, and the Islamic veil in particular, emerged to take center stage during the founding years of the Turkish state. A new body of literature that recently emerged examining the role of women in the modernization project in Turkey asserts that women's images, and particularly the Islamic veil, played a crucial role in the foundation of the new Turkish state and the institution of official nationalism.[17] Yeğenoğlu suggests that it is possible to discern "the fundamental contours of the project of nationalism" by examining the "discursive articulation of the veil."[18] In the 1920s, the Islamic veil took a central place in official discourse, where it was used as the symbol of backwardness, "barbarism," and the oppression of women by the Ottoman state. Atatürk himself condemned the practice of veiling in the following words:

> In some places I have seen women who put a piece of cloth or a towel or something like it over their faces . . . when a man passes by. What is the meaning and sense of this behavior? Gentlemen, can the mothers and daughters of a civilized nation adopt this strange manner, this barbarous posture? It is an object of ridicule. It must be remedied at once.[19]

It was through such rhetorical techniques that the veil was projected as a mark of the oppressive Ottoman-Islamic rule that had subjected the nation, represented by the female body, to backwardness, barbarism, and uncivilized, degrading conditions. This rhetorical device allowed the projection of the immediate past as a catastrophe from which the national subject needed to be liberated and guided toward a better future. Hence, the unveiling of the female body came to be the ultimate sign of the emancipation of women and the liberation of the nation to achieve the advancement and progress it deserves. By creating such a narrative of subjugation and liberation, the new state itself acquired the role of the liberator who would guide the nation toward civilization.

Unveiling the female body also served to reset the boundaries of the public and the private, which in turn served the creation and institutionalization of a sense of secular, modern nationhood. One of the most potent images that has destroyed Islamic norms of publicness and privacy and instituted in their place secular norms has been the image of women in bathing suits on the beach. The bathing suit ensures the public exposure of the parts of the female body that were deemed private under Islam and hence covered by the veil. Therefore, no piece of clothing other than the bathing suit could so fully symbolize the abolishment of the authority of Islam over the female body and put in its place the authority of secularism. Therefore, images of women in bathing suits were abundantly used in photographs, cartoons, and illustrations during the formative years of the republic.

The image of women wearing bathing suits on the beach, or in state-sponsored beauty pageants and on other similar occasions, symbolized Turkey's radical break from the Ottoman-Islamic ways to embark on a path toward a West-oriented, secular modernity. This state-sponsored parade of images of women in their bathing suits was justified with a rhetoric of liberation of the body/nation from the oppressive authority of Islam.

The visibility of women in the public sphere gained a new significance during the early years of the new republic. The state was actively promoting the appearance of women in public places, wearing modern clothes, engaged in modern activities. Photographs of women lawyers, women parliamentarians, women pilots, women in military training, and women in athletics were proliferating in publications sponsored by the government.[20] Married couples in secularist elite circles were demonstrating new forms of public visibility by showing up in public places as "man and wife," a previously uncommon practice, organizing flamboyant dance receptions wearing elegant European dresses and suits, arranging evening gatherings

Figure 1. The image of women on the beach in their bathing suits was one of the most vigorously promoted images symbolizing Turkey's devotion to Westernization (*Servet-i Fünun*, back cover page, 1925).

at coffee saloons, becoming members of prestigious golf and horseback-riding clubs, and so on.[21] The image of the "new woman" of this period was that of "the woman who appeared in Republican ballroom receptions and similar gatherings organized by cultural centers (*halkevleri*) and associations, together with men and dressed in Western style clothing, thereby displaying 'modernity.'"[22] Mustafa Kemal himself did much to promote the image of the "new woman" as a "symbol of the break with the past" by personally encouraging women's public visibility and making personal appearances together with his wife and adopted daughter at social occasions and official ceremonies.[23]

In sum, in the early years of the republic the presence of women in the public sphere was actively promoted by the new state as a mark of modernity, secularism, and civilization. Such a state-sponsored feminization of the public sphere also served to strengthen the patriarchal basis of state power, where men's power and authority is measured by the control they are able to exercise on women and their bodies.

Female Public Visibility and Political Agency

During the 1920s and 1930s, the secularist state not only promoted the proliferation of the images of Westernized women in the public sphere, but also adopted some important legislative measures involving women's place and status in society. The pluralistic women's movements of the late Ottoman period, which had reflected a wide range of ideas including secularism, nationalism, and reformist Islam, were consolidated by the new Turkish state in 1924 as the Turkish Women's Federation, which endorsed the secularist ideals of the state.[24] The civil code of 1926 gave women equal rights in inheritance and marital affairs, and in 1934 full suffrage was granted to women. As a result, Turkey had eighteen women parliamentarians elected in 1937, at a time when women in several other countries in Europe lacked even the right to vote.[25] Drawing on these developments, Göle notes, "It is the construction of women as public citizens and women's rights (even more cherished than the construction of citizenship and civil rights) that are the backbone of Turkish modernism."[26]

According to the Turkish feminist scholar Şirin Tekeli, the granting of full suffrage and allowing the presence of women in the parliament were strategic moves on the part of the state to show Europe that Turkey belonged to the world of Western democratic societies.[27] This point is attested by the following words of Mustafa Kemal Atatürk, commenting on the granting of full suffrage to women:

> This decision has earned Turkish women a higher status than that of the women of other nations. In the future, it will be necessary to search for covered and veiled women [only] in history books. . . . By participating in

general elections, Turkish women are now using the most important of all rights. This right, which is denied to women in many civilized countries, is now fully available to Turkish woman. She will use that right effectively and confidently.[28]

This and similar statements made by Kemal Atatürk resonated so widely among secularist women, organized under the Turkish Women's Federation, that its leader, Latife Bekir, said, "In Turkey, woman has been called by Atatürk to rid herself of the veil and take her place alongside men."[29]

As illustrated here, the words of both Atatürk and Bekir established a direct link between political participation and the wearing of the veil: if women were to have a presence in the public sphere, it could be and had to be achieved by taking off the veil. It was explicitly made clear that the "most important right" available to women could be exercised only if the mark of Islam, that is, the veil, was removed. What is crucial here is that the mark of secularism (i.e., the image of the modern woman in the public sphere) was being defined as an erasure of the mark of Islam (i.e., the image of the Muslim woman wearing the veil). In other words, modernization and the constitution of the new national subject were to be achieved through the removal of the veil from women's bodies. Atatürk himself referred to the practice of veiling as a "barbarous posture" or an "object of ridicule" that needed to be remedied.[30] These interventions illustrate how in the early years of the republic "the unveiling of women became a convenient instrument for . . . the construction of modern Turkish identity as opposed to backward Ottoman identity."[31]

This is why today in Turkey the first generation of women who grew up under the secular state feel so threatened by the increasing presence of veiled women in the public sphere. It is especially this generation of educated women, who were brought up to believe that their presence and status in society as doctors, lawyers, teachers, or scholars is predicated upon the absence of the mark of Islam, particularly the veil, in the public sphere.[32] It is mostly this generation of women who are organizing around associations such as that called The Promotion of Modern Life and actively protesting and demonstrating against political Islam and the headscarf in Turkey today.

The rights and privileges granted to women in the early years of the republic undoubtedly contributed to an expanded presence of women in the public sphere. There is no doubt that women benefited from these rights handed down by the state, but it soon became obvious that the new secular state was more concerned with its ability to control and manipulate images of women displayed in the public sphere than with their actual presence. The Women's People's Party, founded by autonomous women's groups in 1923, was denied authorization by the state. The Turkish Women's Federation, which was formed in 1924 and had campaigned successfully in support of secularist reforms, was disbanded in 1935, only a year after full suffrage was granted to women.[33] After these initial years of the republic, Turkey did not have an autonomous women's movement until the 1990s, and the number of women in the Turkish parliament never reached the level that it was in 1937 (eighteen parliamentarians, constituting 4.5 percent of the Great National Assembly, the highest percentage ever). As Kandiyoti notes, "Women's emancipation under Kemalism was part of a broader political project of nation-building and secularisation. . . . The authoritarian nature of the single-party state and its attempts to harness the 'new woman' to the creation and reproduction of a uniform citizenry aborted the possibility for autonomous women's movements."[34] However, it should be noted that the percentage of women in elite professions, such as medicine, law, and academics, has been saliently high in Turkey. Even though the expanded visibility of women in the public sphere was largely enabled by the modernizationist aspirations of the state, this tightly defined and controlled visibility nevertheless gave rise to a substantial presence of secularist, Westernized women professionals and intellectuals.

Although the enhanced presence of women in the public sphere has been occasionally interpreted as the granting of political agency to women,[35] the new public visibility of women operated to deny agency to the bearer of these identities. To the contrary, it was through constructing images of women and displaying them in the public sphere that the male secularist elite was able to achieve political agency. The degree to which the state was able to forge these images and monitor and manage their performance in the public sphere allowed the intervening subjects to constitute themselves as political agents capable of staging such well-orchestrated performances. As women's bodies became sites from which national identity was forged and displayed to the public, the secular state constructed itself as the political agent that is able to dress and undress women's bodies, to regulate and control their presence and visibility in the public sphere, thereby establishing its own identity as secular, modern, and Westernized. The bearers of these identities, women, did not have a say or agency in the construction of these identities, and when they did attempt to voice their autonomous concerns, as in the case of the Turkish Women's Federation, they were silenced.

The Hat Law: The Male Body and State Power

Codes and regulations involving public attire and dress have been some of the most effective and controversial means through which the Turkish state has undertaken its modernization and Westernization plans. The most obvious and effective intervention with regard to the body was the Hat Law of 1925, which abolished the wearing of religious garb and the fez by men and instituted the hat as the required headgear for bureaucrats and civil servants. This law was recognized as one of the crucial "revolutionary steps" undertaken by the founder of the republic, Mustafa Kemal Atatürk. The justification of the Hat Law read as follows:

> The issue of headgear, which is completely unimportant in and of itself, is of special value for Turkey, which wants to become a member of the family of modern nations. We propose to abolish the hat worn currently, which has become a mark of difference between Turkey and other modern nations, and replace it with the hat that is the common headgear of all modern civilized nations.[36]

Thus regulating and controlling public attire and dress was employed as a strategy that would erase marks of difference between Turkey and "modern nations" and institute marks of similarity in the quest toward the constitution of a new "modern, civilized" nation. Clothing was acknowledged to be an inscription upon the body of the national subject of a mark of modernity, civilization, and Westernism. In a speech Atatürk made when he introduced the Hat Law, himself wearing a top hat, he justified this deep involvement of the state in the clothing of its citizens with the following words:

> Gentlemen, . . . I tell you as your own brother, as your friend, as your father, that the people of the Turkish Republic, who claim to be civilized, must show and prove that they are civilized, by their ideas and their mentality, by their family life and their way of living. In a word, the truly civilized people of Turkey . . . must prove in fact that they are civilized and advanced persons also in outward aspect. . . . This grotesque mixture of styles [of our dress] is neither national nor international. . . . My friends, international dress is worthy of and appropriate for our nation, and we will wear it. Boots or shoes on our feet, trousers on our legs, shirts and tie, jacket and waistcoat—and, of course, to complete these, a cover with a brim on our heads.[37]

In these statements, the endorsement of the Western style as the "international" norm of civilization shows that civilization was understood as a universal norm rather than the specifically European values and standards that constituted it. The adoption of European-style clothing was seen as an important indicator that the "people of Turkey" were being transformed into a civilized nation that was capable of meeting the universal norms and standards of a modern lifestyle.

What is significant about the Hat Law is that it primarily targeted statesmen, bureaucrats, and civil servants. It was through the bodies of male political subjects that the state was instituting a new sense of nationhood. Nevertheless, such regulations on clothing as the Hat Law are often given as examples of a type of intervention related to women's bodies that has emerged as the "discursive instrument" with which boundaries of the nation have been drawn and its relationship to its various others, such as Islam, have been established.[38] There is no doubt that this type of intervention related to women's bodies functioned as such an instrument, but it is important to acknowledge that the Hat Law involved only men's clothing, since this illuminates the different ways in which the male and the female bodies were implicated in nation- and state-building efforts. While interventions related to the female body invariably sought to alter and manipulate women's public visibility, the Hat Law did not involve the public visibility of men. It did not target the establishment of new norms of publicness, nor did it attempt to regulate the clothing of all men. Rather, it involved the clothing only of state officials and civil servants. Hence, the Hat Law was about the image and the authority of the state itself.

The first intervention involved the body of Atatürk himself and was performed by himself when he made his public statement introducing the Hat Law wearing an elegant suit, a shirt, a tie, and a top hat. This performance was not only a display of a new national identity, but also a declaration of a new sense of statesmanship and a modern sense of governance in contrast to that of the Ottoman state, which had failed to undertake such a revolutionary break from traditional forms of governance. Atatürk, as the head of state and the embodiment of state power, was in civilian and "international" clothing that marked upon the state the sign of civilization, modernity, and progress. Addressing the nation as their "brother . . . friend . . . , father," Atatürk constituted the state as the modern patriarch who has the will, power, and knowledge to direct the nation toward progress and civilization. Hence, the Hat Law was an important intervention with regard to the male body that served to insert a distance between the republic and the Ottoman state, which was projected as barbaric, incompetent, and despotic, and therefore to constitute the new state as modern, competent, and liberal.

The Hat Law also involved the institutionalization of secularism. As discussed in the introduction, secularism in Turkey was established by bringing all Islamic authority, practice, and knowledge under the strict and direct control of the secular state. This institutionalization of secularism involved tight control of the public visibility and presence of Islam. While official Islam was given a limited and tightly controlled place in the public sphere, autonomous Islamic discourses were suppressed and kept out. The Hat Law not only banned the fez, but also outlawed the wearing of religious garb and the turban by men except for the staff of the Directorate of Religious Affairs and the imams of mosques. The unauthorized wearing of religious garb was severely penalized, not so much because secular authorities were against Islam per se, but because such "imposters" were confused with government-appointed religious officials and thereby "undercut the authority of the authorized personnel."[39] In other words, this regulation sought to ensure that the only presence and visibility of Islam in the public sphere was that of the official version. It is interesting that the Hat Law was a part of the same set of interventions that sought to construct a new secular, modern national subject that, on the one hand, unveiled and de-Islamized the female body and, on the other, brought such an exemption to the wearing of Islamic garb and turbans. In other words, while the state was unveiling the female body with one hand, it was dressing up certain male bodies with Islamic garb with the other. This peculiarity again points at the different ways in which male and female bodies were employed in the state- and nation-building processes. Again, the male body was employed as the bearer of the mark of the authority of the state to institute secularism, which was understood and implemented as an absolute control over the practice, knowledge, and visibility of Islam in the public sphere. The authorization of the wearing of Islamic garb and turbans by the officials of the Directorate of Religious Affairs while it was forbidden to anyone else served to constitute the state as the only authority over Islam and ensured that the only presence of Islam in the public sphere was the state-sanctioned official version.

The First Beauty Queen: The Nationalized, Secularized, and Unveiled Body

During the 1920s and 1930s, images of Westernized Turkish women were proliferating not only in the local but also in the global public sphere. Images of the "modern Turkish woman" were appearing in European journals and magazines, displaying the dramatic changes taking place in Turkey.[40] One instance of this was the organization of the first beauty pageant in 1929 by the secularist, semiofficial newspaper of the state, *Cumhuriyet* (Republic). On 7 February 1929, the newspaper said, "Who is the prettiest woman in Turkey, beautiful enough to go to the international competition? If all citizens give this issue due concern and take it upon themselves as a national duty, the competition we are organizing to find the most beautiful woman in Turkey will yield beneficial results."[41]

This undertaking was a major step for Turkey's secularist elite, who wanted to display for the global gaze evidence that the new republic was indeed capable of meeting the European, bourgeois standards of bodily aesthetics demonstrated through such beauty pageants. But, more important, this was a crucial opportunity for the new state to show that it had such ultimate control over Islam in the country that women who had been veiled just over a decade before could emerge in the public sphere wearing bathing suits and display their bodies to global audiences.

In 1932 the promotion paid off, and the Turkish candidate, Keriman Halis, emerged as the winner in Belgium and became the first Turkish beauty queen to become Miss World. Halis was presented to the Western media as "the granddaughter of the last *şeyhülislam* (top Islamic authority)."[42] This particular presentation of the beauty queen attempted to constitute her past as one that was under the patriarchal authority of Islam, from which she had been liberated by secularism, as demonstrated by the imposition of a bathing suit on her body.

There were multiple interventions with regard to the body of Keriman Halis here, resulting in different layers of inscriptions, some done through clothing, some verbally. The first and most important inscription was the transformation of Halis's body into a national body. By framing the beauty pageant as a matter of "national duty," the secularist newspaper constituted the body of the beauty queen as a *national* body, even before Halis was elected.

The second inscription upon Halis's body was that of norms and standards of modernity. The mere fact that a Turkish woman was able to compete in an international beauty pageant wearing a bathing suit, let alone win it, enabled the new Turkish state to display its power and authority toward the realization of its modernization project. Participation in the international competition allowed the state to show how it had succeeded in achieving modernity, which was, on this occasion, understood as the ability to meet European bourgeois standards of bodily aesthetics and the power and ability to practice those standards through the presentation of women's bodies. This involved the inscription onto Keriman Halis's body of modernity, understood as the appropriation of European standards and norms as the universal.

The third inscription involved the redrawing of the boundaries of the public on the body, thereby instituting the power of secularism to displace the authority of Islam in shaping the national public sphere. Here, the state used the body as a material space on which boundaries between public and private were drawn. By unveiling the female body and presenting it to local and European public audiences, the state demonstrated that the body was subjected to new, secular boundaries. Parts of the female body that had been deemed private under the authority of Islam, such as the hair, legs, arms, shoulders, and neck, were now deemed public under the rule of secularism. Hence, by imposing the bathing suit, a secular understanding of the distinction between public and private was inscribed on the body.

Displaying Halis's body to European audiences wearing a bathing suit was a highly effective means through which the new secular state demonstrated its power to unveil the female/national body and to publicize it in accordance with secular modern norms. The appearance of Keriman Halis wearing a bathing suit before a European audience served to demonstrate the power of secularism to control and open up the female/national body to the European public gaze. The display of the national body to the European gaze was particularly significant since this gaze was taken as the ultimate arbiter of the modernness and Westernness of the new Turkish subject. Furthermore, this European gaze, heavily conditioned by the Orientalist vision of the times, was unquestioningly accepted to be an Orientalizing gaze that saw Turkish women as closed off behind the veil and the walls of the harem. Hence, the presentation of Halis's body in a bathing suit to European audiences came as an exceptional opportunity to show the European gaze that the new Turkish state had indeed liberated the female/nation from the confines of the harem and the veil and had inscribed secular, modern, Western norms upon the body of the national subject.

The fourth inscription was that of establishing the constitution of Islam as the culprit that had confined the national body to oppressive, backward conditions, thereby turning Halis's body into a site of political encounter between Islam and secularism. By presenting Keriman Halis as "the granddaughter of the last *şeyhülislam*," Islam was reinscribed on her nationalized body as that which had been erased by secularism. This inscription of Islam as the trace of something now absent served to constitute the nation's past as that which had been confined to the patriarchal authority of Islam, but one that had been freed by secularism. It was this inscription in particular that was an exemplary instance of a modernizing intervention that framed the nation's past as an oppressive desolation under the authority of Islam and constituted the secular state as the agent of modernity that had liberated the nation from such adverse conditions. Through the presentation of Halis's nationalized, secularized, and modernized body, the state presented itself as having ultimate control over women's bodies, which were represented as once having been under the strict control of Islam, but now having been brought under the undoubted and demonstrable control and authority of secularism.

Many years later, this pageantry became a matter of scrutiny for Islamist writers. Writing on this issue in the 1990s, one of the prolific Islamist women writers in Turkey, Cihan Aktaş, noted, "It is particularly revealing to see that the first Muslim girl to participate in a beauty pageant in the Western-Christian world wearing a bathing suit was elected the beauty queen of the world."[43] According to Aktaş, the "Western-Christian" jury had elected the "Muslim girl" to demonstrate the victory of the Western world over Islam. Aktaş sees this secularist performance not as an act of secularization of the national body, but rather as the opening up of the Muslim body by the secular state, which had subjected it to conquest and violation by the "Western-Christian" other.

This evaluation by Aktaş was a final, post hoc inscription on Halis's body sixty years after the pageant. Aktaş rewrote the pageant not as a victory, but as a defeat. In Aktaş's account, the pageant was a site where the body of a "Muslim girl" was exposed, allowing it to be conquered and violated by the "Western-Christian" gaze. This account of the pageant maintains that Keriman Halis's body was indeed a national body, but one that was inherently and naturally Muslim. Therefore, the imposition of the bathing suit upon this body is read not as its secularization and a display of modernity, but as a secularist intervention that exposed the Islamic body and subjected it to violation and conquest by the "Western-Christian" (public, therefore male) subject. In this respect, this Islamist inscription also used Keriman Halis's body as a site from which Turkey's true national identity could be reclaimed as essentially Muslim, and the secular state constructed as the culprit responsible for the subjugation, defeat, and conquest of the female body of the nation.

In sum, the beauty pageant of 1932 was an outstanding instance where multiple interventions with regard to the body of the beauty queen who had become the embodiment of the nation reveal the ways in which the new state used the female body to institute its project of nationalism and modernity. Later interventions illustrate that the confrontation between

Islamist and secularist national projects has taken place on the ground of the female body, upon which both parties have attempted to instill different discursive contours. These interventions have served to construct a new national subject, as represented by the female body, that is portrayed as in need of liberation and protection, and to establish or contest public-private distinctions as defined by covered or exposed body parts. The framing of the female/national body as in need of a protector and liberator has served to legitimize the transformative interventions and the larger modernization project, and the intervening subject has acquired political agency in the process.

Islamic Delineations of the Body: Unveiling and New Veiling

Constructing the self as a political agent by forging and presenting identities through the manipulation of women's images in the public sphere is not an exclusively secularist strategy. Islamists employed the exact same strategy in the 1990s, equally rigorously forging and manipulating images of Muslim women in the public sphere, thereby constituting themselves as Islamist political agents. Just as the secular state intervened and regulated the public appearance of bodies so as to constitute itself as the sole authority and the guardian of the nation, the Islamists of the 1990s likewise intervened and attempted to regulate the public visibility of women to acquire a similar sort of agency. Similar to the secular state that used the female body as the medium by which to promote and institutionalize its nationalist ideology and modernization project, the Islamists of the 1990s also used the female body to construct a new national subject and promote their own modernization project.

Whereas during its founding years the new state instituted its secularism through the unveiling of the female body, the Islamist elite of the 1990s instituted their Islamism by reveiling the female body, similarly using the body and its clothing as a site from which their nationalist project was articulated. This reveiling the female body was promoted by the Islamists as a sign of liberation of women and the nation from the oppression of the secular Westernizing state that denied the Turkish nation its own true culture and identity. This new Islamist elite of the 1990s, organized around the Refah Party, found political agency in designating the Islamic headscarf as the banner of their political campaign. Although these opposing forces used different frames of reference to form and institutionalize their own versions of national identity, I argue that the secularizing state and its Islamist rivals of the 1990s were equally modernist in generating nationalist modernity projects that employed similar techniques to implement their policies.

The use of the Islamic headscarf as part of the new veiling has been the central focus of political controversies in Turkey since it first became a matter of public debate in the mid-1980s. It was one of the primary reasons for the downfall of the coalition government led by the Islamist Refah Party following the National Security Council decree in 1997 and the cessation of the Refah Party in 1998. Secularist authorities, especially the military, saw the Islamic headscarf as a symbol of the rising threat of political Islam and urged the government to take a series of repressive measures, including tightening of the restrictions on the headscarf in schools and public offices.

The headscarf has become a symbol of political Islam not only in Turkey, but all over the world. The image of the veiled woman has become one of the most powerful tropes of Islamic fundamentalism in the Western media, becoming a more potent symbol of Islam than the mosque.[44] Although the mosque represents Islam as a religion, the image of the veiled woman is more easily associated with Islam as a potentially threatening force, a political ideology that can mobilize women to take up arms in defense of a state ideology, as in Iran. One of the benefits of using the veil as the symbol of political Islam instead of, say, the mosque, is that it allows for the presentation of a particular image of Islam as that which is hidden and mysterious: it is present, capable of action but not open, not accessible; it is behind covers. Hence, the veil allows for the mystification of political Islam, conveniently making it project fear and threat.

How is it that a simple item of clothing has become so loaded with ideological meaning that it not only brings down governments, but becomes an international symbol of a political ideology that is seen as a threat to world peace? It is the disruptive power of the veil that makes it such a potent symbol of an ideology and gives it such a vivid presence under both the national and the global gaze. The Islamic veil is meant to conceal all body parts except the face and the hands, which are the only body parts that can be visible to the public gaze. As such, the veil is a very visible inscription of Islamic norms of publicness and privacy upon the body. The reason the headscarf is particularly controversial is because in the Islamic dress code the headgear is to cover the hair and the neck, which are defined as private, whereas under secular codes these body parts are deemed public. There is no such contrast between the definitions of the public and the private for any other part of the body. For Islamists, to expose the hair and the neck to the public gaze is to reveal a woman's private parts, which are supposed to be revealed only to other women or to her husband in the privacy of her home. Under the heavily patriarchal values of Islam, a woman's private parts can be safeguarded only by her father or her husband, and their protection is the ultimate measure of a man's authority and honor. Hence, by demanding the removal of the veil, the secular state is seen as violating a woman's privacy, and also threatening the honor of her father or her husband, as well as the authority of Islam over her body.

For the wearers the new veiling is seen as an empowering tool that allows women to enter the secular public sphere by maintaining on their bodies the Islamic public-private distinctions. The new veiling is regularly justified by pious women who claim that they feel more secure and less threatened by men when they go out on the street (i.e., into the "public" sphere). For example, a woman writer in the conservative Islamist newspaper *Milli Gazete* notes, "The covering protects its wearer like a shield from being enslaved by all those eyes. It is only after [wearing the covering] that a woman acquires her true identity and belongs only to her husband who rightfully deserves her."[45]

Hence, the new veiling makes it possible for pious women to take up professions such as law or medicine or become active in politics alongside men by covering body parts that are deemed private according to Islam. In fact, the most ardent advocates of the new veiling are those who are sometimes referred to as "Islamist feminists," who claim that the headscarf allows Muslim women to have an active public life alongside men, so it is an important weapon in women's struggle against traditionalism, which seeks to confine women to their homes.[46] Indeed, a majority of male writers and journalists among Islamists voicing this patriarchal/traditional stance persistently declare that a woman's place is in the home, where she should be looking after children and being a good wife to her husband.[47] Hence, Islamist feminists see themselves as having to wage a struggle on two different fronts: one against the secular state, which is trying to either remove their veils or deny them presence in the public sphere, and the other against the traditionalist male-dominant view of Muslim women, which also denies them presence in the public sphere.

These views, which are frequently evoked by those who take up the new veiling, justify veiling as a means to avoid subjecting oneself to the male gaze in public. This view takes for granted that the public sphere is under the domination of the male gaze and that to appear in public, a women needs to protect her body from the probing, insulting, offensive male gaze. The Islamic code of dress, therefore, operates on the rigid assumption that the public is, by default, male. Since publicness is defined by that which is visible to the male gaze, the very act of veiling interpellates the public as an exclusively male subject. The new veiling serves to conceal the female body from the male gaze, and in doing so, it also reconstitutes the body as that which is inherently and naturally an object of male desire. In this respect, the new veiling has the effect of reproducing and naturalizing the power and authority of the male public gaze. Hence, the wearing of the veil ensures that the norms of publicness and privacy are absolutely subordinated to the power of the male gaze, the authority and privilege of which are granted and justified by Islam.

This argument against the new veiling is often raised by secularist feminists in justifying their demands that the headscarf be banned. However, it should be acknowledged that this argument holds true not only for the headscarf, but for any type of clothing that attempts to conceal or hide the sexuality of the female body. Some leftist-feminists of the 1970s for example, would refuse to wear makeup, tight clothes, or anything that would "sexualize" the appearance of women. This is why tight ponytails, loose and shabby clothes, and no makeup were the leftist style of the 1970s. This style was not so different from the Islamic veiling in that they have both been products of the attempt to conceal the sexuality of the female body, so they have both served to reproduce and reaffirm the power and authority of the male gaze, which, it has been assumed, has the natural capacity to define and constitute female bodies as sexual and desirable.

These and other similar attempts to conceal the sexuality of the female body are some of the many strategies by which women have tried to deal with the power and privilege of the male gaze in the public sphere. The headscarf is a strategy similar to that of the leftist style of the 1970s, drawing upon an Islamic frame of reference instead of a secularist one. Secularist-feminist criticism is not justified in singling out the headscarf as submitting to the dominance of the male gaze in public, because several secularist-feminist strategies also present the same dilemma in that they create what they oppose.

Therefore, while unveiling the female body breaks the authority of Islam in dictating the norms of publicness, reveiling it in the secular public sphere serves to reinsert Islamic norms, thereby disrupting the authority and power of secularism. This is how the veil becomes a disruptive force when it emerges in secular public spaces with its own Islamic norms of privacy, thereby unsettling established secular norms that define and constitute the public. When the Islamic headscarf appears in public spaces that are defined around the norm of secularism, such as the university, public offices, or the parliament, it forces an Islamic frame upon the public-private distinction, thereby displacing the secular one. In sum, the unsettling effect of the Islamic headscarf lies in its power to set its own definitions of and boundaries for the public and private, thereby undermining the authority of secularism.

The Islamic Headscarf: From Public Visibility to National Security

Starting in the mid-1980s, the Islamic headscarf came to be the main site of confrontation between Islamism and secularism in Turkey. Since the issue took on a confrontational character in 1987, it remained one of the top matters of public debate and anxiety and was presented as one of the main indicators of the "Islamic threat" in the justifications of various measures against political Islam, including the February 1997 National Security Council intervention. It was also among the top reasons stated as to why the Refah Party was being shut down by the Constitutional Court in January 1998.[48] Within a decade, the headscarf went from being a symbol of religious orientation to a top-priority national security issue.

The Islamic headscarf is distinguished as a part of the new veiling by the way in which the scarf is tied under the chin so as to conceal not only the hair but also the neck, falling over the shoulders, and worn with loose-fitting long dresses or overcoats. This is justified by reference to the Koran, the Hadith, and Sunni traditions. This type of Islamic attire is almost identical to the new veiling that is widespread in Egypt, which, as described by Arlene MacLeod, also emerged in the early 1980s and is specifically urban.[49]

In Turkey, the religious headscarf first became a matter of public debate in 1984, when the Higher Education Council (HEC) issued a decree stating that students were "allowed to enter classes and walk around [university] premises wearing the turban (türban), which is modern clothing."[50] Previous legislation had been prepared under the auspices of the military regime of 1980, which issued a dress code dictating that students and civil servants were forbidden to wear certain types of clothing, including beards and headscarves, in public premises and universities.[51] Seeing that this stipulation was causing major problems for students wearing the religious headscarf, whose numbers were not higher than 5 percent of the total student body at the time, the HEC found it necessary to provide leeway for these students, so that they could go to class without having to take off any garments. Apparently the authorities at the HEC thought that they could evade the political connotations of the Islamic headscarf by calling it a turban and defining it as "modern clothing." The word türban also meant headscarf, but it was commonly used to refer to the fashionable type of headscarf seen in the Parisian fashion shows, which, the authorities must have hoped, would be the least easily associated with Islamism. This rhetorical strategy was mainly an attempt to deny and erase any and all political meanings that the headscarf would bear, and instead establish it as a piece of secular "modern clothing," making it appear less threatening and even tolerable in the overbearing secularist discourse of the state.

By 1987, it was obvious that this rhetorical strategy had failed miserably. Even though the secularist media were now using the word *türban* to refer to the Islamic headscarf, the result was not the anticipated de-Islamization of the headscarf, but rather an Islamization of the word *türban*. The increasing numbers of students wearing the Islamic headscarf, now called a turban, on university campuses were attracting intolerant and aggressive responses from various secularist circles including university administrations and individual professors, who were personally asking these students to leave their classrooms.[52] The secularist media, especially the radically secularist *Cumhuriyet*, were making every effort to rid the word *türban* of the Islamic connotations it had acquired, so as to reinforce the authority and power of secularism to define the terms of public discourse, including the meaning of the headscarf. On 7 January 1987, the lead story of *Cumhuriyet* was "A Formula for the Turban," with an illustration that showed exactly how the permissible turban could be worn.

The picture shows a woman with a headscarf tied behind her neck, and the article notes that as long as the headscarf was not tied under the chin, it could be considered "modern clothing." The next day, a front-page piece titled "The Turban Cannot Be Worn for Religious Purposes" asserted:

Figure 2. "A Formula for the Turban" showed exactly how the permissible turban could be worn, tied up behind the neck and not under the chin (*Cumhuriyet*, 7 January 1987).

According to fashion designers, the turban is being misconceived. Experts point out that female university students whose pictures are appearing in newspapers are not wearing the turban but the *"sıkmabaş"* headscarf, and they add that the turban cannot be worn for religious purposes. The head-scarf is used to cover up the hair completely, and is tied under the chin. . . . Yet the purpose of the turban is not to hide the face but rather to reveal it completely. . . . Usually the hair is visible, sometimes let loose under the turban, or hanging down in curls from above it. The turban does not have a religious purpose. It is a chic, but a daring piece of fashion wear.[53]

In a similar attempt, a university dean tried to differentiate the modern turban from the religious headscarf by providing a prescriptive description of the turban: "1) Part of the hair must be visible in the front; if it is not visible, the turban must be pulled back so that it is visible; 2) some hair must be visible at the back; 3) the ear lobes must be visible."[54]

As these interventions illustrate, secularist officials and the media at-tempted to reframe and depoliticize the Islamic headscarf by revealing

Figure 3. "The Turban Cannot Be Worn for Religious Purposes" showed the ways a permissible turban could be tied (*Cumhuriyet*, 8 January 1987).

body parts, namely the hair and the neck, that are deemed private under Islamic codes, thereby keeping it from doing exactly what the Islamic veiling is supposed to do. Had these interventions succeeded, secularist authority to dictate the boundaries of the public and the private would have been maintained. However, secularist circles tried hard but failed to maintain the authority of secularism, and the Islamic headscarf continued to appear in public spaces covering the female body in accordance with Islamic notions of publicness and privacy. Whether called a *türban*, *sıkmabaş*, *çarşaf*,[55] or veil, the headscarf was increasingly worn by female students to cover their hair and necks as an explicit endorsement of the Islamic norms of publicness and privacy, and not as the fashionable "modern" and secularized turban tied behind the neck.

Therefore, the headscarf resisted secularist attempts at appropriation by establishing itself as undoubtedly Islamic. Realizing that the attempt to appropriate the headscarf into secularist discourse had failed, in December 1986 the Higher Education Council passed another decree that annulled the previous one on the grounds that "the turban had actually replaced the headscarf and it came to symbolize certain ideological orientations."[56] The new decree stated that students should wear "modern clothing" at all times on campuses and that interpretation of what "modern clothing" meant was for university administrations to decide. It was right after this decree, during January 1987, that the headscarf-turban dispute reached its peak. While most university administrations were adopting policies to ban the wearing of the headscarf on university campuses, the ambiguity of the definition of "modern clothing" was creating anxiety and frustration for all parties, particularly for students who were denied access to classes because of their questionable attire. When the head of the HEC, İhsan Doğramacı, was questioned about what "modern clothing" meant, he answered, "Go and look at Europe, whatever you see there is modern clothing."[57]

In most universities across the country, students were being forbidden to enter university premises and attend classes unless they took off their headscarves. The students responded with resistance and various demonstrations, protests, and petition campaigns. However, secularist circles had no intention of yielding to their demands for the removal of the ban. A prominent columnist writing in the secularist *Cumhuriyet* reflected the resolute and deep-seated hostility of the secularist discourse regarding the headscarf:

> If these young girls must cover their heads then they can quietly stay home and wait for a bigot husband like themselves! In that case no one would

have anything to say against them. In her home she can cover her head, or any other part of her as tightly as she wants. What do we care, what does the society care! But those girls who say, "*I want to have an education, I want to become a doctor, a lawyer, an engineer, a chemist, a state official or a teacher,*" there is only one path we can show them and that is the path of modern civilization.[58]

These words reflect the thoughts of many other unyielding secularists, who firmly believed that Islam should be confined to the realm of the private. What was at stake here for secularists was "modern civilization." In other words, the public visibility of Islam through the headscarf was perceived as a potential loss of modern civilization, which was, for the columnist, constitutive of the public sphere, the modern professions, and secularism.

Within secularist discourse, the activism of the students in defense of their headscarves was increasingly perceived as a direct threat to the state and the secular Constitutional system. A columnist wrote that, "the head-scarf battle is in fact a rebellion against Atatürk's reforms and the principles of the republican state Atatürk established."[59] Student groups protesting the "turban-ban" were frequently referred to as "proponents of the Shariat [Islamic Law]."[60] Another columnist wrote, "the turban has become the symbol of the pro-shariat movement and of antisecularism in our day."[61]

Facing such uncompromising hostility and coercion by secularist circles, the students nevertheless refused to leave their headscarves at home. They wanted to explicitly bear their Islamic identity *and* become lawyers, doctors, engineers, or teachers. They were insistently coming to school wearing their headscarves, and were either being turned away at the gate or were asked to leave the classrooms. In May 1987, fifty-eight students of the theology department at Ankara University received disciplinary suspensions for going to school with headscarves. The use of other restric-tive, disciplinary, and legal measures against the students ensued across the country. These measures triggered a wider and more resolute response from the students. Between 1987 and 1989, the number of demonstrations and protests grew. Refusing to take off their headscarves, students under-took petition campaigns, boycotts, and hunger strikes.[62]

Contrary to secularist expectations, these students did not resort to Koranic references or to requirements of a pious Muslim lifestyle in defense of their choice to wear the headscarf, but rather evoked liberal democratic values, namely freedom of conscience and individual rights. Their refer-ences to liberal democracy and individual rights did not necessarily indicate a genuine devotion to liberal values; however, they did indicate an endorsement of these values as the acceptable norm in politics.

As a result of the growing number of protests, in 1989 (and again in 1991) the Higher Education Council gave in and removed all restrictions on clothing, but this decision was annulled both times by the Constitutional Court. The decision of the Constitutional Court, which is still active today and is the basis of the ongoing restrictions on the headscarf, read as follows:

> The headscarf and the particular style of clothing that accompanies it, which lacks a modern appearance, is not an exemption but a tool of segregation. This situation, which is the display of a pre-modern image, is increasingly becoming widespread, and this is unacceptable in terms of the principles of secularism, reformism and the Republic. Using democratic principles to challenge secularism is the abuse of freedom of religion.[63]

As these words suggest, the appeal to a discourse of liberalism and democratic rights by the wearers of the headscarf has indeed left the secularist authorities on the defensive. This has resulted in more such articulations, where the principle of secularism is placed above and beyond democratic values, suggesting a form of secularist authoritarianism.

This decision set the tone for the subsequent interventions regarding the headscarf, and encouraged some university administrations to pursue tight regulations against students with headscarves. The public debate and ongoing demonstrations, changing regulations, campaigns, and protests continued until the National Security Council decree in February 1997, which called for a ban on the headscarf for all students and civil servants. This resolution was later fully endorsed by the government.

The Headscarf as the Banner of Islamism

Within less than two decades, the headscarf gained so much discursive momentum that it not only became the focus of some of the most effective demonstrations and protest movements in Turkey, but also became one of the main reasons for the shutdown of the Refah Party, which had won the highest percentage of votes in the 1995 elections; provoked the mobilization of various secularist circles and later the army to take action; and compelled the negotiation of the constitution.

While most scholarly research and media attention regarding the headscarf focuses on understanding why women wear this particular piece of clothing, it is quite obvious that the political effects of the headscarf go far beyond the specific intentions of the wearers. This study does not use ethnographic information on women taking up the new veiling and does not seek to make a claim about what such veiling means for the wearers. Even though this may come across as a further silencing of the voices of the wearers, it can be even more problematic to make generalizations about the reasons for wearing the veil based on the views of a particular group of veiled women. There are probably as many reasons why the veil is worn as there are wearers. Giving voice to and thereby privileging one or two of these meanings will inevitably silence the other, less potent meanings. That is why this study does not attempt to provide any "original" voices of the wearers of the veil. Instead, the analysis builds on the assumption that a lot more can be understood about the headscarf and its constitutive effects if the headscarf itself is made the object of study, and not the women who are wearing it. The methodology I pursue here focuses on tracing the effects of the headscarf as it appears in public displays and negotiations, rather then uncovering the reasons why women wear it.

It seems that the initial appearance of the Islamic headscarf in secular public spaces in the mid-1980s was the result of a spontaneous action rather than one that was orchestrated by Islamists as part of a political project. Regardless of whether it was worn solely in the name of Islamic piety or was adopted as the expression of some political ideal, the headscarf has given an undeniable visibility and presence to Islam in the secular public sphere. It was the wearing of the headscarf in a particular manner that came to be recognized as the mark of an Islamist ideology, and its appearance not just anyplace, but on the university campus—a monumental space of modernity and secularism—made it an issue of public controversy. In accordance with the official understanding of secularism, what was intolerable to secularist authorities was not that the headscarf represented Islam per se, but that this was a particular visibility of Islam in the public sphere that was not in compliance with official Islam and was not under the control of secularism. Emerging in secular public spaces as the sign of an autonomous interpretation of Islam that challenged the official version, the headscarf single-handedly undermined the authority of secularism over the public sphere.

However, the wearing of the Islamic headscarf did not remain this autonomous and spontaneous intervention in the public sphere. Soon after the headscarf controversy reached its peak in the late 1980s, the Refah Party emerged on the scene with a political program that designated the headscarf issue the top-priority item on its agenda. Members of the Refah Party were suddenly seen at rallies and public meetings declaring the party the gallant defender of the rights of students with headscarves who were being harassed by secularists. The Refah Party used the opportunity to define the headscarf controversy as a battle between secularism and Islamism, thereby turning the headscarf into the standard marking the battlefield on which their own battle would be fought. In other words, the Refah Party hijacked the headscarf from the women wearing it and declared it the symbol of their political ideology. Islamist writers started to call "all Muslims" to rally behind the headscarf, which, according to a columnist, was "akin to the national flag."[64]

Later, when Islamist circles were reassembling around the new political party, the Fazilet (Virtue) Party, formed after the shutdown of Refah Party in 1998, the Islamic headscarf was considered as a possible official party symbol.[65] The reason that this idea was later dropped was because, in the words of the Fazilet Party's leader, Recai Kutan, "it made the party look too feminine." It is telling that the headscarf, which was elevated to the status of the "national flag," was nevertheless seen as a mark of femininity with which the political elite of the party did not want to identify. The political agency had to remain masculine and unmarked.

Those in secularist circles, who were more than ready to designate the headscarf as a sign of the threat of Islamism, unhesitatingly accepted this new framing of the headscarf controversy by the Refah Party and acknowledged the headscarf as the undeniable symbol of political Islam. Hence, a new political paradigm was created that regrouped all political alignments around the secularist-Islamist divide, thereby designating it as the main axis of politics in Turkey. The faint voices of veiled women who were declaring that their headscarves were not an expression of a political ideology and that some were in fact against the Refah Party's political objectives were totally subsumed by and lost to the pervasiveness of this new paradigm.

Therefore, the image of the veiled woman started to be promoted in the public sphere by the Refah Party as a symbol of Islamist nationalism. The enthusiasm with which Islamist circles employed these images was demonstrated in the public rallies and gatherings of the Refah Party, where women were gathered up in the front and media attention was drawn to them. It was through the insertion of such images of veiled women into the public performances of the Refah Party that Islamism started to emerge as an alternative nationalist ideology. The promotion of the image of the veiled woman was surrounded by a powerful campaign that not only inscribed new national meaning on the female body, but, more important, produced a counterdiscourse of modernity within which a new nationalist ideology took shape. Designating the female body as the symbol of the nation, this new Islamist discourse used its medium to produce an alternative notion of nationhood. This nation was inherently and unarguably Muslim, and therefore its people deserved to live in accordance with Islamic values, norms, and principles. However, according to the Islamists, the secularist state had used and abused the female body as a symbol of its Westernization and modernization efforts to such an extent that it had come to represent everything but the Turkish woman, alienated from her own body and her own home, where she naturally belongs.[66]

Proliferating in publications, newspapers, and other sources of the Islamist media, this discourse produced the notion that the Turkish woman had lived a relatively happy life under the Ottoman state, where "her real place was her home and her basic duties were to be a mother, rear children and obey her husband in accordance with Islamic principles."[67] The secular state was projected as having subjected the female body to alienating and corrupting conditions by tearing woman away from her home and forcing her to take on careers and assume an equal place alongside men in the public sphere. By doing so, the Westernizing and modernizing interventions of the state had undermined woman's essential function as a mother and creator of the nation and had torn her away from her rightful cultural/Islamic roots. Hence, the secular state was incriminated for failing to protect motherhood, thereby undermining the very source from which the nation is generated, and alienating the nation from its true Islamic national culture. Islamists, on the other hand, were projected as the true protectors and saviors of the nation, who, by restoring the rightful status of woman in society as a mother, would restore the true cultural basis and source of the Turkish nation and bring it under their own guardianship.

The Refah Party's project was nationalist because it produced a new understanding of nationhood based on what it claimed was a common Ottoman-Islamic culture that the people of Turkey shared. As further illustrated in subsequent chapters, the Refah Party leadership promoted the idea of an Ottoman-Islamic civilization as Turkey's "true national culture" and national identity. The party's project advanced a new understanding of nationhood with a new national history, but the national community in question was made up of the existing citizens of the Turkish Republic living in the established national boundaries. In other words, the Refah Party's ideology did not challenge the boundaries of the established national community, nor did it seek to contest the basic constitutive principle of nationhood itself. Instead, it sought to come to power to govern and transform the existing "Turkish nation" and targeted all its citizens regardless of religious or political affiliation, not just pious followers of the Refah Party or members of the larger transnational Islamic community (the *umma*). They merely competed with secularists to govern the same nation. The female body, for them, also represented the Turkish nation, albeit conceptualized with a different identity, one that is essentially and primarily Muslim.

The Refah Party pursued a strategy similar to that of the founding state in promoting images of women to secure its own agency, but eventually they discouraged women's agency. The party's leadership, which had actively promoted the image of the veiled woman in all of its political campaigns, did not give a single administrative post to a woman during the 1994 local elections, nor did it promote women's candidacy in the parliamentary elections of 1995. The Islamist political elite found agency by vesting the headscarf with its own ideological meaning and manipulating the image of the veiled woman for its own political project. In other words, using the medium of the female body to achieve its goals, the Refah Party usurped the Islamic headscarf in order to develop and advance its new nationalist project. This intervention related to the female body was one that reveiled it so as to challenge the authority of secularism. Just as the unveiling of the female body during the founding years had allowed the new state to develop and advance its nationalist project, the reveiling of the female body by the Islamists in the 1990s enabled the Refah Party to formulate and promote an alternative, Islamist, nationalist project. Just as the public visibility of "modern women" in the early years of the republic had served to vest the state with political agency and to deny agency to women themselves, the headscarf had the exact same effect for the women wearing it. It served to vest the Islamist leadership with political agency at the cost of agency for the wearers of the headscarf. Just as the secular state had incriminated the Ottoman rule during the nation's founding years, this time the Islamists condemned the secular state as the culprit responsible for this harm done to the nation. Again, similarly, this strategy allowed the Islamists to establish themselves as the only agents capable of the protection and transformation of the nation toward a better future.

The Male Body, Erbakan's Versace Ties, and Islamic Haute Couture

Similarities between the new state of the founding years and the Islamists of the 1990s do not end with the mutual designation of the female body as the embodiment of the nation, interventions related to which served to create and promote a new national ideology. The male body was also employed toward similar goals, namely the construction of statesmanship as a modern, civilized, and competent mode of governance.

The Islamist intervention with regard to the male body was not nearly as pronounced as that of the Hat Law, but it nevertheless served similar purposes. During the mid-1990s, when the Refah Party was rising to prominence, its leader, Necmettin Erbakan, started to appear before the media in fashionable suits, noting his Versace ties, which soon became his trademark.[68] Similar to Atatürk, who had made a public appearance wearing a suit and a top hat, thereby inscribing on his own body the norms of "civilized" modern governance, Erbakan also used his own body to create an image of modern and competent Islamist statesmanship.

Erbakan's suits and trademark ties served a twofold function. First, they served to vest the Islamist elite with agency and ascribe to it the qualities of a competent leader who was capable of ruling and transforming society toward a new Islamist nationalist ideal. Whereas the Refah Party's political discourse advanced a new nationalist ideology that redefined the Turkish nation as an Ottoman-Islamic civilization, Erbakan's fashionable suits with Versace ties projected the leaders of this movement as modern subjects who not only knew the ways of Islam but were also equally competent in adopting modernity, along with Western values, ideals, and norms.

Second, this intervention with regard to the male body of the Islamist leadership served a crucial function toward unsettling the dominant view of Islamism as backward, "uncivilized," fundamentalist, incompetent, and lacking taste and culture. Refah circles were very much aware of the kind of snobbery they had been subjected to by secularists, who saw secularism and Westernism as the prerequisites for acquiring high-class "refined" tastes and cultural standards. Islamist writers often wrote critical remarks about the snobbery of secularist circles for their scornful accusations that Islamists lacked taste and cultural refinement. A columnist criticized secularists for just sitting there and scorning Refah Party circles for being "dressed like funeral parlor attendants" (*cenaze levazımatçısı kılıklı,* an idiom used to refer to men with a miserly and inept appearance) instead of doing something useful with their time, as Refah circles did.[69] This secularist snobbery that targeted the Islamist male subject sought to deprive the Islamists of the competency and agency of political leadership. In the face of such deprecation, Erbakan's fashionable suits and ties served to confute the image of the "funeral parlor attendant," instead projecting an image of the Islamist elite as competent and equally capable of displaying refined tastes and high cultural standards.

It was not only Erbakan's clothes that unsettled secularist projections of the Islamists as uncultured and lower class. In 1994 Erbakan threw a lavish wedding for his daughter at the Sheraton Hotel in Istanbul that was attended by hundreds of guests, among them models who had recently gone pious and started to wear Islamic headscarves with elegant garments. These models were still working in fashion shows, albeit ones that were organized by the newly emerging Islamic fashion industry. Images of these beautiful models attending the wedding dressed in elegant garments and highly stylish head coverings, wearing makeup and accompanied by their good-looking and equally elegant fiancés or husbands, scandalized secularist circles. These women in the new veiling and wearing makeup were not only in the company of men, but were sometimes even seen hand in hand with their male companions. These images were certainly incompatible with the dominant view of Islamic apparel as projecting a "barbaric posture" or the "funeral parlor attendant" look criticized by secularists. The parade of elegance and a refined sense of affluence at the wedding made it impossible to mark Islam as uncivilized, traditionalist, lower class, or tasteless.

The same year, the newly emerging Islamic fashion companies started to run large ads in newspapers and magazines portraying beautiful models wearing elegant dresses and stylish headscarves in compliance with the Islamic dress code. Tekbir Giyim, the leading company in Islamic fashion, started to hold Islamic fashion shows where top models would display the latest designs in what came to be Islamic haute couture.[70] The audiences consisted of both men and women watching the beautiful models as they walked up and down the catwalk, all in makeup and often wearing garments that were relatively tight-fitting. Note that the new veiling is supposed to involve loose-fitting dresses and overcoats so as to hide the contours of the female body, and makeup is certainly in defiance of the Islamic code.

The emergence of Islamic haute couture not only bewildered those in secularist circles, who were disarmed by the display of the possibility of such Islamic modernism, but also elicited an angry reaction from among Islamist circles. A majority of Islamist intellectuals, writers, and journalists flared at the companies that produced such garments and turned the headscarf from "an item of identity and political struggle" to an item of "fashion and high society."[71] They saw this transformation as a degeneration of Islamic attire and a dilution of the Islamist struggle.

Regardless of the reactions they elicited, these Islamic fashion shows played an important role in the creation of a new order of class hierarchies within an Islamic frame, which redefined norms of class status and broke

Figure 4. Models displaying the latest
in Islamic fashion (downloaded from
the *Tekbir Giyim* Web site, http://www
.tekbirgiyim.com.tr, 18 October 2003).

the claimed monopoly of secularism on high culture. In other words, the
emergence of Islamic haute couture served not only to destroy the secularist image of Islam as backward, barbaric, lower class, and lacking cultural
taste and aesthetic values, but also to advance the image of an Islamic
high culture. Through interventions with regard to both male and female
bodies, a new Islam-based standard of class distinction and an alternative
high culture were produced. Even though this development was criticized by Islamist intellectuals, there is no doubt that it served to further
strengthen Islamist political ideology by demonstrating that Islamism is
equally capable as secularism of producing an alternative high modernism
and normalizing it as a new mode of national high culture.

Uncovering the Islamic Body: The Case of the "Veiled Marilyn"

The clash between Islamism and secularism took a new and sensational
turn after the eruption of the Fadime Şahin scandal in January 1997. The
incident started with the arrest of the leader of a controversial mystical
order, Müslüm Gündüz, while he was in the privacy of his bedroom with

a woman. The arrest caught him while he was still in bed, when the police broke in with a large crowd of cameramen and reporters of the secular media. The next day pictures of the half-naked Müslüm Gündüz were all over the newspapers. The woman who had been in bed with him was Fadime Şahin, who was unofficially wed to him through an alleged private religious ceremony, the legitimacy of which was recognized neither by civil authorities nor by Islamic circles.[72] Fadime Şahin later "came out" and made public appearances on prime-time secular channels with her own version of the story, became the first woman with Islamic attire ever to become a media star in Turkey, and remained the top story in both the Islamic and secularist press and other media for several weeks.

Analysis of the Fadime Şahin case allows for the simultaneous examination of several themes raised in this study. It involves the contestations and redrawing of distinctions between public and private, the mapping of secularism and Islamism onto the public and the private realms, the designation of the female body as a site of the construction and negotiation of national identities, and the constitution of the secularist public gaze as the gaze of the male national subject. But, most important, it demonstrates how the female body is strategically used not only by the state but also by the media as a sign of the vulnerability and fragility of the national body that needs to be rescued and protected, thereby establishing the intervening subject as the heroic leader vested with agency and authority. In other words, Fadime Şahin became the damsel/nation in distress who needed to be rescued by the heroic knight/state (or other political power), in this case the secular media, which reestablished its authority to organize, monitor, and guide the life of the nation.

Analysis of the events that unfolded around the Fadime Şahin scandal reveals the significant function of the Islamic veil not only in symbolizing an ideology, but also in projecting Islam as a field of mystery, obscurity, and even perversion that operates to authorize the secular media to probe and intrude. The secular media often uses the word *veil* as the mark of the private. The two Turkish words used are *örtü* and *çarşaf*, which mean "covering" and "sheet," respectively. Therefore, the secular media often uses the phrase *what is behind the veil* to refer to what is covered up and closed to the public. The private is evoked here as that which is closed to the public gaze, but this closure takes the public as the reference and is not a finite closure in and of itself. In other words, the private realm is designated and defined by the public gaze, and therefore, any place, any idea, or any body or body part can be designated as closed to the public gaze and belonging to the realm of the private. Precisely because of this ambiguity and uncertainty surrounding the distinction between the public and the private, there is always a tension, an anxiety, around the "private," since it always bears the potential to be opened up and exposed. Hence, the private sphere turns into a site of desire, a site that the public gaze first recognizes as closed so as to mark its own difference as the open, the unenclosed, the public, but at the same time also constitutes the private as a site bearing mystery, desire, and allure. "Under the covers," "behind the curtain," "underneath the veil" are some of the images evoked by the secular media, which serve to constitute the private as that which is closed but also desirable and mysterious to the probing and overbearing gaze of the public.

Because Islam has already been confined to the private realm by the secular state and the media, it also emerges as a site full of mystery and desire, as well as sexuality, which is conveniently hidden and secured from the secular public gaze by nothing other than the veil. When the public visibility of women's bodies is added to the powerful mark of Islam, the headscarf, it is the body of the Islamic woman that comes to represent so many things at once. The mystery of Islam (especially mystical orders that have thrived on secrecy and concealment), the mystery of the private, and the mystery of concealed sexuality all converge on the body of the veiled woman, turning it into a site of desire, political confrontation, and interventions of both the Islamist and the secularist kind. These converging "mysteries" of the veil, concealing the private, Islam, and sexuality, have been confined to the realm of the private and mystified so as to constitute the gaze as public, male, and secular, vested with political agency desiring and able to lift the cover. The scandal that unfolded around Fadime Şahin is an outstanding instance illustrating this ongoing moment of the constitution of the secular public subject.

On 28 December 1996 the evening news programs were covering a rather odd story of the kind that had all the right elements for sensational journalism: sex, scandal, politics, and Islam. The police were breaking into an apartment to arrest Müslüm Gündüz, the leader of a controversial mystical order, the Aczmendis, to be interrogated about some of his public speeches. What was out of the ordinary was that the arrest was being made in Gündüz's bedroom, while he was in bed with a woman, whose identity was not revealed at the time. The arrest was being made in the company of a crowd of reporters, cameramen, and news photographers, who were taking shots of Gündüz while the police were preventing him from hiding away from the cameras.

Gündüz was already a popular figure in the secular media, having attracted attention because of the unconventional ways of the Aczmendi order. The Aczmendis wear large turbans and heavy gowns, have long beards, and carry long scepters, claiming that this was exactly the way the Prophet Mohammed was dressed. This order, with a small number of close-knit followers, claims to be a mystical Islamic order following the teachings of Said Nursi,[73] with Müslüm Gündüz standing as the leading sheik. However, within the network of popular Islamic mystical orders in Turkey, some of which have roots in Anatolia going back to the thirteenth century, the Aczmendi order is relatively new (established in 1987) and is not recognized as fully legitimate by the other well-established and popular orders, such as the Nakşibendi or the Nur movement. In particular, their insistence on carrying out some of their ritualistic meetings (zikir) publicly in mosques rather than in lodges (dergah, places designated particularly for ritualistic meetings of mystical orders), is seen as an improper abuse of mosques and an inappropriate public display by the more conventional Islamic circles. But it has been due to their spectacular and exaggerated appearance, their carnivalesque public displays, and the unsettling speeches of their leader[74] that the Aczmendis have been able to attract so much media attention.

The conditions of Gündüz's arrest and the appearance of his half-naked photographs in the secular press elicited an angry response in the Islamic media. The collaboration between the media and the police to break into a private bedroom was seen as an outrageous invasion of privacy and an act of "media terrorism."[75] Columnists were writing in fury, protesting the violation of Gündüz's right to privacy. However, no one was saying anything about the violation of the privacy of the woman who was with Gündüz and was subjected to the same demeaning circumstances. Gündüz claimed that she was his wife under an unofficial yet religiously legitimate wedlock, but the legitimacy of the wedding was later disputed by Islamic authorities. No one paid attention to this nameless figure in the background trying to hide from the cameras, and no one would have even remembered her presence if it had not been for a news program five days later, when she made a dramatic appearance in a live interview.

On 3 January 1997 at 7 p.m., television audiences across the country witnessed quite an unusual news story. A veiled woman was being interviewed in the studio, telling her story in tears. The woman was Fadime Şahin, a twenty-four-year-old university graduate and the alleged wife of Müslüm Gündüz, who was talking about how she was tricked into this fraudulent marriage, how she had joined mystical orders to seek religious enlightenment, how her ill-fated path had led her to the wrong people, who took advantage of her ignorance and naïveté. Apparently, Fadime

Müslüm Gündüz merkez dergâhın önünde.

Figure 5. The Aczmendis wear large turbans and heavy gowns, have long beards, and carry long scepters, claiming that this was the way Prophet Mohammed was dressed (*Radikal,* 14 January 1997).

Şahin had previously been a member of another mystical order similar to the Aczmendi group, whose leader had "forcefully married her."[76] Seeking help, advice, and redemption, she went to Müslüm Gündüz, who told her that he could help save her from her "evils within," but unless they were connected by the marital bond, he could not be in the same room with her or talk to her. When Fadime Şahin questioned his reasoning, he assured her that it was only a formality, that it would be a nonofficial religious marriage and that his strict religious convictions necessitated such a precondition. However, after the questionable ceremony, Müslüm Gündüz threatened her into having sex. While Fadime Şahin was telling this part of her story in tears, the camera zoomed close to her face, dramatizing her tears and creating a very intimate sight.

In the following days, secular newspapers and television stations reported that viewers from all over the country had called in to say that they felt sorry for Şahin, that they cried with her, and that they were furious about the things that were going on in these clandestine mystical orders. Şahin was lined up for interviews with other stations and newspapers, and she made similar appearances on various programs in the subsequent weeks. Within a matter of days Fadime Şahin appeared on every major news program of the secular stations, her pictures and interviews were on the front page of every newspaper, and a large group of cameramen and reporters were camping on her doorstep for days. For almost two months, Şahin's story remained right at the top of the agenda of public debate. Her story triggered discusson of various other issues, ranging from the problems of religious marriage to the legitimacy of mystical orders. The secular media had made Fadime Şahin a star, the first veiled media star in Turkey. While Müslüm Gündüz was tried and sent to prison for a variety of different charges, Fadime Şahin made a small fortune with the interviews she gave. A year later, at the end of 1997, the media were still talking about her when she published her memoirs revealing the details of her experiences with the mystical orders and how their leaders deceived her through false marriages in order to have sex.

In Turkey, it was quite uncommon, if not unprecedented, for a woman to publicly announce her sexual experiences during a news program. It was also unprecedented for a veiled woman to have so much air time on a news program (Şahin's confessional appearance lasted close to thirty minutes) to talk about anything, let alone her personal affairs. There have been several other cases of rape or scandalous affairs with political repercussions in Turkey, but none of the women involved were invited to television studios for live, half-hour interviews during prime-time news programs.

The reason that Şahin became an exception was precisely because she was veiled and was willing to allow the secular media to peep into the closed and "veiled" world of Islam. In a way, Fadime Şahin was helping the secular media to lift the veil—off of the covered world of Islam and also off of her body. This intervention of the secular media is well articulated by the Islamist writer Cihan Aktaş, who criticizes the media for abusing Fadime Şahin's story in order to present itself as a "hero and savior" of Muslim women. Aktaş writes that in the secular media

> the Muslim woman is imagined as an object waiting to be saved from the Muslims and the burden of the veil. The confessional regrets of women who perceive Islam as a religion for men are presented as religious sermons. This sermon continues as a publisher designates these women as "those who are standing up against oppression" and announces that "Muslim women are removing the veil of silence that conceals the world of Islam." . . . In this savior mentality, the "headscarf" is presented as a mistake and a deviation, whereas the wearer of the headscarf is presented as a victim waiting to be saved. In this "rescue" operation, the real party that is being saved is obviously the "savior" itself.[77]

Here Aktaş draws attention to the constitutive function of the way in which the secular media covered the Fadime Şahin story. By presenting itself as the savior of "abused Muslim women," an image that was constructed through displays of Fadime Şahin, the media constituted themselves as the secular male hero that steps in and saves unfortunate, victimized women from the deceitful, abusive, and aggressive hands of Islamist men. Here there were three different subject positions involved. The probing gaze of the media constructed the image of the "veiled woman" as the helpless, vulnerable female whose headscarf fails to protect her body from being subject to abuse and violation. They also constituted the Islamic male subject as the aggressive, deceitful threat to the vulnerable body of the female. By positioning these two images of the Islamic male and female subjects against each other (incarnated in the bodies of Müslüm Gündüz and Fadime Şahin, respectively), the media were able to constitute themselves as the secular male subject who has the power and agency to step in and "save" the helpless abused woman from the clutches of the aggressive Islamic male subject.

In the secularist construction of the story, both the Islamic female body and the Islamic male subject were presented as hiding behind the concealing veil of Islam, which failed miserably in both cases. It failed to protect the body of the female from abuse, and it failed to conceal the clandestine world of Islam from the probing gaze of the secular media.[78] In this respect, it is quite meaningful that one of the secularist newspapers covered the Fadime Şahin story with the headline "What Is Underneath the Covering?"[79] By presenting the veil as a covering imposed by Islam to protect itself from the probing gaze of the secular male subject, the secular

Figure 6. "The Veiled Marilyn" (*Aktüel*, 22 January 1997).

media found agency and power in removing the veil. Drawing attention to this point, Cihan Aktaş notes that "a woman who carried her veil as the articulation of freedom and confidence, rather than as an act of covering up and closure, would not have been a news event."[80]

The way in which the secularist male gaze made itself a heroic (and lustful) conqueror for lifting the veil and looking at what it concealed is revealingly illustrated in the way in which the popular weekly magazine *Aktüel* covered Fadime Şahin's story.[81] The picture on the cover was a collage photo, which had Fadime Şahin's head on the body of a model wearing the same overcoat, but with a wind blowing from below throwing open her coat and revealing her legs, in a pose reminiscent of a famous photo of Marilyn Monroe.

The story was titled "The Veiled Marilyn," and the subtitle on the cover read: "We've Become Peeping Toms as a Nation: Our Eyes Are in Fadime's Bedroom." This illustration on the cover of *Aktüel* was displayed on every newsstand all over Turkey. Every copy stood as yet another constitutive moment of the national secular male gaze, a testament to its power to probe into "Fadime's bedroom" as well as her private life, her soul, and her body. The secular male subject found agency and power in opening up the Islamic female body to the public gaze.

However, the conquest of the Islamic body by the secular male gaze was not quite fully successful. Various subtle and explicit attempts of the secular media to get Fadime Şahin to remove her headscarf failed. Stories were published about her decision as to whether to unveil. Photographs of a woman without a headscarf appeared with claims that they were of Şahin, all of which turned out to be fake.[82] In an interview conducted a year after the incident, the reporter insistently asked her questions such as "Why are you still wearing the headscarf?" and "Is it because of pressures from your family, because of your social circles, or because of the media?" and speculating, "It looks like you are going to take it off soon."[83] In response, Fadime Şahin said she was wearing the headscarf not for anyone else, but for Allah, and that she would not take it off because "it does not have any weight, [it is not a burden]," and it is a part of her.

Fadime Şahin remained veiled and popular, whereas Müslüm Gündüz ended up in prison serving a sentence for abusing religion and involvement in illegal organizational activity against the secular state.

3

Cities, Squares, and Statues:

The Use of Public Space in the Making of the Nation

An essential component of nationalist projects that seek to institute a new sense of nationhood and define a new national subject is the construction of national space. The institutionalization of a sense of nationhood requires that the nation be thought of as a finite community of people living on clearly demarcated land. The sense of singularity and unity that is so essential to the making of a nation is relevant not only to the people constituting the nation, but also to the land upon which they live. Therefore, the creation of a sense of unified territory becomes a vital component of nation building, such that what are otherwise disconnected and arbitrary places come to be imagined as a unified, monolithic, single piece of land on which a single nation resides and over which a single state rules. In other words, nationhood is not only about the collective imagination of a national community, but also about the imagination of national space. Hence, cities, spaces, and places take the center stage in the construction of a new sense of nationhood or in the emergence and advancement of alternative nationalist projects.

The use of social space in the creation of a nation-state is most explicitly evident in various monuments, museums, memorials, monumental structures, and statues scattered around a city. There is not one city in Turkey that does not have at least one square with Mustafa Kemal Atatürk's statue at its center, marking not only the center of the city but also the center of the nation. As the founder of the Republic of Turkey, Atatürk is an assertively promoted symbol of the nation, whose picture is present in every public office and every school, with busts or statues in squares, public buildings, and schools throughout the country. Atatürk's mausoleum, Anıtkabir, was completed in 1953 in Ankara as a memorial that would "represent the Turkish nation in the name and person of Atatürk,"[1] thereby locating the center of the nation in the new capital city. Allegiance to the Turkish nation and its constituent principles, namely secularism and Turkish nationalism, came to be measured by allegiance to these iconic images of Atatürk, the symbol of the nation. Therefore, acts of vandalism against Atatürk's busts and statues are taken as assaults against the nation and the state and are often treated as acts of violence against the nation and the state.

The placement of such statues and monuments in city spaces is one of the interventions that seek to create new spaces or rearrange, relocate, or rebuild existing ones, serving several functions. First, such interventions seek to give material form to a nationalist project. A new sense of nationhood comes to life and is reified through the erection and placement of symbols of the nation in urban spaces. The placement of monuments and icons of the nation becomes one of the essential means through which the national ideology finds material presence and authority in public life. The placement of such marks serves to organize and reconstitute public life around national norms, thereby nationalizing the public sphere.

Second, such interventions serve to establish the victory and authority of the official national ideology over its alternatives. The designation of Ankara as the capital city in 1923 to replace Istanbul was itself a declaration of the triumph of the new secular nationalist ideology advanced by Atatürk against Ottomanism, its main contender, which was centered in Istanbul. Similarly, the monuments and statues placed in significant city spaces stand as testaments to the victory of official nationalism over its contenders. The particular object that is selected as representing the nation (for example, Atatürk's iconic figure), the ways in which it is displayed, and how it is evoked in official nationalist discourse frames the whole display as a victory and prevalence of one nationalist ideology over others. In this case, the prolific presence of Atatürk's image signifies the prevalence of secular Turkish nationalism over its contenders, such as Islamist and Kurdish challenges. For example, in 1996 an officer of the Turkish military (an adamantly secularist institution) personally supervised the erection of a statue of Atatürk in a local square in Sultanbeyli, one of the districts of Istanbul, whose inhabitants had voted predominantly for the Islamist political party, the Refah Party. In this case, the placement of Atatürk's statue came as a forceful imposition of secular nationalism in an Islamicized district in an attempt to reestablish the power and authority of secularism as an uncontestable norm and defining mark of the nation. The iconic figure of Atatürk has become the most potent symbol of official nationalist ideology not only for the state, but also for contending ideologies. For example, Atatürk's statues and busts are often subjected to vandalism by radical Islamist protesters, who recognize them as symbols of secular Turkish nationalism as well.

Third, interventions related to places serve to create a sense of unified national territory. This function is particularly evident in the making of the capital city. The mere declaration of a capital serves to project the nation as a singular entity that can have only one center, and it allows for the demonstration of the consolidation of state power, which in the case of Turkey is to govern the nation through a single representative body, the parliament, housed in the capital city. Also, in the case of Ankara, the making of a new capital city served the homogenization of urban space and national land, with Ankara functioning as a model national city after which various other towns and cities across the country were designed. Furthermore, interventions that inscribe the signs of the nation on public places imbue them with national meaning, thereby connecting those particular locations to the larger national territory. The erection of a statue of Atatürk in the central square of a city not only serves to solidify the city around its center, constituted by the sign of the nation, but also connects it to the national territory, thereby constituting it as a part of the larger national land. Likewise, Atatürk's mausoleum at the center of Ankara not only constitutes the city as consolidated around a nationally defined center, but also serves to constitute the city as the center of the larger national territory, marking it as the capital.

Fourth, interventions related to places are one of the most effective means through which the intervening subject constructs itself as the ruling power. The state constructs itself by opening up new spaces, closing others, inscribing them with the marks and symbols of state power, and organizing urban space in accordance with official national ideology. Therefore, interventions in places become self-constitutive acts. The state intervenes to control space, to dictate the meaning of urbanity, to shape the evolution of the public sphere, and to suppress contending ideologies. It does so by strategically placing squares, parks, statues and monuments, cultural centers, and public buildings; by monitoring architectural styles; by dictating urban design and development agendas. Through such interventions, the state acquires agency and power to control and dictate the norms that guide daily public life, thereby constituting itself as the agent of modernity that inscribes the nation into space.

This chapter explores the making and negotiation of Turkish modernity and national ideology through the use and arrangement of cities and urban spaces. After discussing the role of Ankara and Istanbul in the formation of the new state and the institutionalization of a new national ideology, I examine the ways in which public places in Istanbul became the medium through which Islamism produced and attempted to institutionalize an alternative nationalist ideology. In its interventions in various sites of the city between 1994 and 1998, the Istanbul city administration, run by the Islamist Refah Party, formulated and promoted an alternative nationalist ideology that defined the Turkish nation as an Ottoman-Islamic civilization in contrast to official Turkish-secular national ideology. This Islamist alternative challenged the official ideology, which took West-oriented modernity and secularism as a constitutional basis, by producing and displaying the national subject as essentially Eastern, Ottoman, authentically local, and Islamic. This alternative identity later lost ground and eventually fell out of public circulation after the popular Mayor Recep Tayyip Erdoğan was removed from office in 1998, but remained as the ideological basis of the Islamist movement gathered around Erdoğan that later split from the Refah/Fazilet Party and reorganized in the Adalet ve Kalkınma (AK) (Justice and Development) Party.

Just as official nationalism involved the use of cities and public spaces as some of the main sites for the establishment of a new sense of nationhood, in the 1990s the Islamists also made use of city spaces to construct an alternative sense of nationhood. I argue that both secularists and Islamists used similar strategies to implement their nationalist ideologies when they designated a particular city as the center of their notion of nationhood. In the case of secularists, this city was Ankara, which was declared the capital city in 1923 and was quickly built from scratch with the vision of the founding nationalist ideology. The new state diverted a large chunk of its scarce resources to the creation of a modern, secular, national city out of an insignificant little town. For the Islamists of the 1990s, the city that represented the heart and soul of the nation was not Ankara but Istanbul, which was declared the center of the Ottoman-Islamic civilization that marked the true identity of the Turkish nation. In both cases, the immediate past or the present conditions of these places that were treated as the temple-cities of their respective national ideologies were portrayed as in dire need of an emancipator and protector. In both cases, the intervening subjects constructed themselves as the agents of liberation and transformation who had the will and power to bring their designated national city under their guardianship and introduce the needed changes.

In its founding years the new state built the city of Ankara as a new place wherein the nation could live the "modern, civilized" life that it deserved, which had been denied to it under the Ottomans. The Ottoman state was projected as the main culprit responsible for the calamity that the nation had suffered, particularly when it left the national land defenseless and opened it up to conquest by the colonial powers at the end of World War I. This projection of the Ottoman as the evildoer and the national land as the victim allowed the new state to construct itself as the political agent that had valiantly come to the rescue of the land and the nation, for which it provided a new sense of place and a new sense of belonging.

Islamists pursued a similar strategy in the 1990s when they started to project an image of Istanbul as the capital of the Ottoman-Islamic civilization and the center of the "real" Turkish nation in contrast to Ankara. The secularist state residing in Ankara was projected as having deprived the nation of effective governance and detached it from its own cultural roots through imitative and alienating Westernizing policies. The city of Istanbul was portrayed as the heart and soul of the nation, which had been subject to oppressive and dismal conditions and lost its true identity, and could be restored only by the Islamist leadership. I argue that these Islamist interventions related to places were similarly modernizationist in producing a discourse that defamed the present conditions of the nation and established the Islamist party as the agent of modernity that sought to liberate and transform the nation and guide it to its rightful place in the future.

A crucial element in the implementation of both the founding and the Islamist nationalist ideologies was that they evoked not only local but also global audiences. The implication of a global audience is not a coincidental offshoot of the formation and display of national identities that happen to take place in globally exposed locations; rather, this global dimension is *constitutive*—and in that respect, essential—in the making and implementation of official and alternative national ideologies. In other words, these subjectivities are formed and staged the way they are and in those particular locations precisely because of the presence of the global gaze in those places. It is through acknowledgment and affirmation by the global gaze that national identities come into being and seek to attain legitimacy and recognition.

Centering the Nation: Ankara and Anıtkabir

The use of cities and city spaces in the building of a new nation-state in Turkey was prevalent throughout the initial years of the republic. Starting in 1923, the building of a new state involved not only the establishment of new state institutions but also the development of a new sense of nationhood and the creation of a nation over which the state would rule and through which it would legitimize its power and authority. The image of this new nation found shape through various means, ranging from the writing of a new national history to the making of new social and political institutions, starting with the constitution. One of the important media for the creation of this new sense of nationhood has been the use and rearrangement of cities and city spaces.

First and foremost, the changing of the capital from Istanbul to Ankara was one of the crucial steps declaring the identity of the new Turkish state. The new nation was being founded upon new norms that celebrated Turkish nationalism, in contrast to an Ottoman identity, and endorsed a West-oriented, secular, and modern political system in contrast to an Islamic model. The centering of the nation around such new norms found its expression in the declaration of Ankara as the new capital of the republic in 1923. The center of the city, which later became Ulus Square, was designated by the placement of the National Assembly building where the republic was declared into being in 1923 by Mustafa Kemal Atatürk. Hence, the center of the capital city and of the new nation was constituted by this act of declaration.

Ankara was chosen as the capital not only for geographic or strategic reasons. It was important that Ankara did not bear any significant marks of Islam and had not played an important role in either Ottoman or Islamic history. Although it had developed in the sixteenth and seventeenth centuries as a small town of commerce and agriculture, it had lost most of its population to a famine and then a big fire at the end of the nineteenth century. It was only after the introduction of the railroad that the town found life again. Therefore, what of this small town had been carried into the twentieth century was very much a product of modern times. For the founders of the new republic, no other place could better serve as the site at which to establish a new secular state that wanted to distance itself as far as possible from its immediate precursor, the Ottoman state, and to build itself as a new and modern state totally dissociated from Islam and Ottoman times. Ankara bore no visible Islamic-Ottoman mark, therefore serving as an ideal location for the building of a city that would rise as the embodiment of the secularism, modernity, and a West-oriented sense of civilization that constituted the main principles of the founding ideology. In the proposal submitted to the Grand National Assembly in 1923 that would establish Ankara as the capital, it was said that Ankara would better serve as the administrative center of the republic when "the foundational basis of the new Turkey" was taken into consideration.[2]

The building of Ankara started with the city center, the central square from which the rest of the city would expand. Marking the center of the nation, this square was initially given the name Hakimiyet-i Milliye Meydanı (National Sovereignty Square), but it later became Ulus Meydanı (The Nation Square). Ulus Square stood at the intersection of İstasyon (Station) Avenue and Atatürk Boulevard (constituting the city's north-south axis), marked at its center by the Victory Monument and encircled by buildings and other structures representing the key axes of the new republic. These included the parliament building, the Ankara Palas Hotel, Sümerbank (a state-owned textiles and apparel company), and Türkiye İş Bankası (the Turkish Business Bank, Turkey's first private bank, founded with state support in 1924).[3] The final landmark, which faced the square from the bottom of Station Avenue, was the central train station, where railroads from all over Turkey converged when they were completed by 1933. This placement of the train station down the road extending in front of the parliament building accentuated the national significance of Ulus Square, which was now located not only at the intersection of the main axes of the city, but also at the point of convergence of national territory.

The parliament building was significant both because it was the gathering space for the nation through its representatives and because its courtyard was used as the central ceremonial and meeting place, particularly for the head of the state to address citizens and announce important legislation and various reforms. This area was also used for the public execution (hanging) of the Independence Tribunal convicts, who were condemned for resisting or opposing Atatürk's reforms, for collaborating with the occupying forces and the Ottoman ruler in Istanbul during the war, or for leading insurgencies—often based on Islam—in Anatolia.[4] These public executions were performed using state authority and power to incriminate alternative political ideologies and projects, particularly Islamism and Ottomanism.

Hence, the parliament building representing state power and authority gave Ulus Square its most prominent meaning as the political center of the nation, where the state would call its nation into being and constitute itself as its legitimate ruler. Standing nearby was Ankara Palas, which was a hotel commissioned by Atatürk himself to serve as the official guesthouse and represented the state's commitment to modernization, understood at the time as adhering to the universal norm of civilization. Ankara Palas became the main social space of the new republic, where the West-oriented secular modern lifestyle of the republican elite was engaged in and displayed. The annual Republic Banquets held on 29 October to commemorate the foundation of the republic, New Year balls, and other similar occasions held there became the main axis of social life in Ankara, where the new republican elite gathered to display the new national culture and lifestyle. Atatürk himself was often the central figure at these receptions and banquets, dressed in fashionable tuxedos and top hats, accompanied either by his wife or one of his adopted daughters, dressed in elegant evening gowns.

The state textile company Sümerbank and the first private bank, Türkiye İş Bankası, stood on the other side of the square, which together represented the state's resolve to build an industrial base for a national economy. These two buildings stood near the parliament as testaments to the commitment of the state to tend to the economic well-being of the nation, and they pointed to yet another failure of the Ottoman state to do so.

The most prominent structure on Ulus Square was the Victory Monument, which inscribed the most potent sign of the nation on the square. Standing tall at the center of the square, the monument was completed and erected in 1927 to commemorate the war of independence that had been fought and won under the leadership of Mustafa Kemal Atatürk. The rules for the competition that was used to find a design for the Victory Monument had specifically stated this theme and pointed out in its thematic description that the monument should reflect Turkey's great victory not only against the outside enemy (namely the European colonial powers), but also against the enemy inside, which had been the "Ottoman rule in Istanbul that conspired [against the Turkish nation] in collaboration with the enemy."[5] Reliefs and several quotations from Atatürk's speeches carved on both sides of the monument depicted the war fought against both these enemies. These inscriptions were yet another framing of the Ottoman state as the culprit responsible for the catastrophe that the Turkish nation had suffered, and located the source of this suffering in Istanbul, where the Ottoman ruler resided. The Victory Monument carved this incrimination of the Ottoman rule and of Istanbul into stone and inscribed it in the heart of Ankara.

Standing at the center of the monument is the iconic figure of Atatürk in military outfit, riding a horse on top of a tall pedestal overlooking the city that extends downward from underneath the monument. The height and the strategic positioning of this monument placed the newly emerging city under the gaze of Atatürk, as if he was closely monitoring the growth of the new city under his feet, overseeing the development of Turkish modernity and nationalism in the direction he ordained.

Below the equestrian figure of Atatürk, three figures stand in the three lower corners of the pedestal representing the Turkish nation: two soldiers and a peasant woman carrying a cannon on her shoulders. This peasant woman later became a prototypical figure and proliferated in numerous national monuments, poetry, paintings, and narrations of the War of Independence. On the front face of the bottom platform were the figures of two wolves, making a reference to the gray wolf, an idol appropriated from ancient Turkish mythology, which were later removed when the monument was moved to a new location on the square. The wolves made reference to the ethnic roots of official nationalism, which locates the origins of the Turkish nation in pre-Islamic central Asia. The two soldiers and the peasant woman represented the "unnamed heroes" who had selflessly served their country and took their place on the Victory Monument alongside Atatürk as the gendered archetypes of the ideal citizen. During the inaugural ceremony, the spokesperson asked the spectators to "look carefully, because everyone would see themselves" in these three figures, and he described one of the soldiers as representing the wisdom and agility of the nation, the other its gallantry and valor.[6] The figure of the peasant woman standing at the back was singled out as "the Turkish woman, carrying the cannon to the front, holding it as if she is holding her baby; because she knows that the cannon means life to her child, pride to her husband and honor to her nation." These portrayals are typically gendered constructions of modern patriarchal citizenship, which assigns differential roles to men and women. For men, the most honorable national duty is to serve as soldiers to protect national territory, whereas for women it is motherhood, which earns them the ideal citizen status. Note that motherhood can either be in the form of bearing children or in the form of bearing and caring for—but not using—the sign of masculine power (the cannon). Therefore, the Victory Monument establishes norms of national belonging where the feminine mark of citizenship is established as the reproduction and preservation of the nation, whereas fighting for one's country becomes its masculine mark.[7]

Many years later, with the expansion of business and public buildings toward the South, the center of Ankara was relocated around Kızılay. But when Atatürk's mausoleum, Anıtkabir, was built in 1944, it emerged as the undeniable symbolic center of the city and the heart of the nation.[8]

A year after Atatürk died in 1938, a parliamentary commission was set up to oversee the building of the mausoleum, and the commission decided on Rasattepe for its location. This place, which later took the name Anıttepe (Monument-Hill), was chosen precisely because it was in a very central location and also on one of the few hills in the area, which would allow for the monument to be visible from all around the city. A member of the commission said:

> Rasattepe is like a star in the middle of a crescent reaching from Dikmen to Etlik [the southern and the northern corners of the city, respectively]. If Anıtkabir is built here, it will be as if the city of Ankara has opened its arms wide to welcome Atatürk into its bosom. Hence, we will have Atatürk rest right in the middle of the star of the crescent on our flag.[9]

Therefore, what used to be an ordinary piece of hill came to be laden with much national significance, as it was designated Atatürk's burial site. The mausoleum was to become an inscription upon this hill, marking it as the center of the capital and the country, as well as the center of the national flag, which mapped the nation upon the city of Ankara, at the heart of which Atatürk's body would be resting.

Among twenty-seven projects whose designers were competing for the building of the monument, the Onat-Arda proposal won, both because both architects were Turkish and because theirs was the only project that "reflected the antique roots of Anatolia" rather than Ottoman-Islamic traditions.[10] The architectural plans for the mausoleum were changed many times after the project was initially accepted, eventually yielding an eclectic architectural style that makes it difficult to associate with a specific locality or culture. This style and design was congruent with the dominant understanding at the time, which took modernity as a universal standard that is beyond the confines of time and any given style.[11] Therefore, the architectural style of the monument reflected the endorsement of modernity and its universalist principles. Yet the idea of a "mausoleum" itself made reference to pre-Islamic and especially Greek-Anatolian traditions, and this cultural specificity certainly expressed a deliberate disassociation from Islamic references. In other words, the endorsement of modernity and universalism found expression in a sharp distancing of the new national norms and principles that dictated a new lifestyle, urban design, and aesthetic values from Islam and Ottoman traditions. Therefore, the mausoleum has been a firm articulation of the secular, modern, national aspirations of the new nation-state, marking the center of the capital city, Ankara.

Even though Anıtkabir is a burial site, which is a sacred location that would customarily be under the jurisdiction and authority of Islam, there are no religious inscriptions or any sign of Islam on any part of the monument. The only place that makes a reference to Islam is the burial chamber where Atatürk's body rests, which is oriented toward the *qibla*, the holy direction toward which prayers are oriented in Islam. However, this chamber is underground, below the symbolic sarcophagus, a pre-Islamic, ancient Greek-Anatolian form of burial, before which visitors pay homage to Atatürk and the nation, and official ceremonies are held. Furthermore, visiting the burial chamber is nearly impossible in that it requires a special permit from the chief of the military staff that is very rarely given. In other words, the only reference made to Islam in the mausoleum is buried underground, is hidden from and inaccessible to regular visitors and the public at large. Therefore, the mausoleum stands as an articulation of the triumph of the secularist ideology of the state over its Ottoman-Islamic contender, expressed through the ability and authority of secularism to totally displace and remove the marks of Islamic and Ottoman influences on this burial site of the utmost national significance.

The careful removal of Ottoman-Islamic influences from the national space of the mausoleum is reflected in its internal design and wall decorations as well. All inscriptions on the walls, mostly quotations from Atatürk's various speeches, are in the new Turkish alphabet, which uses Roman letters introduced by Atatürk himself, replacing the former Arabic script. The designs and carvings on the walls are mostly from Anatolian rug designs, which represent secular rural life and are not associated with Islam. The burial chamber located underneath the mausoleum is made of marble brought from different Anatolian cities; and the red marble coffin in the middle is surrounded by brass pots, each carrying a sample of soil brought from every province of Turkey and Northern Cyprus. This collection of marble and soil samples that are brought together around Atatürk's body no doubt signify the territorial unity of the nation and place at its center the iconic body of Atatürk, which has become the embodiment of the foundational ideology. In other words, Atatürk's burial chamber is a monumental articulation of a nation unified around the founding principles of modernity, Turkish nationalism, and secularism.

Even though the building of Ankara as the new capital city was an absolute priority for the new state, nationalization of the land did not stop there. Other towns across the country needed to be transformed into national cities as well. Unlike Ankara, most of these towns had thrived under Ottoman rule and bore several Ottoman and Islamic characteristics.

The typical Ottoman town would be clustered around a central public square marked by the main mosque, which would be surrounded by the marketplace, shops, inns, and lodges. Hence, in Ottoman towns Islam constituted the central organizing force around which a sense of community took shape and public life was organized. The founder of the republic decided to use Ankara as the model city after which other towns would be designed and transformed into national cities. Just as the Ulus Square was designated in Ankara, a new location was designated in each of these towns to become the city center and displace the former center established around the main mosque. Just as the Victory Monument marked the city center in Ankara, each of these new city centers was marked by a similar statue or a monument of Atatürk and invariably named Republic Square.[12] As in Ankara, the placement of these monuments was accompanied by the building of new governmental and municipal buildings, police headquarters, and other offices representing the secular power of the state, as well as the central train station. While other insertions in these new city centers primarily served a metaphorical function, nationalizing the city and making it part of the larger national land, the placement of the train station near each Republic Square served to physically connect the city to the rest of the national land and particularly its center, the capital.

This relocation of city centers by insertion of the marks of Turkish nationalism and state authority not only dislocated the central role Islam had played in defining cities and their communities, but also allowed the establishment of a new sense of secular-national community in its place. The standardization of urban design and development across the country, taking Ankara as the model, served to create a sense of national unity and homogeneity consolidated around the "heart" of the nation in the capital city, to which cities across the country were connected via a network of railroads. Among these nationalizing cities and towns, Istanbul proved to be the most difficult challenge due to the pervasive presence of Ottoman state power and the authority of Islam.

Recentering Istanbul: The Taksim Republic Square

Although the center of the new nation was relocated in Ankara, Istanbul still stood as the most important city of the republic, with its historical and cultural diversity, its globally exposed location as the business and cultural capital of the country, and its status of having served as the capital of the Ottoman Empire for almost five centuries. The founders of the republic had declared Ankara the center of the new nation and stood in stark opposition to Istanbul and what it represented, but the world would still be looking at was happening in Istanbul to observe the face of this new republic. Ankara itself bore no significant marks of Islam and Ottoman times, but Istanbul was so full of such marks that it was impossible for them to be hidden or underemphasized in any way. Grand mosques standing tall as reigning monuments of Islam and glorious palaces and mansions testifying to the imperial authority of the Ottoman state were visible from all over the city. Laced with water fountains, tombs, small mosques, lodges, and monuments, every street, corner, and square of the old city was heavily laden with Ottoman and Islamic marks. This pronounced presence of symbols and marks of the Ottoman-Islamic reign made the articulation of the new national identity in the city difficult. When the Ottomans had conquered the city of Istanbul in 1453, they had expressed their triumph and ultimate authority over the formerly Byzantine city by simply overtaking the center of the city and the central symbol of state power, Hagia-Sophia Church. Hagia-Sophia was then converted into a mosque, and a bigger mosque was built right across the square, so as to overshadow this central monument of the East-Roman imperial authority with Ottoman power (namely, the famous Sultanahmet Mosque, also known as the Blue Mosque, which is the only mosque in the world with six minarets). Hence, what had been the center of the Byzantine Empire became the center of the Ottoman Empire with the inscription of the marks of Islam upon the central square. For the next five hundred years, Sultanahmet Square remained the center of the city as well as the empire, expanding with the main monuments of Ottoman reign.

The new Turkish Republic chose a different venue. Instead of overtaking or overshadowing such monuments of Ottoman dominion, the new authorities of the secular republic decided to relocate the center of the city to a neutral location and inscribe the symbols of the new republic on a clean slate. This location was Taksim Square, a place that was on a hill, sufficiently far from Sultanahmet yet still within the city limits, from which the grand mosques of the "old city" were not visible. The only significant structure in Taksim that gave the square its name was that housing the city's water distribution system, built in 1732. This building was the only structure in the area related to Ottoman rule and did not have any religious significance. There were no significant marks of Islam or Ottoman political power in the area. Furthermore, Taksim was adjacent to the district where a majority of the non-Muslim population of the city lived and was in fact surrounded by Istanbul's main churches and synagogues, which served these communities. Hence, what was visible around Taksim Square were signs of non-Muslim cultures and European influences rather than mosques and signs of an Ottoman presence. In other words, relocation of the city center to Taksim allowed for sufficient distance to be set between the new city center and the Ottoman-Islamic center both in geographic terms and in cultural terms.

The old city center, Sultanahmet Square, gradually became a tourism enclave, which was neatly packaged and presented for the tourist gaze as part of the old and distant past as if to deny its existence outside of this enclave. The Hagia-Sophia Church/Mosque was turned into a museum, together with the Topkapı Palace and several other structures in the area, where once the imperial power of the Ottoman dynasty had reigned. The museumification of Sultanahmet Square represents the power of the secular republic to enclose the Ottoman era and its culture and confine them to a spatially as well as temporally remote area. What had been the center of a vast empire for five centuries was suddenly designated an adjacent district that no longer bore any political viability or national significance for the newly forming secular republic.

The designation of the Taksim area as the new center of Istanbul was to be marked by the erection of a national monument at its center. The famous Republic Monument was built and erected in 1928. Thereafter the official name of the place was Taksim Republic Square, which designated the new center of Istanbul by the inscription on it of the mark of the nation, the Republic Monument. This monument has two sides, one composed of a group of soldiers and generals, depicting the War of Independence, and the opposite side depicting the founders of the republic, both groups led by the central figure, M. K. Atatürk, whose image stands at the front of each group. On the military side, Atatürk is in his military uniform, and on the side depicting the political leadership, Atatürk and his cohorts are in modern civilian clothing. Therefore, the monument signifies the formation of a new independent state founded not only upon a military victory, but also upon the norms of modernity and secularism.

This central monument is the mark of Turkish national identity that designates Taksim Republic Square as the center of the city and establishes Istanbul, which was once the capital city of the Ottoman Empire, as a city reconstituted in accordance with the new founding ideology and remolded to fit the image of the national model city. It is in this secularized-nationalized space that Islamist circles wanted to build a monumental mosque, which turned into an aggressively promoted and severely disputed project soon after the Islamist city administration came to power in 1994.

Figure 7. The proposed mosque would overshadow the Republic Monument that marks the center of Taksim Republic Square and also the Atatürk Cultural Center in the back. Photograph by Zeynep İnanç.

In the political climate of the 1990s and the early years of the new millennium, it is not only the Republic Monument that makes Taksim Square the locus of secular nationalist ideology. Other monuments and structures around the same square concertedly turn the place into a display of official nationalism and modernity. One of the significant structures that overlooks the square is Atatürk Cultural Center (Atatürk Kültür Merkezi, or AKM), a prestigious facility including concert halls, theaters, and exhibition halls that serves as the home of the Istanbul Symphony Orchestra and the State Opera and Ballet Company. With its repertoire devoted to Western classical music and ballet, its modern architecture, and its name derived from the iconic founder, Atatürk, AKM stands as a monument of official Turkish modernity that recognizes and adopts the standards of European high culture as the universal norm of civilization. Another more recent addition to the square has been a McDonalds, which has been taken not so much as an insertion of American cultural imperialism, but more as an affirmation of Turkey's access to global cultural flows and its ability to incorporate one of the most salient symbols of Western popular culture. It is in this square that is overdetermined by the symbols of Turkish secular nationalism and a West-oriented modernization project that the Islamist plan to build a new mosque in 1994 created so much annoyance among state authorities and secularist circles.

The Taksim Mosque: Insertion of Islam into Secular Space

The victory of the Refah Party in the local elections of 1994, which brought an Islamist administration to power in the local government of Istanbul for the first time in the history of the republic, elicited widely discrepant reactions from Islamists and secularists. While secularist circles that took it as an omen of an approaching Islamist coup d'état experienced the election as one of the most shockingly disastrous moments in Turkish history, Islamist circles celebrated it as "the victory of the 'other' Turkey."[13] There was one thing that both secularists and Islamists agreed upon: the 1994 local election marked a turning point in Turkish history; nothing would ever be the same again.[14]

However, even though the 1994 election was seen as a historical landmark, this was not the Refah Party's first electoral victory. Earlier, in the 1989 local elections, the Refah Party had been victorious in prominent Anatolian cities, including Konya and Sivas, and in the 1992 partial elections, it had emerged as the party receiving the highest percentage of votes.[15] Yet none of these previous victories had been considered historical turning points. What made the Refah Party's victory in 1994 such a significant historical moment was that it took place in Istanbul, a city that occupies a crucial place in both secularist and Islamist imaginations of the Turkish national identity.

There are several reasons why the city of Istanbul occupies such a central role, involving complex historical, economic, sociological, global, and cultural dimensions. What is of particular interest here is the global dimension, because it is what makes the city of Istanbul the site from which Turkey's national identity is projected and contested both for local and for global audiences. In other words, it is not in the capital, Ankara, but in Istanbul that the national public sphere is constituted as the site from which Turkey's national identity is projected for the gaze of the global subject, which now has a daily presence in Istanbul through the flow of tourists, international businesses, global media, and other international travelers. This is why Istanbul is recognized and presented as a "world city" in both secularist and Islamist discourses.[16]

The shock and panic that characterized the secularist response to the Islamist victory in 1994 were partially conditioned by an awareness that the most significant national stage in Turkey would no longer be under the control of secularism. Having an Islamist political party in the city administration of Istanbul would mean that the display of Turkish national identity as secular and West-oriented would be seriously undermined by an increased Islamic presence in public spaces. Indeed, the Islamist administration undertook several changes in public places under its jurisdiction, which challenged secularist norms in many ways.

It is in this context that the Islamist city administration, only three months after it came to power in 1994, promoted the project of building in Taksim Square a new mosque that they aspired to make one of the tallest and largest mosques in the Middle East.[17] The announcement of this project elicited an uproar from the secular media, which started an aggressive campaign against the project, condemning it as "unfeasible," "ideologically motivated," "destructive to the environment," "aesthetically repulsive," and "damaging for tourism."[18]

The secularist opposition was not against the idea of a new mosque in itself. Several other mosques had been built in Istanbul, and none of these had become controversial. But Taksim Square is not just anyplace; it is the center of Istanbul, circumscribed by the monumental structures of official Turkish modernity and secular nationalism. For secularists, it was unthinkable for the Republic Monument, with the figure of Atatürk at the fore and standing right at the center of the square, to be overshadowed by a huge mosque.

The controversial Taksim Mosque project was rebuffed many times by various governmental and nongovernmental agencies before it was withdrawn by the Islamists, turning the matter into a hostile public dispute between Islamist and secularist circles. Secularists argued that there was no need for a new mosque in the Taksim region and that the Islamist proposal was motivated by purely ideological/confrontational goals.[19] Islamist circles, on the other hand, claimed that the Taksim region had more churches and synagogues than mosques, which privileged the non-Muslim population living in the area to the detriment of the majority, who are Muslim.[20] The editor of *Cuma*, an Islamist weekly publication, wrote, "Secularists are against the building of a mosque in Taksim only because they want to oppress Muslims. . . . Whoever opposes the building of the Taksim Mosque is not only an undeniable enemy of Islam, but also an unmistakable despot who fails to recognize freedom of conscience."[21]

The fact that the Taksim Mosque project became the object of a highly charged political controversy suggests that this mosque, as a place for praying, was not only about meeting the demands of religious practice or about the insertion of an Islamic artifact into a public space, but primarily about the articulation of an alternative national identity. This point was explicitly articulated by Mayor Recep Tayyip Erdoğan, who referred to the Taksim Mosque as the "symbol of the nation." In response to a question as to why the city administration was so insistent on building a new mosque in Taksim in spite of the objections and protests of secularist groups, the mayor said:

> Tourists who come to Taksim don't even understand that they are in a Muslim country. . . . Symbols allow you to make a statement to the observers. For example the Dome Cathedral in Cologne or the Brandenburg Gate in Berlin are such symbols. . . . Nations put forth their identity through their art. A tourist who comes to Taksim should be able to see what the art of a foreign country looks like.[22]

This statement by the mayor made it explicit that the building of a mosque in Taksim Square was about the articulation of the Islamist version of the Turkish national identity, to be placed on display for tourists. In this context, the mosque emerged as a part of a spectacle displayed for the global gaze, constituting the national subject primarily as Islamic rather than ethnic-Turkish and secular. The evocation of the tourist gaze, which was frequently done by city officials and the Islamist media, constituted the West, particularly Europe, as the audience whose gaze was upon Turkey through its tourists. A new mosque in Taksim Square was to be a statement made for this audience, a statement that would constitute the national identity as essentially Islamic, and at the same time reaffirm the Euro-Western as the spectator for which that identity was to be displayed.

The city commission that would supervise the Taksim Mosque project expressed a similar concern with the global gaze during discussions on the location of the mosque. The commission decided on the park next to Atatürk Cultural Center and insisted on a particularly tall and large structure so that it would be the most impressive monument on Taksim Square and would be saliently visible when viewed by tourists on boats touring the Bosphorus Strait.[23]

In these interventions, the strategy pursued by the Islamists was one that sought to insert a potent symbol of Islam into a space that was already designated as the center of the city, as determined by the signs and symbols of official nationalism. Instead of designating an alternative location or claiming, for example, Sultanahmet Square, the Ottoman center, as the alternative city center, Islamists chose to compete for the same space with secularists to frame and reshape the center of the city in accordance with their own nationalist project. Furthermore, this intervention sought not to divest the square of national significance or to actually remove and replace the existing monuments of Turkish nationalism, but instead to overshadow them with a larger and more visible Islamic insertion. This strategy suggests that the Refah Party's primary objective was not so much to challenge and change the established nation-state system, or to contest the idea of nationhood itself, but rather to compete with secularists to govern the same nation living in the same land. The only difference between the Refah project and that of the secularists was that the Refah Party sought to introduce a new definition of the Turkish nation as an essentially Ottoman-Islamic community to replace the official version that constituted it as ethnically Turkish and secular. In its interventions in Taksim Square, the Refah Party merely wanted to redefine the national meaning of this central space by inserting a mosque, thereby seeking to place a new constitutive core at the heart of the nation.

In sum, the controversy over the Taksim Mosque project was over Turkey's national identity. What was at stake in this dispute between secularists and Islamists was whether or not Turkish national identity would incorporate and use Islam as a self-defining mark. The adamant secularist reaction against the project reflected the obstinacy of secularists against granting Islam a visible presence in the Turkish national identity. On the other hand, the aggressive promotion of the project by Islamist circles reflected a desire to insert Islam into national space—both the nationalized space in Taksim Square and the conceptual space of the nation wherein the national identity was formulated. Therefore, the Taksim Mosque became an attempt to inscribe Islam upon secular-national space, and emerged as the articulation of the Islamist version of nationhood as part of an alternative nationalist ideology that designated the national space of Taksim Square as the appropriate place to establish itself as a contending nationalist project.

Following the National Security Council (NSC) decree in February 1997, which called for strict measures to be taken against the rising influence of political Islam, a series of public lawsuits were opened up against the Refah Party and its leaders that eventually resulted in the shutdown of the party, the removal from office of Istanbul's Mayor Erdoğan, and the banning of the top leaders of the Refah Party from active politics for five years, including Erbakan and Erdoğan. The remainder of the party organization reconvened under a new party, the Fazilet (Virtue) Party, which again won the mayoralty at the local elections in 1999 in Istanbul. However, the NSC crackdown had been effective: the new city administration formed after the removal of Tayyip Erdoğan not only withdrew the notorious Taksim Mosque project, but actually went further, placing a huge sign in Taksim Square paying homage to the republic. During the celebration seventy-fifth anniversary of the founding of the Turkish Republic in 1998, the city administration placed an unmistakable sign in the square, right across from the Republic Monument, that read: "Long Live the Republic, On Its 75th Anniversary—Istanbul Metropolitan Municipality."

This inscription marked the end of the period of the Islamist city administration under Erdoğan's leadership. Even though the same party remained in power in the administration, the discourse around the promotion of an Ottoman-Islamic identity was removed from public circulation, all relevant publications and articles on the municipality's official Web site were discontinued, and funds allocated for the promotion of this discourse in conferences, seminars, meetings, and gatherings were cut.

Placing Istanbul under the Global Gaze

The Taksim Mosque controversy was only one among several points of contention that arose between the secular state and the Refah Party, as these became increasingly salient after the Islamist city administration came to power in 1994. As the mosque project revealed, it was fast becoming apparent that secularists and Islamists had very different notions

Figure 8. The sign placed by the city administration that saluted the seventy-fifth anniversary of the republic. Photograph taken in May 1999.

of what the "Turkish nation" was. One of the occasions where this conflict was played out as an explicit confrontation was Habitat II, the Second United Nations Conference on Human Settlements, which took place in Istanbul in June 1996.

From the start, Habitat II was perceived as a perfect opportunity for a carefully packaged and prepared display of Turkish national identity for the global gaze by all parties involved. In relation to the conference, thousands of foreign media representatives, state officials, international business delegates, and members of various nongovernmental organizations (NGOs) from all over the world would be visiting Istanbul within a two-week period. TOKI (the General Residence Administration), a state institution appointed by the government to host the conference, used the slogan "Six billion people from the world are coming to Istanbul" in its campaign to publicize the conference in Turkey. The campaign did not focus on informing the Turkish public as to what the largest international conference ever to be organized in Istanbul was about; it did not even sufficiently address the main theme of the conference, settlement and housing issues. Rather, it focused on creating an awareness that Istanbul was going to become globally visible to the whole world, that is, to "six billion people." Thus, the most salient feature of the conference became this idea that the whole world would be watching Istanbul.

As a result, the ever-present awareness that the global gaze was upon Turkey was elevated to unprecedented levels, and preparations took on a frantic pace. While the officially designated conference site was undergoing major construction in preparation for various meetings, including the convention of the United Nations General Assembly, the public attention was not so much on the conference site as on the adjacent area, where visitors would go on short excursions to see Istanbul. The adjacent area was Taksim Square and the Beyoğlu district, which is the heart of the city's entertainment and night-life with its cafes, restaurants, bars, clubs, theaters, concert halls, and shopping centers. In preparation for the conference, the whole Taksim-Beyoğlu region underwent a major amelioration, from the installation of new lampposts and trees down to the renewal of all the cobblestones on the sidewalks. The public sphere in Istanbul was getting ready to display itself for the global gaze.

But of course there was absolutely no agreement as to how Turkey was going to be presented in this display, and, more important, *who* was going to do this presentation. This dispute, referred to as a "crisis of representation" in the media, took shape when the state institution TOKI and the city administration of Istanbul engaged in a public conflict over who would be the official host of the conference.[24] Although TOKI was assigned by the government as the official host, the mayor of Istanbul, Erdoğan, stated that the rightful host should have been the city administration, since it was the city that represented civil society, and not the state, especially in relation to issues of settlement and housing. The mayor claimed that the government had designated TOKI "in order to prevent the pro-Islamic Refah Party from playing a prominent role in this important international seminar."[25]

Even though the city administration could not officially host the conference, it organized parallel events, some in conjunction with the conference, but mostly on its own initiative with its own resources. This "parallel Habitat conference"[26] included several exhibitions, publications, and panels, where the city administration could "promote Turkey . . . [using its] own cultural resources," thereby implying that the official host representing the secular state was not promoting Turkey's real cultural identity.[27]

The involvement of the city administration in the Habitat II conference was no small undertaking. The city allocated a total of 2.5 trillion Turkish liras (amounting to about 3.7 million U.S. dollars at the time) for the conference, including the cobblestone renewal and other city improvement projects. As a part of the "parallel Habitat conference," the city spent $540,000 for the exhibitions and concerts; $300,000 for a "Habitat II International Academic Seminars" conference, which included close to fifty panelists, more than a dozen of whom were invited from different parts of the world; and a total of $892,000 for the promotion of Istanbul, including the creation of several documentary films, music CDs, and publications, which were made available to the visitors.[28]

The reason that the city was so insistent on hosting the conference and diverted such a large amount of its resources to the organization of these events was because the Islamist administration saw the conference as an unprecedented opportunity to display the Islamists' own vision of Turkey for the global gaze. The mayor noted that this international summit which was to meet in Istanbul was

> an important opportunity to promote Istanbul and Turkey to the whole world. . . . The fact that thousands of foreigners are coming to our city encouraged us to prepare "with the thoroughness of a housewife." We have to show our traditional hospitality, and accommodate our guests in our city in the best way possible. This is also an important opportunity in terms of showing the kind of vision we have regarding Istanbul.[29]

It is quite revealing to see here that the mayor was not only constituting the Turkish host as a "housewife," but also referring to Istanbul as if it was in the domestic (private) sphere. The mayor did not hesitate to represent the Turkish national subject as a woman in her house who was about to host some visitors for whom the national/female self was to be displayed. The mayor's words constituted a global audience who would be watching, assessing, and evaluating the Turkish "housewife" subject and her hosting skills. This reference confirms the argument made earlier that the national public subject is reified in the form of the body of the female, who is to be prepared and presented at her best for the approval of the global gaze. The awareness of becoming visible under the global gaze resulted in the perception of the self as a female on display and the national public sphere as a private realm within the larger global public sphere that would be exposed to the global gaze. In the process, the Islamist elite is constituted as the true agent of this intervention, which had prepared the national subject and presented it to the global gaze in accordance with her "true" cultural identity.

Locating the Authentic National Culture in Istanbul

One of the sites through which the city administration displayed its own view of Istanbul for "six billion people from around the world" was the daily newspaper *Habitat Days*, published by the city both in English and in Turkish and prepared for and distributed exclusively at the Habitat II conference. In this publication, Istanbul was presented as a city that is deeply rooted in the traditions of Ottoman-Muslim culture, in which the city finds its "true identity."[30] It was also presented as being under siege, threatened by massive but mismanaged urbanization, imitative modernization, and Westernization. For example, according to a columnist, the true spirit of Istanbul, which constitutes its identity, "spreads out from mosques and minarets, from the domes and from the tombs of its saints [*evliya*]. . . . With this identity, Istanbul is primarily an Islamic city," a city where traditional practices are "falling victim to Coca Cola and Pepsi."[31]

In most of the articles written about Istanbul, the true identity of the Turkish national subject was located in architectural styles; in everyday practices including those surrounding food, clothing, and music; and in social, political, and educational institutions that were associated with Islam and Ottoman times. For example, mosques were presented as reflecting the "true self" of the nation as opposed to modern high-rises, as was şerbet (a soft drink based on fruit juices, popular in Ottoman Istanbul) as opposed to Coca Cola and Pepsi; Ottoman-style water fountains as opposed to water sold in plastic bottles; and Ottoman architecture, reflected in tombs and tekkes (dervish lodges), as opposed to five-star hotels or the Bosphorous Bridge (the bridge built in 1973, connecting the European and the Asian continents).[32] In other words, cultural objects, daily practices, and urban structures associated with the Ottoman era were picked out and quarantined as symbols of Turkey's true identity, framed as being under the threat of Western influences. On the other hand, technology, consumerism, capitalism, and West-oriented modernism were framed as the consequences of the imitative Westernizing policies of the secular state, which alienates the nation from its own culture.

The identification of the national culture with Ottoman-Islamic practices was reflected in the form of nostalgia for what were presented as Ottoman traditions and institutions. Another article that appeared in *Habitat Days* complains:

> The centralist policies have standardized the deformation of our urbanization. Today . . . there is no sentimental and spiritual relation between the city and the man living there. We have very few (maybe no) monuments as a heritage to future generations. Our cities have no identity [because] we couldn't preserve the traditional identity.[33]

A photograph of one of the recently urbanized districts of Istanbul that was published with this article depicts a scene overcrowded with residential buildings, some incomplete (for example, lacking windows and frames). Presented as a typical scene of modernity in Istanbul, the photograph consists of a series of buildings that all look alike, without any uniqueness, or lacking "identity" as the author puts it. A mosque, barely visible among the crooked buildings, stands as the mark of nostalgia that the author is grieving about, which has been overwhelmed by the crooked and incomplete modernity of the city.

In his analysis of the effects of the Ottoman *millet* system on everyday life in Istanbul, a writer praised this system of multiculturalism whereby "communities based on different religions and sects were recognized as separate legal systems, each enjoying the right to practice their own laws, traditions and beliefs under the administration of their leaders."[34] In contrast to the highlighted fairness and peacefulness of the *millet* system, another writer referred to the republic as "official Turkey," consisting of the centralized state, politicians, and political parties that are "artificial products" of the new system.[35] The artificiality of "official Turkey" was contrasted with the "other Turkey," which "had the training of an empire for centuries" and faces "real problems," not artificial ones imposed by the state.

In this series of articles that appeared in *Habitat Days*, Istanbul was displayed as a city under siege, its true identity located in Islamic and Ottoman traditions that are undermined to the point of destruction by West-oriented modernity and the secular state. This image of Istanbul is illustrated in a cartoon that appeared in a special Habitat II issue of the Islamist monthly publication *İzlenim*, which depicts an old mosque, itself protecting what seems to be the only piece of green left in the concretized city, that has been overwhelmed by and suffocated under overbearing modern high-rises.

This theme was repeated throughout various publications and documents of the municipality, including those at its official Web site. The official Web site of the Greater Municipality of Istanbul was set up in late 1997, with information about the activities of the administration, as well as detailed information about Istanbul, including the Refah Party's version of its history. Most of the informational articles presented at the Web site had been previously published in various documents of the city, including

Figure 9. An old mosque, protecting what seems to be the only piece of green (*İzlenim* 33–34 [May–June 1996]: 42).

a CD-ROM with information on Istanbul that was prepared for the Habitat II conference. At the municipal Web site, Istanbul was depicted as a city whose true identity is located in Ottoman-Islamic traditions and has been eradicated by the building of the modern nation-state and the formation of the republic:

> With the onset of the Republic, Istanbul has lost its status as the capital city of an empire. What was once the capital of three empires in a row, became just another big city of a nation-state. Again with the Republic, Istanbul lost its status as the center of the caliphate of the Islamic World. With the closure of *tekkes* and *zaviyes* [dervish lodges] the richest mystical spheres in history moved out of daily life of Istanbul. All these destroyed Istanbul and its identities, which were the products of hundreds of years of experience. Istanbul, which is primarily a city of history, has been torn away from its history and its historical riches (cultural, religious, social, architectural, folkloric . . .).[36]

In this and other similar presentations of Istanbul, the city administration displayed the city as the true capital of the nation, which has been corrupted and depraved by the secular republic. Istanbul was presented as the "eternal capital city" of the "Islamic-Ottoman civilization," which constitutes the true national identity as distinct from and inherently foreign to the Westernizing influences of the secular state.[37]

Davut Dursun, an influential intellectual among Islamist circles, who wrote for *Habitat Days* as well as various other publications of the municipality, provided an outline of views about the identity of Istanbul. In his article titled "Which Istanbul?" Dursun asserted that there are several different Istanbuls.[38] The first is the Istanbul of the Byzantine period, or Constantinople, which was the capital of the East Roman Empire until 1453. The effects of this period, he argues, are still present in Istanbul through various historical artifacts around the city that are very much a part of daily life. The second is the "Islamic-Ottoman Istanbul," which, according to Dursun, existed in the period that made Istanbul a global city. For Dursun, the salient markers of this Istanbul are "those unique mosques, *medreses* [religious schools], beautiful palaces, civilian architectural works, fountains, tombs and other masterpieces." Alongside these two "historical Istanbuls" is a third Istanbul, which was formed as the economic, financial, and trade capital of the country after the nineteenth century. This Istanbul is present "not with its mosques, minarets and tombs like the Ottoman-Islamic Istanbul, but with the symbols of the modern times such as modern business centers, high-rises, places for entertainment, big hotels or financial centers." According to Dursun, "The essence of Istanbul is the part that reflects the Ottoman-Islamic identity," which is being eradicated both by the state and by civilian initiatives.

Dursun's article appeared in *Nehir,* a monthly Islamist journal that had published a special issue titled "Istanbul: The City in Search of Its Identity."[39] One article after another in this issue dealt with the ways in which the city was devastated and demolished, as reflected in the titles "The Ravished Situation of Istanbul" and "Istanbul: The Lost City." In these articles, Istanbul was depicted as an essentially "Ottoman-Islamic" city, which is threatened both by the modernizationist and Westernizationist interventions of the secular state and by the degeneration brought by mass immigration and rapid urbanization resulting from poor and incompetent governance.[40]

The incrimination of the secular state for the devastation it had brought to the nation proliferated in Islamist publicity, including at the official Web site of the city administration, where it was noted:

> One of our priorities is to open up Istanbul's cultural riches to our people. As a result of the cultural crisis that we have been living for two centuries [with the onset of Westernization] our people have been torn away from these cultural riches. [Under these conditions] cultural life has become alien to its own people and history, and cultural activities have become a means to undermine our own cultural roots.[41]

This narration evokes the "people" as the national subject on whose behalf the Refah Party administration was speaking, and who had been alienated from "its own" history and culture by Westernizing and modernizing interventions of the secular state. It was this rhetoric, which defined Istanbul as an essentially Ottoman-Islamic city and the "true" capital of the nation victimized by the centralized Westernizing and modernizing secular state, that informed the ways in which the city administration reimagined and projected the city. This rhetoric also established the Refah Party as the political agent that would rescue the nation from the devastation inflicted upon it by the secular state and lead it toward its future, where it could become the glorious civilization and global power that it deserved to be. In publicizing its cultural activities at its Web site, the city administration remarked, "Our aim is to make Istanbul one of the main cultural capitals of the world, and to make it the center of the Turkish and Islamic world."[42]

The discourse of the city administration established Istanbul as the true center of the Turkish nation, redefined as an Ottoman-Islamic culture, and projected the secular state as having subjected the city to corrupting and

Figure 10. "Istanbul: The City in Search of Its Identity" (*Nehir* 18 [March 1995]).

degenerating influences that tore the nation away from its "true" identity and rightful cultural/Islamic roots. Islamists, on the other hand, were projected as the true protectors and saviors of the nation, who, by restoring Istanbul's true identity, would restore the true cultural basis and source of the Turkish nation and bring it under their own guardianship.

In sum, interventions in city spaces and public places allowed the Refah

Figure 11. "Istanbul: The Lost City" (*Nehir* 18 [March 1995]: 16).

Party to develop and advance its new nationalist project. These interventions designated Istanbul as the true capital of the Ottoman-Islamic civilization and framed it as under siege and threatened by the Westernizing secular state. Just as the designation of Ankara as the new capital during the founding years had allowed the new state to develop and advance its nationalist project, the designation of Istanbul as the alternative capital by the Islamists in the 1990s enabled the Refah Party to formulate and promote an alternative, Islamist, nationalist project. Just as the building of Ankara as the model national city had served to construct the new state as the agent of transformation and the new guardian of the nation, the reframing of Istanbul as the bearer of the authentic culture and identity of the nation served to vest the Islamist leadership with political agency. Just as the secular state condemned the Ottoman-Islamic rule as the culprit responsible for the suffering inflicted upon the nation and the occupation of its land, the Islamists likewise incriminated the secular state for harm done to the nation and for the loss of its identity. This strategy similarly allowed the Islamists to establish themselves as the only agent capable of protecting and leading the nation toward a better future.

The Çamlıca Restaurant: The Construction of Authenticity

The construction of the national subject as Ottoman-Islamic was perhaps most carefully forged and displayed in Çamlıca Restaurant, a large facility owned and run by the city administration. The Çamlıca premises, including a restaurant, a coffeehouse, a large tea garden, and smaller flower gardens surrounding the restaurant, are highly popular. With a magnificent view of the Bosphorus Strait, overlooking the Sarayburnu cape on which Topkapı Palace is located, as well as the Bosphorus Bridge, which connects the Asian and the European continents, Çamlıca draws a substantial number of tourists, serving more than twenty thousand people a day on summer weekends. Its customers are mostly inhabitants of Istanbul, but tourists from all over the world constitute a substantial portion of its clientele as well.

Under previous city administrations, the restaurant had been run by a private contracting company that managed the site as an expensive patisserie/cafe. When the city took over the management of the site and reopened it in August 1995, Çamlıca had undergone quite a transformation. The city administration's primary goal was to display there what they believed to be authentic Turkish culture. Consistent with the Refah Party's policy to develop and advance a new national identity that took Ottoman-Islamic culture as its basis, the Çamlıca premises were renovated, from the rearrangement of the gardens and the complete redecoration of the restaurant to the creation of a new menu and the addition of an "Ottoman Coffee House." What emerged was a restaurant heavily decorated with ornaments, paintings, inscriptions on the walls with Ottoman calligraphy, furnishings, and other decorations that were thought to reflect Ottoman and Islamic objects, styles, and forms, thereby creating quite an Orientalist image.

The restaurant was redecorated to create a nineteenth-century Ottoman atmosphere, the menu was changed to include various distinguished dishes from the Ottoman cuisine, and the music played in the garden was changed from Western classical to classical Turkish music. Prices were reduced more than one-third to attract a larger crowd and appeal to lower-income customers. The most salient inscription of Islam in Çamlıca was the banning of all alcoholic beverages, which were replaced by various traditional soft drinks, tea, and coffee. Under all of the Refah Party's Islamist city administrations, restrictions on alcohol have been a strictly observed policy, and in the Istanbul administration this regulation was introduced through a circular in 1994 that banned alcohol on all premises owned or managed by the city. Alcohol was not served even at the banquets, official dinners, or gala receptions of international performances, exhibitions, or concerts held at any of the municipal premises. Even though this policy was harshly criticized by secularist circles for being "uncivilized" and making Turkey look bad and backward in the eyes of

Figure 12. Scene from the Çamlıca restaurant after the renovations. Photograph taken in July 1997.

Europeans, city officials prided themselves on this policy for providing "safe and privileged public spaces for the people of Turkey to enjoy and not just the [secularist] elite."[43] Again, it is possible to observe at work here the Refah Party's rhetorical strategy, which identified the upper-class Westernized (and alcohol-consuming) elite as secularists who had been alienated from the "real" (and Muslim) people of Turkey. The banning of alcohol and the lowering of prices on the Çamlıca premises were policies that publicized this image of secularists as a Westernized and degenerate elite who had been estranged from "the people."

However, what made the Çamlıca premises an exceptional and an exemplary social space was neither the banning of alcohol nor the price cuts. Rather, it was the removal from the menu of sodas and all carbonated beverages, claiming that they were foreign and alien to the Turkish culture. And this was regardless of the fact that Turkish-brand sodas and carbonated beverages are available in Turkey, often at substantially lower prices. Under the new management, the only beverages served at the restaurant were to be traditional soft drinks such as şerbet (fresh fruit juices that are presented as a part of the Ottoman cuisine).

Another novelty at Çamlıca was the creation of a rural Anatolian display in the garden, where women in peasant clothing baked fresh rural pastries (gözleme). This rural touch was rather impossible to pass off as authentically

Islamic, because it did not embody anything that is specifically Islamic or Ottoman. The enhanced rural atmosphere in the middle of the garden had a different authenticating function, one that situated authenticity in a kind of "primitiveness" of the rural. The rural was presented as that which is the least touched and transformed by modernity, owing to its remoteness. The pastries were cooked on sheet-metal (*sac*) stoves with wooden utensils, representing proximity to nature, genuineness, and purity, in contrast to technology, modernity, and urbanism. The reproduction of the rural as that which is spatially distant from modernity within a very urban location created the effect of authenticity, thereby constituting the cultural practices displayed there as authentically local. In other words, the display of the image of rural as untouched by urbanity and modernity serves to authenticate this very urban and modern display of an Ottoman-Islamic identity.

At the opening ceremony, the mayor of Istanbul, Recep Tayyip Erdoğan, said:

> The Çamlıca premises have been renovated in accordance with the principles of national identity, national culture and national character. Here, alcoholic or not, foreign beverages will not be served. Our people will enjoy Turkish beverages and Turkish meals. . . . What I ask of Istanbullians is to protect this and other similar sites without ruining the beauty of the

Figure 13. The pastry (*gözleme*) stand at Çamlıca. Photograph taken in July 1997.

environment. If we can do this we will again be number one in the competition of civilizations.[44]

Removing carbonated beverages from the menu caught the attention of the secular media. After all, Coca Cola was a powerful symbol of American cultural imperialism in the leftist discourse of the 1970s. Therefore, removing carbonated beverages from the menu was immediately taken as a political statement comparable to leftist positions. Indeed, the Islamists had done something that leftists had been unable to accomplish during the 1970s. However, a closer examination suggests that the similarities between leftism and Islamism should not be carried too far. After the secular media made a huge fuss about banning carbonated beverages at a tourist site, the city responded in its bimonthly publication:

> Our goal here was to create a truly authentic place. Tourists coming from Europe and other places are mostly interested in such authentic, original sites. Surely they will not be interested in seeing other cultures, standardized five-star hotels or night clubs. . . . They do not have to come all the way here to see [their own cultures].[45]

This justification does not express a sense of the danger posed by cultural imperialism and a need to protect the local culture from its erosive effects. It does not reflect a concern with preserving the self against destructive threats. Had such a concern been the case, the city would certainly not have been eager to attract more tourists. Tourists and the Western culture they represent were not seen as a threat to the self; on the contrary, they were the targeted audience in the display of the authentic local culture. It was the gaze of the tourist for which this authentic local culture was being displayed. What the Islamist city administration was concerned with was what the West, which was coming to see Istanbul through the tourist, would see there.

Instant Coffee, Self-Service, and French Chairs

In Çamlıca Restaurant, while city officials attempted to present the "authentic Turkish culture" through a carefully forged display of an Ottoman-Islamic culture, slippages in these attempts reveal the forged nature of the identity that was placed on display, which ended up subverting the claims to authenticity of the place. Carbonated beverages were successfully removed from the menu, but something quite unauthentic slipped through; the menu included instant coffee! A large board placed near the counter in the garden listed the beverages available. The bottom line read, in capital letters, "NESCAFE," which is a brand name but has become the generic term for instant coffee in Turkey. Here was a restaurant that claimed to be authentically Turkish and was serving generic instant coffee in a country famous for its Turkish coffee.

"NESCAFE" was not the only extrusive sign that stood out as a misfit in the display of authenticity and tradition. Another extrusion was the word written on signs hanging around the restaurant: "Self-Servis," which is a mutated spelling of *self-service* based on the Turkish pronunciation of this English term. These signs invited visitors to approach the "rural" counter right in the middle of the garden to enjoy the authentic pastries prepared fresh and baked by women in peasant clothing, the authenticity of which was severely undermined by the sign reading "Self-Servis" placed right next to the counter.

Furthermore, at the Ottoman Coffee House, which was a small building attached to the side of the restaurant, there was a picture on the wall representing an authentic Ottoman coffee house with a divan-style seating arrangement where wide, cushioned benches were lined up against the wall so as to have all customers facing the center of the room and chatting away as they sipped their Turkish coffees.[46] While the illustration on the wall stood as yet another insistent effort to verify the authenticity of Ottoman culture by emphasizing historicity and tradition, the actual furnishing of the coffee house had no resemblance whatsoever to the representation on the wall. The chairs and tables in the coffee house were of nineteenth-century French style and were arranged in an orderly fashion, dividing the space so the guests could sit separately, in contrast to the Ottoman divan-style seating, which preserved the singularity of the social space, enhancing communal interaction.

According to the managers, the designers decided to have the not-so-comfortable and not-so-sociable French chairs instead of the original comfortable divans "so that tourists would not relax too much and stay too long."[47] This utilitarian reasoning had conveniently surpassed any concerns with authenticity.

The Çamlıca Restaurant case is one of the revealing instances whereby an alternative national identity was forged and displayed for the public gaze, presenting the nation as authentically Islamic and Ottoman. Even though the city used these interventions to carefully attempt to forge an identity and present it as authentically local, inevitable slippages revealed the forged nature of these displays and their unfounded claims to authenticity. The unauthentic slippages, such as the instant coffee, the French

Figure 14. The Ottoman Coffee House with French chairs and divided seating arrangements. Photograph taken in July 1997.

chairs, and self-service subverted the construction of the national identity as a homogeneous and naturally self-contained subjectivity. Rather, they defied the externality of the West to the performance of the Islamic-Ottoman subject and served to create a display of hybridity rather than authenticity, with various representations of rural Anatolia, the Ottoman heritage, diverse culinary practices, and Islamic traditions, as well as marks of modernity, Westernism, and secularism, combined in a heterogeneous conglomeration. They transformed the display of a claimed authenticity into a staging of heterogeneity, combining bits and elements from multiple worlds that could no longer be reduced to any single particular identity, nor was it a discernible mixture of identifiable categories. In other words, interventions to construct an Islamic-Ottoman identity in the Çamlıca Restaurant only resulted in a display that escaped neat categorizations and further blurred the boundaries that delineate the Islamic self from the secular or Western other.

However, even though these slippages seem to have subverted the concerted efforts of the city officials to create a sense of authenticity, they in fact served the larger goals of the Refah Party to establish Islamism as a viable alternative modernization project very well. First of all, these slippages allowed the framing of the larger display as modern, within which scenes of rurality, authenticity, locality, or historicity were carefully orchestrated to produce the desired effect. Hence, the unauthentic insertions allowed for the creation of a sense of authenticity and genuineness without making the whole scene look rural or primitive. Second, they allowed the intervening subject to constitute itself as modern and a master of all worlds, both rural and urban, both modern and traditional, both Western and Eastern. By serving Nescafe alongside Turkish coffee, displaying a modern sense of efficiency (self-service) coupled with authenticity (the rural display), and employing utilitarian reasoning (the use of French chairs) as the organizing force behind the display of locality (the Ottoman Coffee House), the intervening subject demonstrated that he was a competent agent of modernity who could orchestrate such a display of authenticity and locality without himself becoming traditional, rural, or completely Eastern. On the contrary, these inscriptions allowed Islamism to constitute itself as modern.

Islamic High Culture: East Meets West at the CRR Concert Hall

With its sophisticated design and technical capabilities, the Cemal Reşit Rey (CRR) Concert Hall was another important asset of the city administration as an important resource for carrying out its interventions. When it was first built, the CRR Concert Hall was valued as one of the shrines of Turkish modernity and secular elite culture. It is a large-capacity concert hall technically and spatially well equipped to host symphony orchestras and other performers of Western classical music. For most of its patrons, every concert is another confirmation of the Westernism of Turkish modernity, another reaffirmation of Turkey's proximity to Europe. Anticipating that the Islamist administration would ruin this monument of secular modernity by Islamizing it, the secular patrons of the concert hall were not happy when the Refah Party took over the management of the CRR.

Soon after the Islamist city administration came to power, the director of the concert hall, Filiz Ali, resigned in anger, refusing to work with an Islamist administration. The Friends of Music Association, constituted of devoted secular patrons of concert halls, held angry meetings protesting the new administration and what they believed to be a policy of "Islamization" at the CRR. They believed that the new administration would gradually curtail the quality and quantity of Western classic music concerts and replace them with Islamic rituals and chanting.[48]

The Islamist administration did undertake some changes at the concert hall, most of which were unprecedented in such shrines of secularist elite culture. Suitable rooms were converted into prayer chambers (*mescit*); the serving of alcohol was banned on the premises; receptions that had previously been held at openings, where alcoholic beverages were served, were cancelled; and the repertoire was changed from exclusively Western classical music to include Turkish classical and folk music concerts. The Islamist administrators saw these changes as "natural" and necessary so as to open up such sites to the "public" instead of keeping them reserved for the exclusive use of a privileged secular Westernized elite.[49] The secularist patrons, however, were outraged by what was an unacceptable intervention with regard to their turf. For the first time ever in that concert hall, women dressed in Islamic attire and wearing headscarves started to come to concerts and continued to do so in spite of the disapproving gazes and intolerant gestures of the secularist patrons.

The change in the concert hall's repertoire was indicative of a shift toward a non-Western notion of culture and civilization and away from the dominant standard of Western high culture. But it was not an attempt to move away from Western culture itself. This policy was rather strikingly embodied in a special production initiated by the city administration, a production that brought the Ottoman military band (*mehter*) together with an internationally renowned jazz artist, Okay Temiz.

The concert was conceived to serve as a platform where the East and the West could meet and enter into a dialogue in musical terms. During the concert, both the *mehter* and the jazz band displayed their own sounds, then tried to converse with each other, and finally attempted to perform by producing each other's sounds. The *mehter* group played the "Turkish March" by Mozart, and the Swedish saxophone player from the jazz band performed a *peşrev* (a section of Turkish *fasıl* music comparable to an overture).

It would not be accurate to categorize the *mehter*-jazz concert as an overt attempt to Islamicize the public sphere, as was anticipated by secularist circles. Rather, the concert reflected a desire to bring what is perceived as the "East" and the "West" into mutual recognition and dialogue to negotiate and learn about their differences without attempting to overpower each other.

A matter of controversy here was having the *mehter* and the jazz band represent the East and the West, respectively. *Mehter* music dates back to the sixteenth-century Ottoman military establishment and has a respectable position within the larger Turkish classical music tradition. However, what constitutes the repertoire of *mehter* music today was established during the late-nineteenth and twentieth centuries, long after Ottoman Westernization and modernization had begun.[50] Therefore, *mehter* music had already been transformed by European musical influences. Some of the most popular pieces played by *mehter* bands today are marches, which take the Western classical musical scale as their base.

Just as the *mehter* is not quite authentically Eastern, the jazz band that is taken to represent the West is not quite foreign either. The band discussed here was formed by a Turkish percussionist, Okay Temiz, who has been performing for international as well as Turkish audiences for years. One of his important accomplishments as a percussionist has been the incorporation of the highly complex rhythms from Turkish music into jazz.

What was thought of as the East and the West that were being introduced to each other at the *mehter*-jazz concert at the CRR Concert Hall had met a long time ago and had already transformed each other. The former acquaintance between Ottoman and European cultural and musical practices did not cast a shadow over the attempts of the city administration to celebrate mutual recognition and dialogue between what are segregated into the East and the West, but it did cast a shadow on attempts to establish the Western as that which is external and foreign and the national self as authentically Eastern. In other words, the efforts of the city administration to demonstrate its desire to bring the East and the West into dialogue with one another ended up once again reproducing Orientalist binaries and constituted the East and the West as mutually exclusive civilizational clusters.

The changes introduced at the CRR Concert Hall and in its repertoire expressed a desire to bring the East and the West together, but in order to do so, they were first separated and repackaged as two distinct entities. However, even though the apparent goal of these musical interventions was to create amiable relations between the reified categories of East and West, they served a more subtle function toward the establishment of Islamism as a modernizing force. Most important, these interventions brought Islamic circles into public spaces of Western high culture that had until then been under the strict monopoly of secularism. They allowed for the projection of an image of Islamism as capable of producing its own elite, who are educated and cultured enough to appreciate and consume fine art and Western music. They served to demonstrate that Islamists were equally capable of successfully directing a highly acclaimed concert hall and hosting internationally renowned symphony orchestras, jazz bands, and dance companies alongside Turkish orchestras performing the work of Turkish composers and concerts of classical Turkish music. As in the case of other interventions carried out by the Islamist city administration, these also allowed the intervening subject to constitute itself as modern and a master of all worlds, both Eastern and Western, both Ottoman and Turkish, both traditional and modern. They also served to constitute Islamism as a modernizing force with its own upper-class elite and its own high culture.

4

Performing the Nation:

Public Contestations of National History

Just as modernization and nation-building involve interventions related to bodies so as to constitute a sense of nation as a single, monolithic body, and interventions related to places so as to create a sense of a unified, single national land, they also involve interventions related to time so as to create a sense of a homogeneous, linear, and singular national history. The singularity and linearity of time are such firmly established principles of modernity and nationalism that time has come to be perceived as a naturalized, taken for granted, and invisible component of politics. The concerted efforts of nationalist projects to institute and normalize a sense of a single, linear, national time are often sufficiently successful that the constructed nature of history becomes invisible and national time becomes naturalized. And yet the creation, homogenization, and nationalization of time are by no means natural processes. These processes involve the writing, dissemination, publicizing, and performance of national history.

Creation of a national time is such an essential component of nationalist projects that the building of a new nation can be realized only to the extent that a sense of homogeneous, uniform time that dominates and shapes all perceptions of the past, present, and future can be successfully instituted and normalized. This essential feature of nation-building projects is acknowledged by Benedict Anderson, who draws attention to the generation of a sense of "simultaneity" as a necessary precondition for the making of a national community. According to Anderson, "an American" who has no idea what his fellow nationals are up to at any one time "has complete confidence in their steady, anonymous, simultaneous activity."[1]

Therefore, interventions related to time involve the creation of a sense of simultaneity such that the nation can be imagined as a totality living on the same time line, sharing the same past, present, and the future. As Anderson notes, "The idea of a sociological organism moving calendrically through homogeneous, empty time is a precise analogue of the idea of the nation, which also is conceived as a solid community moving steadily down (or up) history."[2] This effect is achieved through a variety of different mechanisms, only one of which is the newspaper, as acknowledged by Anderson. Perhaps even more effective is the television, which ensures that "the whole nation" is watching the same news coverage at the same moment, particularly when an event of national significance, such as a natural disaster, war, or some important international competition, is involved. Hence, the very act of turning on the television and tuning into a national channel becomes an act of initiation into citizenship and of becoming part of the nation. By addressing a large number of people exactly at the same time and subjecting them to the same narration of some "national" incident, television enables the simultaneous interpellation of multiple national subjects, thereby conjuring a national community.

Print and broadcast media play crucial roles in the creation of a sense of belonging to the national community by enabling an imagined linkage in the present time between subjects who are otherwise disconnected in space and totally ignorant of each other's existence. However, the construction of a sense of national belonging also involves the formation of an imagined linkage between subjects who are separated in time, sometimes by centuries. In other words, if a nation is to be imagined into existence as a singular entity moving in "homogeneous, empty time,"[3] a national subject living in the present has to be made to feel connected to events and people who are otherwise disconnected not only in space but also in time. This imagined linkage involves not simultaneity but the instillation of a sense of continuity across time. This sense of continuity can be ensured only by making the past available in the present. One of the most effective ways in which this is achieved is through commemorative practices that memorialize some nationally significant event in the past and engage the national subject in the present. By partaking in such commemorative practices, participants are initiated into national history and provided a sense of connectedness to the past and to the people who have lived in that past. Hence, commemorative practices are pivotal in the formation of imagined linkages between people who have lived decades or centuries apart, thereby constituting the nation as an entity that has a continuity above and beyond time. In this chapter I am particularly interested in the commemoration of the founding moment when a new nation-state is created and around which a new national history is woven.

This chapter explores the mechanisms through which national history is created and normalized during the foundation of a new nation-state, and the emergence of alternative histories as produced and performed by contending nationalist projects. I illustrate that the writing of the official national Turkish history, which was written by a committee convened under the leadership of Atatürk, inscribed the Turkish nation into time, defamed the Ottoman and Islamic past, established Atatürk as the founder of the republic, and set the founding moment as 29 October 1923. I then examine the unofficial commemoration of the conquest of Istanbul on 29 May by Islamist circles in Turkey, whose large-scale demonstrations and parades celebrate an alternative history that contests official secular history. The celebrations of 29 May not only glorify the Ottoman past, but also make a connection between the conquest of Istanbul and a prophecy made by the Muslim prophet Mohammed, thereby making the event a part of Islamic history as well. I argue that these Islamist projections of Turkish history serve to construct an alternative national identity that is Ottoman and Islamic, evoking a civilization centered in the city of Istanbul as opposed to the secular, modern Turkish republic centered in the capital city of Ankara.

The unofficial celebration of 29 May emerges as a disruptive interjection in time, an event that forces the public to think of its past in terms of centuries instead of decades. Suddenly the celebration of national time, which had exclusively concentrated on the two decades between 1919 and 1938, warps into the past and locates a national moment in the fifteenth century. The projection of this alternative national history serves to incorporate Ottoman times into the national memory, unsettling the secularist constructions of national history centered on the Kemalist/republican era of the twentieth century. It undermines secularist conceptions of the modern nation-state and calls into question the official date of the founding of the Turkish nation, set as 29 October 1923.

The commemoration of 29 May also addresses broader questions about the making and contestation of national identity through daily practices in public life. As discussed later, such commemorative practices show how the making of national history involves a series of contested and negotiated interventions in public life. Like interventions related to bodies and places, modernizing interventions related to time involve a similar rupture between the immediate past, which is projected as "catastrophic," and the idealized future, toward which the intervening subject is to guide the nation. These interventions involve the restructuring of time around a founding moment, whereby the state emerges as the author and creator of a new national history. The celebration of the founding moment through commemorative practices not only serves to perpetuate the linear time of the nation, but also implicates the public in the making of national history. In these modernizing interventions, the new state emerges as the agent of modernization that sets out to build a new society (nation). It is through these acts of intervention that the state constitutes itself as the agent of modernity. As such, these interventions have a self-constitutive function, where actions produce the actor and not vice-versa.

Just as official nationalism involved the insertion of a founding moment around which a new national history was written, in the 1990s the Islamists produced a different founding moment around which an alternative national history could be written. I argue that secularists and Islamists used similar strategies to implement their nationalist ideologies when they designated a particular founding moment around which to constitute a new national history. In the case of secularists, this moment was 29 October 1923, when the new republic was declared into being. This moment came to be the central point of national time and the main axis around which public memory would be built through the commemoration of Republic Day every year on 29 October. As for the Islamists of the 1990s, a new founding moment was located on 29 May 1453, when the Ottoman sultan Mehmet II conquered Istanbul and brought the Byzantine Empire to an end. This new founding moment became the anchor point around which an alternative national history was written that saw the Turkish nation as an essentially Ottoman-Islamic civilization. In each case, the founding moment became the locus of commemorative practices around which a new sense of nationhood was advanced and projected. In each case, the nationalist ideology that constituted the basis of interventions unquestioningly upheld the same standard equation of the nation-state, which equates one nation with one state with one history. In each case, the writing and performance of national history served to project the nation as suffering some malefic conditions from which it needed to be liberated and brought under the guardianship of a new leader. In each case, the intervening subjects who inserted the nation into time constructed themselves as the authors of this new national history and the agents of liberation and transformation. Therefore, I argue, Islamists are just as much a force of modernization as secularists were in the founding years.

The Founding Moment: Inserting the Nation into History

The writing of national history is an act by which a nation-state declares itself into being, locating itself as both the author and the agent of that history. The formation of a nation-state is marked by a beginning, a founding moment, often celebrated as a day of independence or a national liberation day. In Turkey, the advent of the modern nation-state is celebrated on 29 October as Republic Day, commemorating the day when the National Assembly declared the new republic into being in 1923. Because the Ottoman period does not play a constitutive role in official national history, there are no official days of commemoration referring to incidents that took place under the Ottoman Empire. All official national commemoration days in Turkey are related to various events that took place under Mustafa Kemal Atatürk between 19 May 1919, when Atatürk first started organizing the resistance movement in Anatolia, and 10 November 1938, the day that Atatürk died, which is commemorated as National Mourning Day.

Conquest of Istanbul Day, widely celebrated by Islamist circles on 29 May, is not an official holiday. Although it is officially recognized as a day of historical importance, it is not evoked as a constitutive moment of national history. Every year a small official ceremony is held, at which representatives from the military, the municipality of Istanbul, and the governor's office visit Fatih Sultan Mehmet's tomb and make short speeches to a group of soldiers gathered for the occasion. Public attendance of these ceremonies is not usually encouraged, and until 1994 the occasion did not attract any media attention. Until the Islamist celebrations became public, the secular media did not acknowledge 29 May as a day of national significance, and the date usually passed as just another ordinary day, with no particular visibility in the public sphere.

After the Islamist city administration of the Refah Party came to power in 1994 in Istanbul, 29 May started to be celebrated publicly by Islamist circles every year, with parades, firecrackers, public concerts, symposia, and a night full of festivities at the İnönü Stadium, attended by around thirty thousand people from all over Turkey. Although the form and style of these celebrations resembled national commemoration days in other parts of the world, the peculiar thing about these 29 May celebrations was that the state played no role in their organization, because the date is not officially recognized as a national holiday. Between 1994 and 1998, when the Refah Party was shut down, the festivities were jointly organized by the city administration of Istanbul and the National Youth Foundation (Milli Gençlik Vakfı), an Islamist nongovernmental organization affiliated with the Refah Party that has branches in almost every major city in Turkey. These celebrations were open to the public, and they targeted not an exclusively Islamic-communal audience, but a national-public audience, which was evident from the ways in which 29 May was evoked as a moment in national history. This fact was explicitly articulated in the demands of Islamist circles for the recognition of 29 May as an official national holiday, which were an expression of the ambition to give the Ottoman past a constitutive role in the national history and identity.[4] These demands and the unofficial celebrations of 29 May by the Refah Party receded after the party's shutdown in 1998, but the acknowledgment of 29 May as a day of national significance continued in the Islamist press.

The controversy surrounding the status and place of the Ottoman Empire in the writing of Turkish national history has been one of the main controversies of Turkish national identity. While the official national history has been built on carefully forged boundaries separating and distancing the Turkish national experience from its Ottoman predecessor, Islamist challenges to official national history have been proposing alternative national identities as essentially Ottoman and Islamic, thus raising demands to incorporate Ottoman history within the national memory.

The formation and ongoing reproduction of identities, whether they are personal, communal, or national, involve some sort of a making of history, be it diary-keeping in the construction of personal identities or the writing of official histories in the making of national ones. The construction of history serves to locate the national subject in time, which is ascribed a particular continuity. Within this continuum, identity is consolidated around an essential quality that is claimed to manifest itself as a sameness over time, an integrity that transcends and endures the destabilizing effects of temporal change. In the construction of national identities, this ascribed essential quality may be located in ethnicity, race, blood ties, language, culture, or historical experience. Hence, the composition of national histories involves the creation of time frames in which such constitutive qualities can be instilled as traceable, continuous, and enduring features. Ana Maria Alonso reminds us that in the writing of history, "defined as specific sorts of performances or texts through a series of framing devices," what may appear to be a historical truth is in fact an effect of the ideologically motivated reconstructions of time.[5] Alonso notes that "the way such reconstructions are framed configures their truth value by bringing into play the ideologically constituted status of different forms of knowledge." National histories involve the employment of such framing devices that restructure time, within which the nation can be inscribed as a historical truth.

It is particularly in the creation of national identities that history becomes highly controversial, a site where claims to the singularity, holism, and the natural boundedness of national history are guarded with much higher stakes. If the writing of national history is a vitally constitutive act through which the national subject is written into being, then the conservation of that history as naturally bound, singular, and factual is crucial for the ongoing reproduction of the national subject and one of its embodiments, the nation-state.[6] In other words, it is the very existence of the nation-state that is at stake when the axioms of national history are opened up to contestation and negotiation. Since the nation-state is predicated upon the notion of a singular nation consolidated around a unitary state, the equation "one state = one nation = one history" has to be preserved at all costs. Therefore, the writing of national history inevitably involves the employment of various mechanisms and strategies to naturalize and objectify history, thereby rendering it uncontestable and nonnegotiable. Drawing critical attention to the role of the national historian in objectifying history, Prasenjit Duara notes, "What appears as the delineation of an evolution of a nation is a complex project of repressions and recreations, the sublimation of the other in the self. To us, in our subject positions as modern historians, the assumed transparency of linear History blinds us to its rhetorical strategies for containing these repressions, for preventing a rupture in the body of the nation."[7]

One of the distinguishing marks of national identities is the inherent ambivalence that Homi Bhabha refers to as the "double-writing" or the "double-time" of the modern nation. The national subject that declares itself into being through the writing of history presents itself as having an eternal presence that is validated by its historicity and great age; at the same time, it also projects itself as new and modern. Hence, the nation-state always faces the anxiety of projecting itself in double-time, in the past and in the present, both old and new, eternal yet also novel. According to Bhabha, "The political unity of the nation consists in a continual displacement of its irredeemably plural modern space, bounded by different, even hostile nations, into a signifying space that is archaic and mythical, paradoxically representing the nation's modern territoriality, in the patriotic, atavistic temporality of Traditionalism."[8]

The anxiety that arises out of the double-writing of the nation is articulated not only in "signifying the people as an a priori historical presence,"[9] but also in attempts to present the nation-state as new and modern. One of the vital mechanisms through which the effect of newness is produced involves the creation of a temporal rupture, a break from the immediate past that serves to mark the onset of the nation-state in a new beginning or a "founding moment." This intervention related to time gives time a form by creating a turning point that marks the end of the old and the beginning of the new. It is at this moment of historical rupture that the nation-state inserts itself into being. As John Gillis notes, "People who have never seen or heard of one another, yet who regard themselves as having a common history . . . are bound together as much by forgetting as by remembering, for modern memory was born at a moment when Americans and Europeans launched a massive effort to reject the past and construct a radically new future."[10]

The inscription of a "founding moment" is crucial to the formation of the nation-state for two reasons. First, this inscription serves to structure time in such a way that it is reconstituted as linear, singular, and national time, turning it into the one and only continuity that frames all events and moments in relation to the founding moment. From then on, time *becomes* national history. In other words, it becomes difficult, if not impossible, to conceive of a past that was not national, or at least that did not exist in reference to national time. From then on, the histories of persons, associations, groups, practices, and ideas take their place in time always in reference to linear time as oriented around the founding moment, thereby becoming a part of the nation. In her investigation of the centennial and bicentennial celebrations of the American Revolution, Lyn Spillman states that this "founding moment" was crucial in the constitution of American national identity, not only in that it served as one of the key symbols of the American nation, but also in that it "became a central theme which could ease the introduction of other topics."[11] Spillman illustrates how during the bicentennial celebrations newsletter writers would always construct their stories in reference to the founding moment even when their topic was something not directly relevant to the revolution, such as community history, or, say, Italian influences on the architecture of the period. As illustrated here, the founding moment serves to both homogenize and nationalize time in such a way that all particular histories are subsumed under it, becoming a part of the one and only time of the national community.

Second, this inscription serves to constitute the state as a national subject vested with the ability (agency) to intervene and inscribe the nation into time. The founding moment of a nation-state often marks a triumphant war of independence, a civil war, or a revolution. Nationalist discourses are laden with narratives of emancipation and liberation from colonialism, expansionism, traditionalism, feudalism, autocracy, despotism, or fascism. In any case, there is always an enemy from which "the nation" is saved, at the "founding moment," by "the founders," for "the people." The new nation-state is presented as a new beginning for "the people," who have existed all along, but who were saved from the ruinous circumstances that immediately preceded the founding moment. This is why the immediate past is often demonized and the nation is situated in the distant, ancient past, barely traceable by historical record. This is why the discourse of nationalism (of the modern nation-state) presents the nation as simultaneously modern and ancient. As Duara notes, "While on the one hand, nationalist leaders and nation-states glorify the ancient or eternal character of the nation, they simultaneously seek to emphasize the unprecedented novelty of the nation-state, because it is only in this form that the people have been able to realize themselves as the subjects or masters of their history."[12]

In sum, the "founding moment" of the nation-state, often celebrated as an independence day, republic day, or day of liberation, serves to constitute "the people" as a national community living under one time as one nation; the immediate past as evil, threatening, and destructive to "the people"; and the new state as the heroic national subject that assumes the agency to step in and save "the people" from their malefactors. The multiple functions of the founding moment are illustrated in the following excerpt. The first official Turkish national history, *The Outline of Turkish History*, which was prepared and published in 1930 by the Turkish History Committee, which had been convened under the leadership of Mustafa Kemal Atatürk, concludes with the following sentences:

> The sons of Osman [the Ottoman dynasty] had long lost the ability and the honor to rule the Turkish nation. During the Armistice the Turkish nation encountered the worst devastation that it had ever faced in its history, which is as old as the history of the whole world. Almost no one contemplated the possibility of overthrowing the enemy armies and establishing an independent national Turkish State. [But] knowing the heroism of the Turkish nation in battlefields, the hardships it is facing and its needs, Mustafa Kemal took on the leadership of the nation and initiated an opposition in Anatolia (1919). . . . Mustafa Kemal, who saved the Turks from the sons of Osman and the worthless Caliphate, formed the Republic (29 October 1923). The Gazi [Mustafa Kemal],[13] who was elected as the

president of the Republic, engaged the Turkish nation on a path of true advancement and progress.[14]

In this paragraph alone, this national history constitutes (1) the Turkish nation as having a history "as old as the world"; (2) the immediate past as the worst catastrophe that the nation had ever faced; (3) the Ottoman dynasty and the caliphate as the agents of this devastation; (4) Mustafa Kemal Atatürk as the embodiment of the nation-state and the heroic savior of the nation; and (5) the founding moment of 29 October 1923 as the historical rupture that marked the beginning of the new nation-state and the end of the preceding calamity.

This historical inscription is a good illustration of the "double-time" of the nation. National time as structured by the national historians locates the nation in the ancient, so far back that it cannot be any older—"as old as the world" is as close as one can get to "eternal." This is a rhetorical strategy that serves to present the nation as a naturally bound, singular entity that has an existence above and beyond time, enduring temporal change, and preserving its incorruptible essence. Its existence is thereby rendered uncontestable and nonnegotiable. On the other hand, the political agent who has inscribed the nation into and above time has also set the nation upon a new path of "advancement and progress," thereby reconstituting it simultaneously as eternal and timeless and as novel and modern, that is, in double-time.

In Turkish national history, the effect of novelty and modernity (engaging upon a path of "advancement and progress") was achieved by the creation of a historical rupture, a break with the past marked by the founding of the republic on 29 October 1923. In order to create a new beginning, an end had to be created as well, which required the distancing of the nation from everything that marked the immediate past: the Ottoman rule and the caliphate as representatives of the Islamic legal-political system. Whatever Turkey was declared to be in 1923, it had to be something completely new, different from, and better than what had come before. This required the construction of the immediate past as worthless, corrupt, declining—as something that could not possibly be worth celebrating, but should only be forgotten and erased. This is why official Turkish national history deliberately pays only minor attention to the Ottoman period, which ranged from the early fourteenth century to the formation of the republic. And the attention that the Ottoman period does receive is devoted to presenting it as marked by increasing incompetence and corruption. *The Outline of Turkish History*, which locates the beginnings of the Turkish nation in Central Asia sometime around 9000 BC, traces its history up until the early twentieth century in 467 pages. Of this total, the section that covers Ottoman history takes up only 26 pages. In other words, the writing of official Turkish history covered the Ottoman period, which extended about six hundred years, in 26 pages (about 5 percent of the total). This book was later developed into the main compulsory textbook for use in history classes taught in all public high schools throughout the country.

Proliferating through the official national discourse was the view that Ottoman times were a part of the vague past, as if the empire had been a different country with a different people. The changing of the alphabet from Arabic to Roman letters in 1928 was a further and powerful reinforcement of this perception, which served to create the impression that the Ottomans spoke and wrote a different language, thereby inserting and enhancing a cultural and historical distance between the Turkish Republic and the Ottoman Empire.

The presentation of the nation-state as new and modern through the creation of a historical rupture seems to be a common element of most nationalisms. The construction of the French nation-state involved a similar break with the past. John Gillis draws attention to the ways in which French revolutionaries invented the "'Old Regime' by exaggerating its backwardness as well as its injustices, in order to justify their claim that 1789 represented a remarkable leap forward."[15] In other cases, such as that of Britain, where historical memory was not built around a patriotic founding moment, various mechanisms have nevertheless been employed in the making of national history to evoke certain historical periods (such as the industrial revolution) as points of historical rupture, breaks from the past, and changes toward modernity.[16]

Performing History in the Present: National Commemoration Days

The construction of historical memory around a "founding moment" involves not only the writing of official national histories and the preparation of textbooks for national education. More important, such founding moments are celebrated each year as republic days, independence days, liberation days, and other forms of commemorative practice. In other words, the making of history takes place not only in writing but also in public performance and different forms of public visibility. Commemoration days are a means of performing national history in the present, thereby inscribing history into daily life and public memory. The celebration of commemoration days, official ceremonies, ritualistic dramatizations of historical events, parades, and festivals are examples of such performance in the public sphere, whereby the public audience is interpellated as a national subject connected to the present as well as the past.

Commemoration days, which are part of what Gillis refers to as "national memory practices,"[17] serve at least three crucial functions in the construction of national identities. First, they are among the main mechanisms through which national history is inscribed into public life and are instrumental in *constructing public memory*. Commemoration days are a much more entertaining and effective way to elicit public interest and instruct people in national history than, say, history classes in schools. The performance of national history in the public sphere serves not only to incorporate that history into present-day life, but also to interpellate the public as the national subject for which this performance is being displayed. In other words, commemoration days are crucial mechanisms through which the audience is nationalized.

Second, commemoration days serve to locate the nation in time, thereby *historicizing the nation*. Commemorative celebrations constitute "the people" not only as a national community in the present, but also as a community connected to the past. What were once arbitrary and irrelevant events and moments in the past suddenly become relevant, almost personal and constitutive parts of the national self, imbued with new meaning and significance as constitutive of one's national belonging. "History" now means something different than before: a temporal field that is opened up to "the people" so that they can locate themselves in time, far beyond their own life spans. In other words, people who have never seen or heard of one another are bound together as parts of the same national community, not only spatially but also temporally. Someone in the distant past—whether the mythical leader responsible for the founding moment or the anonymous hero or heroine who selflessly fought against the enemy decades or centuries ago—comes to seem as close to a person as his or her immediate neighbors. "Women who carried cannonballs on their shoulders" during the War of Independence in Turkey—a common national theme of various monuments and memorials across the country, as mentioned in chapter 3—can stir up personal sentiments and feelings of connectedness some seventy years later.

Third, commemoration days are also effective in *nationalizing time*. The commemoration of a historical moment on a specific day every year serves to structure public time on a yearly basis, such that public life comes to be arranged around such days, especially if they are legal holidays. Even if the public is not really sure what exactly is being celebrated, or they are not informed, or they do not care, their lives are still arranged around these dates. Participating in the festivities or parades, watching fireworks, going on a family vacation, visiting parents, or even staying home to avoid the crowds—all become means through which the public is implicated in the celebration of the commemoration day. Whatever sentiments they evoke, these days of national significance become constitutive elements in the routine of everyday life, and structure its time on a national basis.

Whether through written histories and textbooks or through commemorative practices, official national history invades public life with a substantial vigor. And yet, in spite of all the strategies and techniques administered to naturalize and objectify this history, it is always surrounded by contestations and negotiations, articulated in many forms. In fact, it is within this field of contestation and articulation of many histories, each interpellating a different national subject, that nationalism becomes possible. As Duara notes, "Nationalism is rarely the nationalism of the nation, but rather represents the site where very different views of the nation contest and negotiate with each other."[18] Indeed, whether the American Declaration of Independence, the French Revolution, the Independence of India, or the formation of the republic in Turkey, founding moments are always also moments of prevalence over contending nationalisms, which are all crucial in the constitution of the founding moment. As such, commemorations of founding moments are always accompanied by contestations, criticisms, and challenges, often posed by contending nationalisms or projects that have been underprivileged by official nationalism. These may turn into alternative celebrations and countercommemorative practices. As I discuss later, the celebration of the conquest of Istanbul emerged as such an alternative to the official celebration of the formation of the secular republic on 29 October. While the 29 May celebrations were established as an Islamist alternative to the secular nationalist project, they served to reproduce an Islamist nationalist discourse that constitutes nationalism as a performative site, much as the official nationalist discourse does. In other words, nationalism should be understood as a field of presentation of contending nationalist projects, where the official discourse of the state has a privileged but not a final or uncontested status. In her study of the multiple articulations of Chinese nationalism, Ann Anagnost states, "The very impossibility of the nation as a unified subject means that this narrating activity is never final. For narrative exemplifies the performativity of language itself, disrupting the closure of any totalizing definition of the national community."[19]

Contestation of official history does not necessarily involve confrontation regarding its validity; rather, it unsettles the assumed naturalness and singularity. In other words, national histories are always contestable and controversial not because they are illusions or misrepresentations of the past, but because they claim closure and totality.[20] In this respect, it might be misleading to follow Ernest Gellner's reasoning when he notes, "The cultural shreds and patches used by nationalism are often arbitrary historical inventions. Any old shred or patch would have served as well."[21]

Treating the constitutive elements of national history as random and arbitrary "shreds and patches" results in overlooking the fact that the choice of one historical moment over another has crucial strategic consequences for the construction and negotiation of national identities. For example, there were several days in Turkish national history that could also have qualified as "founding moments," such as 23 April 1920, when the Grand National Assembly was formed and independence was declared (now celebrated officially as the National Independence and Children's Day). And yet, the founders chose to locate the founding moment not on 23 April 1920, but three years later, on 29 October 1923, the day when the Grand National Assembly declared the Turkish state a republic and elected its first president, Mustafa Kemal Atatürk. One of the crucial differences between these two moments is that, whereas the first National Assembly in 1920 consisted of elements of a much wider political spectrum, including Islamists, Ottomanists, and Kurdish nationalists as well as Bolshevists, the second one in 1923 was much more homogeneously assembled around the principles of secularism and Turkish nationalism under Atatürk's unchallenged authority. The official national history presents the plurality and heterogeneity of the first National Assembly as a problem and an impediment to the realization of Mustafa Kemal's secularist and nationalist ideals, which were finally achieved and declared in 1923.[22] The choice of this as the "founding moment" was obviously far from being random and arbitrary, and is still a crucial point of contention in Islamist, Kurdish, and leftist challenges to the official national history today.

In my analysis of the Islamist contestations of official nationalism, I examine different commemorative acts undertaken by Islamists, which had unsettling effects on the secularist constructions of national history. The celebration of 29 May by Islamist circles was not confined to the community of Refah supporters, but was considered the celebration of a national day, open to the public and accompanied by demands to make 29 May an official national holiday.

Commemorating 29 May: Conquering and Reconquering Istanbul

On 29 May 1996, travelers visiting Istanbul witnessed a rather peculiar celebration. A group of burly men dressed in Ottoman military clothing, some wearing false mustaches, were dragging a decorated sailboat along the asphalt road toward the central Taksim Square. Although it was no easy task to drag the sailboat uphill under the hot sun and the curious gaze of tourists on that summer day, the laboring men nevertheless displayed a solemn attitude of resolve and austerity, as if to remind the observing public of the grave significance of the historical event they were commemorating.

Tourists were not the only people who turned a curious gaze toward this peculiar parade: some inhabitants of Istanbul were equally puzzled, since 29 May was not an official holiday in Turkey. But others knew: this parade was a celebration of Conquest of Istanbul Day, commemorating 29 May 1453, when the Ottoman ruler Fatih Sultan Mehmet (Mehmet II, the Conqueror) conquered Constantinople, bringing the Byzantine Empire to an end. Born to a Christian mother, Mehmet II was twenty-one years old when he led the Ottoman army that seized control of Constantinople after a successful military campaign, which won recognition for the young sultan as a military genius. Realizing that the city was very well protected on the sides facing the Bosphorus Strait and the Marmara Sea, Mehmet II had seventy ships of the Ottoman fleet moved onto land, rolling them over oiled logs from a deeper point on the Strait (Beşiktaş), over the hill around Taksim, and down to Haliç Bay (the Golden Horn), thereby gaining access to the unprotected northern walls of the city. This strategy won Mehmet II not only a definite victory, but also the title Fatih (Conqueror) and recognition as one of the most successful of Ottoman rulers. It was this conquest that the men with false mustaches were celebrating as they dragged the decorated boat through the city some 550 years later.

Celebrations of 29 May usually started with a daytime parade, where dozens of men dressed up as Ottoman soldiers dragged a decorated sailboat, representing the Ottoman fleet, over the asphalt pavements of Istanbul's streets.

The parade was accompanied by a *mehter* band (the military band of the Ottoman army) dressed up in traditional costumes and playing Ottoman military marches. During the evening of 29 May, parades and festivities resumed at the İnönü Stadium, where several demonstrations were held depicting the conquest of Istanbul. An official from the city administration, dressed up to represent Fatih Sultan Mehmet, rode a white horse

543 YIL SONRA İSTANBUL TEKRAR FETHEDİLDİ!
Beyoğlu Belediyesi tarafından düzenlenen 'Temsili Fetih'le 543 yıl sonra İstanbul'un alınışı tekrar gözler önüne serildi. Fatih Sultan Mehmed'in, tarihte ilk kez karada yürüttüğü kadırgalar, Dolmabahçe'den Taksim'e çıkartılıp Kasımpaşa sırtlarından indirildi. Levendler, Fatih Sultan Mehmed ve Hocaları o dönemin kıyafetleriyle temsil edildiler. 100 kadar levendin çektiği üç kadırga yaklaşık iki saatlik bir gayret sonucu Kasımpaşa'ya çekildi ve burada havai fişekler atıldı.

Figure 15. "Ottoman soldiers" dragging a sailboat toward the "Conquest of Istanbul," commemorating the successful strategy of Mehmet the Conqueror (*Milli Gazete,* 29 May 1996).

around the stadium holding up his sword (or his thumb, as he did during the 1996 celebrations). The upheld thumb was the symbolic gesture of the Refah Party, which was widely used during the election campaign in 1994 and later. A representation of the Byzantine city walls was put up, but later toppled by men dressed up as Ottoman soldiers and wearing false mustaches.

Figure 16. The man portraying the Fatih, performing the Refah Party's salute, with thumbs up (*İstanbul* 20 [January 1997]: 35). Photograph by Manuel Çıtak.

During the 1997 celebrations, following the reenactment of the surrender of the Byzantines, the Ottoman soldiers raised the Turkish flag on the walls of the city. After the city was thus "conquered," a woman in white dress, representing the Byzantine city dwellers, approached the man portraying the Fatih, knelt down in front of him, and presented him with a bouquet of flowers. These dramatic performances were followed by *mehter* band presentations, firecrackers, and other entertaining festivities.

Another noteworthy part of the 1996 celebrations was that the evening call for prayers was carried over the speakers in the stadium, after which the performers, organizers, and set technicians, as well as some spectators, gathered on the field and collectively said their prayers.

The dramatization of the conquest and the activities around it abundantly employed various symbols that concertedly constructed a national subject performed as Ottoman, Islamic, and male. While the costumes, the impersonation of Fatih Sultan Mehmet, and the enactment of the conquest were performances of Ottoman identity, the raising of the current Turkish flag on the city walls as the symbol of victory was an unexpected mark that framed the whole performance as a national moment. By raising the Turkish flag instead of, say, an Ottoman banner, the Ottoman historical moment that was being commemorated through the celebrations was evoked as part of Turkish national history. This simple inscription of the symbol of the nation upon an Ottoman past served to incorporate the Ottoman experience within national memory.

Another means by which the celebrations interpellated a national subject was the main slogan of the night, "Biz-Biz-Biz, Fatihin Nesliyiz!" which translates as "We are the generation of the Conqueror" and also means "We are Fatih's kin." This slogan, which was chanted throughout the celebrations and published the next day in most of the Islamist newspapers covering the 29 May celebrations,[23] evoked a community linked to the Ottoman sultan through kinship ties. This was an interpellation of a national subject, invoked as the communal self ("We"), in which Fatih Sultan Mehmet and the present chanters of the slogan were connected not only temporally (across the linear time of the nation) and spatially (as conquering the same city), but also ethnically through blood ties.

A further inscription upon the communal body of this national subject was Islam. Nothing constituted this subject as Islamic more powerfully than the collective act of praying in the stadium, which interrupted the celebrations at prayer time. This interruption was an interjection of the time of Islam, which superseded both the secular time of the nation and the performed time of Ottoman history, suspending the latter two until prayers could be said. The fact that the collective prayers were offered on the field—the same field where Ottoman history and the seizure of Istanbul were being performed—inevitably turned the act of praying into a performance of identity. With the interjection of prayer, Islam dominated the field of performance, thereby emerging as the larger frame within which various other differences were united. The interjection of Islamic time also served to suspend social boundaries such that the performers, the spectators, the top-ranking politicians and leaders of the Refah Party, security personnel, and the men portraying Fatih and the Byzantine and Ottoman soldiers all gathered together on the field to carry out their prayers.

The only boundary not suspended during this unifying performance was that of gender: women, who were already seated in a segregated section of the stadium, offered their prayers in designated prayer rooms (mescit). In sum, the collective act of prayer inscribed Islam onto the performance of identities, underwriting it as the unifying bottom line around which various identities, ranging from Ottoman and national to those related to class and gender, were united.

The Construction of an Islamist National Identity and the Second Conquest

The commemoration of 29 May 1453 as a part of national history has unsettling effects on the official constructions of national identity. Although the public has been taught for years that the history of the modern nation

Figure 17. The performers, spectators, top-ranking politicians and leaders of the Refah Party, security personnel, and those portraying the Fatih and the Byzantine and Ottoman soldiers, all gathered together on the field to carry out their prayers during the 29 May celebrations (*Yeni Şafak*, 27 May 1997).

started in the 1920s with the emergence of Mustafa Kemal as the leader of Turkish independence, the celebration of 29 May inserts a rather out-of-date historical moment from 1453 as another constitutive moment of Turkish national history. This has disruptive effects on the public percep-tions of national time. The disruption unsettles Turkish national identity not only because the scales of national time are thrown off by about half a millennium, but also because the celebrated moment is part of the Ot-toman era, which has been evoked as the "other" against which modern Turkish national identity was constituted. This disruption subverts the mechanisms that present and maintain official national history as natural, objectively and almost fatalistically realized around the founding moment. By interjecting a date that is a part of the Ottoman experience, the forged and contestable nature of national history is revealed and the possibility that there may be multiple founding moments constituting multiple histo-ries becomes credible.

The unsettling and disruptive effects of the Conquest of Istanbul celebrations are evident in the way in which the commemoration of 29 May constitutes a different national subject, one that stands in contrast to the official national identity, defined around secularism and Turkish ethnicity. Even though both secularist and Islamist accounts of the conquest of Istanbul recognize it as one of the most important events of world history and honor Fatih Sultan Mehmet's genius, there is quite a significant disagreement as to exactly whose victory the conquest was. According to the official national history, this was undoubtedly a Turkish victory, narrated as follows:

> The seizure of Istanbul by the Turks brought an end to the East Roman Empire that had lasted around 1000 years. At that time, Istanbul's seizure by the Turks became a worldwide incident. It was acknowledged as an historical landmark ending the Middle Ages and bringing about a new era for civilization and humanity. . . . The conquest of Istanbul by the Turks was, at that time, understood as the defeat of all of Europe and the Christian world by the Ottoman Empire.[24]

In this account, it was the Turks who conquered Istanbul and victoriously inscribed a turning point on world history, and who are therefore presented as agents of history capable of not only putting an end to a thousand-year-old empire, but also opening up a new path for humanity. This nationalist rhetorical strategy, which declares the Turks inscribers of world history, not only locates the newly constituted Turkish national subject in fifteenth-century world history, but also vests it with a universal political agency.

In contrast, the Islamist account of the conquest does not make any reference to the "Turk" whatsoever. In a booklet published and distributed by the Islamist city administration of Istanbul on the occasion of the 542nd anniversary of the conquest, Sezai Karakoç, a leading Islamic writer and poet, constructs a different subject:

> When Fatih Sultan Mehmet conquered Istanbul, the city of Kaisers, he connected his time, his community and his army both to the message of the Great Prophet [Mohammed, who] prophesized during the Battle of the Ditch [that Istanbul would be conquered one day] on the one hand, and to the bearer of hopes for which future generations will be in dire need, on the other. . . . Fatih brought a new time to Istanbul, whose time had corroded. He brought the time of Islam.[25]

In a different article in the same book, Karakoç also writes,

No doubt, our army was heroic. And Fatih was a hero. . . . Fatih was no doubt a genius. But attempting to explain the conquest of Istanbul only with his genius, with the truly ingenious plan to move the ships over land, will not be a sufficient explanation for intellectuals who need to see things from a wider perspective. In reality, the conquest of Istanbul was an encounter between Islamic civilization and Western civilization, in which the West was defeated.[26]

As illustrated in these passages, in Islamist discourse the conquest of Istanbul is presented primarily as an Islamic victory, achieved by the Ottomans. Neither in this text, nor in most other writings on 29 May celebrations, is there any mention of the "Turk" as the victor. In the first of the two earlier passages, the conquest is presented as "connecting" the time and community of the Ottoman Sultan Mehmet II to the time and prophecy of the Prophet Mohammed. Islamist circles acknowledge that the prophet had prophesied the conquest of Istanbul by a Muslim commander. Islamic writing on the conquest of Istanbul is full of references to this prophecy, which connects Mehmet II's victory and the city of Istanbul not to a Turkish ethnic lineage, but to an Islamic and prophetic past. It should be noted, however, that the subject evoked in these passages is still a *national* subject, situated in the "us" implied in the statement "Our army was heroic." In contrast to the official nationalist discourse, this national subject is not ethnically constituted around the "Turk," but culturally constituted around an "Islamic civilization."

The construction of the victorious Islamic/Ottoman subject was common in the Islamist discourse of the Refah Party. At its official Web site, the city administration had a special section titled "The Conquest and Istanbul," where it was noted, "The conquest of Istanbul was the beginning point of the supremacy of Muslims over Europe, which will last for a long duration in subsequent years."[27] By presenting the conquest as a Muslim victory, the city administration's discourse constituted an Islamic subject as the agent of history. Furthermore, this statement explicitly established the conquest of Istanbul as a "beginning point," that is, a *founding moment* that marked the beginning of this alternative national time. Similar rhetorical strategies proliferated through the Islamist discourse on history.

The passages quoted earlier illustrate the rhetoric of the city administration, which connected the conquest of Istanbul simultaneously to the present time, to Islam, and to the agency of the Refah Party itself. Although Islam was presented as the "bearer of hopes" for current generations, it was the Ottoman/Islamic subject, Mehmet the Conqueror, who had brought this hope to Istanbul, and it was the Refah Party that was reviving and reclaiming this prophetic past in the present. In the discourse of the Refah Party that proliferated through such performative interventions, the party was presented as the one and only representative of the Ottoman/Islamic identity, centered in the city of Istanbul. This discourse conflated Islam, the Ottoman past, and the city of Istanbul into a singularity and presented it as the hope for the present generation, and the party as the political agent that had brought all of these forces together under its domain, thereby itself becoming the "bearer of hopes."

The links among the city of Istanbul and its conquest, Islam, Ottoman identity, the Refah Party, and national identity were carefully forged and mobilized quite effectively during election campaigns. During the local elections in 1994, this strategy won the mayoralty of Istanbul for the Refah Party candidate, Recep Tayyip Erdoğan. The campaign presented this young and dynamic candidate as "the new conqueror of Istanbul" and the Refah Party's anticipated victory as the "reconquest of Istanbul."

The notions of "reconquest" and the "second conquest of Istanbul" were evoked quite frequently in the Islamist press and by the Islamist political elite. Celebrations of 29 May were often reported by the Islamist media with the titles "Istanbul Has Been Conquered Again" or "The Reconquest of Istanbul."[28] In his opening speech delivered during the 29 May 1996 celebrations to an audience that included guests from various Muslim communities around the world, the leader of the Refah Party, Necmettin Erbakan, said, "We are on the eve of a new conquest, which merges with the incident that took place 543 years ago. . . . As the Islamic world, we will accomplish this with the help of Allah."[29] Similarly, a commentary that appeared in another Islamist newspaper noted, "This ümmet [Muslim community], which is brought together by an iron will and tekbir [the unity of Allah], will understand the real meaning of fetih [conquest] and make Istanbul once again the capital city of Islam, as it was before."[30]

In these statements the idea of "conquest" was employed to describe an Islamic accomplishment, and thus served to constitute "the Muslim community" as a transnational pan-Islamic movement. It has been argued that such appeals to pan-Islamic ideals, which seek to mobilize various Islamist movements around the globe toward a unified goal, are destined to fail, because the demands and constraints placed by nationalism and the nation-state system inevitably confine such movements within national boundaries.[31] However, rather than contradicting the nationalist objectives of the Refah Party, the formulation of the Islamic subject as a globally constituted community actually strengthened the Islamist-nationalist discourse of the Refah party. The presentation of "conquest" as an accomplishment serving the needs of the Muslim community not only in Turkey, but also throughout the globe, allowed the Refah Party to vest the Islamist movement in Turkey with both a national and a global mission. Within this discursive frame, the city of Istanbul gained further importance as the center of a global Islamic civilization, imbued with meaning and value that went beyond the confines of national borders. The investment of Istanbul with global importance only strengthened the national significance of the city (as evoked in Islamist discourse) as the center of an "Ottoman-Islamic civilization" constituting the core of Turkey's new national identity.

As discussed in chapter 3, within Islamist discourse the promotion of the idea of an "Ottoman-Islamic civilization" does not contradict, but is in fact constitutive of, national identity. The endorsement of the Ottoman-Islamic identity as an alternative nationalism was explicitly illustrated in a speech given by Mayor Recep Tayyip Erdoğan during the third Traditional Youth Festival:

> As the grandchildren of a nation that has always been at the forefront in the quest for civilization, you have to put an end to mimicry. If Turkey is to reach the heights of contemporary civilizations, it can only do so with its own civilization. The youth has to return to its true roots. The poet who wrote our National Anthem, Mehmet Akif Ersoy, did not write his poem in a disco or when he was drunk. He wrote it in Tacettin Dergahı [a dervish lodge], where he disciplined his soul.[32]

The civilization that the mayor referred to here as being Turkey's own is the Ottoman-Islamic civilization, which he presented as constituting the true source of Turkish national identity. The source is to be found not in Western influences and secularism (discos and alcohol), but in Islamic education and traditions (the dervish lodges). By drawing attention to the fact that the national anthem of the republic was written by a devout Muslim, the mayor implied that Turkish nationalism was made possible by an Ottoman-Islamic culture, not by an imitative secularist-Westernist discourse.

Islamist discourse maintains that if the source of true Turkish national identity is Ottoman-Islamic culture, its true capital resides in Istanbul. The municipal Web site noted, "Istanbul is the gem of Ottoman-Islamic civilization and its eternal Capital City. Because of this, Istanbul has a special place in all of our hearts."[33] In contrast to the official national discourse, which constructs the national subject as secular and ethnically Turkish and locates its center in Ankara, the alternative national identity evoked here is defined as culturally Islamic and Ottoman, and centered in the city of Istanbul.

The repeated emphasis on establishing Istanbul as a city at the center of an "Ottoman-Islamic civilization" proliferated throughout the publications, documents, and other promotional materials distributed by the city. This promotion was especially pronounced during the 1996 United Nations Habitat II conference due to the presence of a global audience that had come to Istanbul to attend the conference. The exhibitions sponsored by the city administration for the Habitat II conference included photography, painting, miniatures, examples of the traditional art of book binding, and other exhibits, most of which were presented as "traditional Turkish-Islamic art" and architectural forms practiced under the Ottoman Empire. In a thirty minute video cassette prepared exclusively for members of the foreign media visiting for the Habitat II conference, the opening scene started with the Sultanahmet Mosque, famous Ottoman tiles, and classical Turkish music, while the voiceover presented Istanbul as a city where "history is grasped with every step."[34] What was meant by "history" here was confined to the Ottoman era, which contrasts with the official understanding of history, which locates the origins of the nation in pre-Islamic central Asia. The identification of national history with the Ottoman era and that with Istanbul was a conflation of history and space that allowed for the reimagining of Istanbul as an Ottoman city and the bearer and place of the history of the nation. This rhetorical strategy not only removed the pre-Islamic past from national history but also reframed the time of the republic as a deviation away from it.

In these attempts to identify national history with the Ottoman past, "Ottoman" was understood as a social-political order culturally rooted in Islamic norms and standards, the superiority of which was historically evident in its power to maintain its rule for six centuries and in its glory as a global power. The Ottoman system was presented as being superior to the West not only because it had actually defeated the "West" in 1453, when Istanbul was conquered,[35] but also because it provided a more just and advanced social-political system, framed by Islamic norms, within which diverse religions and peoples (*millet*) lived together in harmony and peace. The decline and collapse of the Ottoman Empire was attributed primarily to Westernization, and the secular republic was held responsible for Turkey's globally weak position, cultural deterioration, and the loss of self that the nation currently suffers.

This understanding of Ottoman history stands in direct contrast to the official national history of the republic, which attributes the decline of the

Ottoman Empire, among other things, to Islam and its resistance to modernization and secularism.[36] Contrary to secularist attempts to dissociate national history from the Ottoman-Islamic past, the Islamist rhetoric of the city administration presented a new sense of national history as essentially located in this past, a past that can be traced in the present through various architectural, cultural, and social practices and monuments of the Ottoman era. It was this image of Istanbul as old, historically rooted in the Ottoman times, constituted through Islamic practices and traditions, that was presented as the real home of the nation. Istanbul, introduced as the real space of the nation, was portrayed as facing the threat of destruction and loss of self and in need of protection against the artificial, imposed, alienating secularist interventions and West-oriented modernizing influences of the state.

This continual emphasis on historicity was prevalent throughout the discourse surrounding the activities of the city administration. The authenticity of the national identity was sought in the degree to which its constituent elements were rooted in history and tradition. It was as if, the more traditional the selected markers of this identity were, the more authentic and real they would be. Therefore, the constituent elements of this alternative national identity were located in traditions, practices, architectural forms, styles, and genres that were linked to Ottoman times. However, since these practices and forms have been recovered from the past to be incorporated into the present, they are also always new. In other words, in order to give presence to things that are associated with the past so as to constitute a new national subject in the present, they are reconstituted, forged, and displayed in the present as representations of the past. Therefore, the city administration diverted its resources to forge an Islamic-Ottoman culture (which was, no doubt, inspired by Islamic and Ottoman architectural, intellectual, and cultural traditions, that is, not fake but forged), which was presented as traditional, historically rooted, and therefore the true source of national identity. In this respect, the promotional activities of the city administration that created an image of Istanbul as an essentially Islamic-Ottoman city were, to a large extent, efforts to forge a past that was constitutive of the present national self. The historicity of this nation was an effect achieved by posing it in contrast to the new, to the recent, to the modern. It was as if things that have appeared recently, such as modern high-rises, discos, and new social and cultural practices, things that do not have a continuity with the past, were inauthentic and foreign and therefore could not be constitutive of the national self.

It is in such a discursive context that the idea of the "second conquest" of Istanbul was introduced as a campaign slogan of the Refah Party. The idea of the second conquest of Istanbul was an effective rhetorical strategy that served to construct the Refah Party as a political agent charged with a historical-prophetic mission to save Islamic civilization from the destructive effects of Westernism. By designating Istanbul as the locus of Islamic civilization, the "conquest" of the city became the only means through which this civilization could be saved. Therefore, the construction of an Islamist subject vested with the agency to carry out a national as well as a global mission required the proliferation of the images of Istanbul as the locus of Islamic civilization, which was projected as being under the threat of destructive alien forces. This was precisely why it was crucial that Istanbul be continually evoked as a city under the threat of degeneration and destruction by forces alien to its "core" Islamic culture. In other words, the construction of the Islamist subject as a heroic political agent was predicated upon the victimization of the city of Istanbul, which was proliferated through the "discourse of reconquest."[37]

The Victimization of Istanbul and the Empowerment of the Islamist Subject

As discussed in chapter 3, the theme of the victimization of the city of Istanbul proliferated in various publications of the Islamist city administration and by Islamist writers. In one article, the state's republican ideology was blamed for "trying to establish Western cultural institutions in Istanbul in order to make it look like a European city."[38] As a result, the author noted, "Istanbul could not preserve its historical and cultural legacy, its distinctive identity." In another article, the real threat to the Ottoman-Islamic subject was presented as what the author referred to as the "Fourth Istanbul."[39] According to Dursun, in addition to the ancient (Byzantine), the Ottoman-Islamic, and the modern-Westernized parts (identities) of the city, a new Istanbul had come about as a result of intense migration from the country and Anatolian villages, constituting the "Provincial Istanbul." It was this Istanbul, where migrants had failed to become Istanbullians but instead had "provincialized" Istanbul, that was indicated as the source of the city's chronic problems. Dursun noted:

> Today this "Provincial Istanbul" is overwhelming both the Byzantine and the Ottoman-Islamic Istanbuls. The most salient mark of the provincial is the lack of standards, rules, laws and aesthetics. And yet, the most important quality of the Ottoman-Islamic Istanbul was having standards, aesthetics,

rules and superior values. These standards and aesthetic forms, which are re-flected in objects, structures, mosques, minarets, tombs, calligraphy, paintings, stones, palaces, everything in the surroundings, does not mean anything to the "provincial." This is the main factor that threatens Istanbul today.[40]

The strategy employed here was a classing technique that privileged the Ottoman-Islamic subject as upper class, with urban "superior values," by marking the "provincial" as the other, lacking taste and aesthetic values. This association of Ottoman-Islamic culture with "superior values" posi-tioned against the value-lacking "provincial" also served to constitute the Refah-Islamist circles as the bearers of this privileged status. This classing of Istanbul was also evident in several other discursive media through which Istanbul was displayed by the city administration. In the official biweekly publication of the city, the "Fourth Istanbul" was explicitly con-demned as the main threat to the well-being of the city. In an article titled "The Southeast in Istanbul," the author wrote:

> We did not want them to come to the city, and we had taken our preven-tive measures. Then the system broke down, and they came to Ankara as parliamentarians. . . . After that their fellow countrymen started to come one by one. And then the barrier collapsed and the cities were flooded. . . . First we pretended not to see it. They brought their songs, we pretended not to hear it. We prohibited their singers to go into radio and television studios. . . . But then technology ruined everything and cassette tapes start-ed to circulate. Once the cassettes were shouting all over the streets, it was no longer possible to avoid hearing them. They brought their *lahmacun*,[41] which started to smell in every corner of the city. We were defeated.[42]

The classing strategy employed in this paragraph is rather complex in that it engages several different markers of lower-class status, conveniently packaged into the constitution of the "provincial other" as the alien infest-ing the city. "Their music," scorned as being too loud, is *Arabesk* music that was banned from television and radio stations until the early 1990s, and "their food," *lahmacun*, which is scorned as being too smelly, is a prominent marker of lower-class, provincial taste, with its heavy onion-garlic spicing. The "southeasterners" are depicted as acting en masse and coming as a "flood," infesting the city with their music and food, in huge numbers.

What is also interesting in this paragraph is the clear demarcation drawn between the Ottoman "we" and the republican other, as well as the incrimination of the new secular state in an unusually implicit way. The "system" that broke down, which marked the onset of this southeastern

(Kurdish) migration, is an implicit reference to the establishment of the republic, when parliamentarians from all over Turkey, including the Kurdish regions, were invited to Ankara. The first sentence in the quoted passage suggests that until the republic was established, the "Ottoman-we" had been effectively governing a complex society, keeping the provincial-other successfully at bay. The formation of the republic is framed as a "breaking-down of the system," thereby once again constituting the secular state as the agent responsible for urban decay and the degeneration of Islamic-Ottoman high culture.

Such images of Istanbul, depicting the city as suffering at the hands of corruption, alienation, and degeneration, proliferated through various Islamist publications and performances. Istanbul was displayed as a place that is open to penetration and destruction, a place that is defenseless in the face of the modernizing and Westernizing influences of the secular state. It was also presented as the central mark of Turkish national identity, defined around an Ottoman-Islamic culture, which was presented as being in dire need of a heroic savior or "conqueror." An Islamist writer, who claimed that Prophet Mohammed had prophesied that Istanbul would be conquered not once but many times, noted, "Fatih Sultan Mehmet saved Istanbul by conquering it, [but] who is going to save the people who are sleeping now? This will happen with the second conquest."[43] Here the "new conqueror" is evoked as the savior of the victimized Istanbul. Therefore, the Islamist subject is endowed with agency and empowered to step in and save Istanbul. By assigning the city a central role in the constitution of national identity, the writer made saving Istanbul an act of saving the nation.

In sum, 29 May celebrations played a crucial role in the construction of the Islamist elite as the guardian and savior of the Ottoman-Islamic nation and the maker of its history. The 29 May commemorations served several crucial functions toward this end. First, as the public performance of an alternative national history, they framed the first conquest of Istanbul in 1453 as an essentially Islamic victory, thereby producing a history defined around a culturally Islamic identity rather than an ethnically Turkish-secular one. Second, they served to establish Istanbul as the true center of this Ottoman-Islamic identity, defined in civilizational terms. Third, they produced images of an Istanbul under siege; threatened by Westernization, imitative and crooked modernization, and urbanization; and in dire need of a savior. Fourth, they promoted the idea of "reconquest" or "the second conquest of Istanbul" not only as a nationalist goal but also a prophetic mission. And finally, this discourse of reconquest served to establish the Islamist political elite organized around the Refah Party as the new conqueror.

The public projection of Ottoman-Islamic national identity emerged as a contestation of official national history. The insertion of an alternative founding moment, 29 May 1453, contradicted the idea that official national history could have begun in 1923. What had been constituted by official nationalism as *external* to national history and belonging to an Ottoman past invoked as the "other," was inserted into public memory as an alternative founding moment. Official national history and its founding moment were destabilized, thereby rendering secular national history visible, contestable, and negotiable. However, while the projection of this alternative national identity served to contest secular national history, it also reproduced and kept intact the ideals of the modern nation-state. The 29 May commemorations emerged as reproductions of an alternative national time that displaced official nationalism, but retained the main nationalist enterprise (one nation = one time = one state). As such, the 29 May celebrations not only produced an Islamic identity in the public sphere, but also served to nationalize Islamic discourse.

As the Islamist celebrations of 29 May gained momentum in the years after 1994, the official 29 May ceremonies also started to gain more media attention. However, since the celebration of 29 May had become so closely associated with Islamism and the Refah Party, the official ceremonies organized by the state were characterized by ambivalence and tension. While the secular state recognized 29 May as a day of historical significance, authorities became quite uneasy about being perceived as celebrating something that bore Islamic references. This tension was openly expressed during the official ceremony in 1997, which took place soon after the famous National Security Council decree issue in February against the rising threat of political Islam. The official ceremony on 29 May, where protocol required that both the mayor of Istanbul and representatives of the military attend the commemoration, became the site of an explicit clash between Islamist and secularist discourses over the conquest. During the routine speeches, whereas the Islamist Mayor Erdoğan asked Allah for the recovery of the freedom of religion that was granted by Mehmet the Conqueror, the military representative said, "We are calling out to the whole world once again, that we are determined to protect the secular and democratic Turkish Republic, which Great Atatürk entrusted to us, with our lives if necessary."[44]

In sum, 29 May is a crucial intervention related not only to public space, but also to public time (i.e., national history). The effect of this intervention, very similar to the effects of others discussed earlier, was a contestation of the power of secularism—in this case, its power to dictate national history in secularist terms. This contestation did not terminate the authority of secularism, but it served to render secular authority visible and negotiable. History emerged as a contested site rather than an established and natural singularity, and the secularist attempts to maintain it as uncontestable and natural were revealed, themselves contested and opened up to negotiation. But at the same time, in revealing an alternative national history, the Islamist interventions reproduced the "one nation = one state = one history" model of the modern nation-state and emerged as agents of an alternative modernization project with an alternative nationalist ideology.

Conclusion

This study began with the premise that modernity is an intervention related to bodies, places, and times so as to displace and induce movement. It is an intervention that displaces by defaming the present so that movement toward the future begins, an intervention that makes the present look so unpleasant that the modern subject is oriented to move away from it toward something better. As such, modernizing interventions involve a two-fold projection. The existing condition is projected as a malady, and the future ideal is projected as a goal toward which transformation is to take place. This transformation is made desirable by projecting it as "advancement and progress" rather than as aimless change. It is in this defamatory and transformative intervention that political agency is created and the modern subject emerges.

Chapters 2, 3, and 4 examined interventions related to bodies, places, and times, respectively, in order to discern the ways in which these media have been instrumental toward the realization of modernization projects and the institutionalization of nationalist ideologies. Chapter 2 discussed the ways in which the female body, designated as the embodiment and symbol of the nation, became a target of interventions for the construction of new or alternative senses of nationhood, whereas the male body represented political power and agency toward the construction of leadership and the implementation of modernization projects. During the early years of the Turkish Republic, the projection of the national ideals upon the body resulted in interventions that allowed the state to impose upon its subjects the image of the modern, secular, Western-looking citizen and to gain political agency in the process. Interventions related to the female body, particularly around the issue of the new veiling in the 1990s, similarly served the construction of an alternative national identity, and also allowed the Islamist leadership of the Refah Party to gain political agency toward the realization of a contending Islam-based nationalist project.

As the wearing of the new veiling became a prominent phenomenon throughout the Middle East in the 1990s, literature studying it also proliferated. These studies examine the multiple meanings of the veil, often providing ethnographic accounts of the reasons why women take up the new veiling, its significance in terms of status and class, its social and economic functions, and so on. This study departs from this line of inquiry by taking the body as a political field and locus of analysis instead of the veil itself, and examines the effects of the veil on the body. It looks at how the veil operates to redraw the public-private boundaries upon the body, thereby challenging the established norms of publicness and privacy. This function of the veil was used both by the founding elite when they unveiled the female body toward the establishment of a modern, West-oriented public sphere where a modern national subject was constructed, and by the Islamists of the 1990s, who reveiled the female body so as to insert new, Islamic norms of privacy in the secular public sphere, thereby disrupting the authority of secularism.

Chapter 3 examined the ways in which interventions related to places operate to give new national meaning to cities and city spaces toward the advancement and institution of official or contending nationalist ideologies. The designation of Ankara as the center of the nation during the founding years of the republic allowed the founding elite to build a new city from scratch where a new sense of nationhood would be instituted. What had been an insignificant peripheral province of the Ottoman Empire suddenly became the center of a new nation, where the monuments of Turkish modernity, secularism, and nationalism proliferated. Modernizing interventions related to places brought about a movement in space, from the old capital to the new, from the old city centers to the new. It was in these dislocating and mobilizing interventions that the new state projected its own modernization project and emerged as the agent that inscribed the nation into space.

By designating Istanbul as the true heart and soul of the nation in contrast to Ankara, Islamists of the 1990s resorted to a similar strategy to advance their alternative nationalist project. Designating Istanbul as the center of the Ottoman-Islamic civilization that constitutes Turkey's "true" national identity, Islamists utilized similar strategies and techniques to unsettle the established norms of nationhood centered in Ankara, and attempted to institute in its place a similarly homogenizing and transformative (and, in that respect, modernizing) nationalist project. Both the founding elite and the Islamists of the 1990s portrayed these "temple-cities" of their respective ideologies as in dire need of guardianship and transformative intervention, and projected themselves as the only agents capable of securing the needed changes.

Chapter 4 examined interventions related to time that locate a "founding moment" around which time is restructured and a national history is written. Such founding moments are the constitutive moments of a nation which become the parameters of national history and are inserted into public memory via commemorative practices such as Republic, Independence, or Liberation Days. Official Turkish history, which was written by a committee convened under the leadership of Mustafa Kemal Atatürk, inscribed the Turkish nation into time, defamed the Ottoman and Islamic past, established Atatürk as the founder, and set the founding moment as 29 October 1923. Since then, this historical rupture that marked the beginning of the new state and the ending of the preceding malady has been celebrated every year as Republic Day. Such commemorative practices not only serve to perpetuate the linear time of the nation, but also implicate the public in the making of national memory.

The unofficial commemoration of the conquest of Istanbul on 29 May 1453 by Islamists relocated the national founding moment in the fifteenth century, thereby reconstituting the national history within an Ottoman-Islamic time frame and unsettling official national history, which was framed around a secular-Turkish time in the early twentieth century. While secularist imaginations of history were unsettled by Islamist interventions, the notion of the nation-state as an overarching, universal category that was predicated upon the conjuring of a homogenous, monolithic nation living in a single, linear time was retained and reinforced. In other words, within the reinforced framework of the modern nation-state, Islamist commemorative practices produced an alternative, yet equally authoritative, nationalist discourse that retained the formula "one nation = one state = one history."

The Normalization of National Ideology into Public Knowledge

The cases analyzed in chapters 2–4 demonstrate that interventions related to bodies, places, and times serve to develop, promote, and institute a new nationalist ideology. The goal of these interventions is to normalize and naturalize this ideology such that it is transformed into public discourse by becoming the norm and standard around which public life is organized and public knowledge is ordered. This is a crucial transformation involving a process of institutionalization of an ideology such that, when it is complete, the partiality of that ideological view comes to be experienced as impartial, factual knowledge. When the perception, experience, interpretation, and assessment of the world come to be dictated by the axioms, categories, and hierarchies of an ideology, its boundaries that set it apart from other ways of seeing and being in the world become invisible, disappearing behind the guise of normalcy and obviousness. In this sense, secularism is an ideology that has been successfully institutionalized in Turkey, in that soon after the foundation of the new state, it was no longer seen as an ideology and came to be regarded as the nonnegotiable and factual norm of public life. It is also in this sense that Islamist interventions in the public sphere in the 1990s contested and subverted the authority of secularism, rendering it negotiable and visible once again.

The cases analyzed here illustrate that the normalization of a nationalist ideology involves the formation of a national public sphere, the creation of a new national subject, the nationalization of land, the writing/projection of a new national history, and the creation of new class hierarchies and a sense of a new national high culture. These normalizing interventions also vest the intervening subject with agency and authority toward the construction of a centralized rule of governance, the building of a new nation, and modernization. Therefore, these interventions have a self-constitutive function, where actions produce the actors and not vice versa.

Observing the interventions of the Islamists related to bodies, places, and times, I have concluded that in Turkey Islamism has advanced an alternative nationalist project that is equally modernizationist to that of secularism and hence has produced what can be referred to as Islamic modernism. As the cases examined here illustrate, Islamists employed quite modernist techniques whereby bodies, places, and times were presented as victims of existing conditions and in need of a savior. This rhetoric called for a remedial intervention that was necessary to save the nation, its land, and its civilization, serving to legitimize Islamist interventions and to constitute Islamists as the agents of this heroic deed. By upholding an alternative set of norms around which the national public sphere was to be reorganized, Islamists produced sets of hierarchical binaries similar to those produced by the secularists, such as backward-advanced, low culture–high culture, provincial-urban, and degenerate-salubrious, that served to create the Islamist subject as an equally viable, modern, and competent competitor to the secularist subject in governing the nation. These Islamist interventions had disruptive effects on the authority of secularism, both because they challenged the secularist basis of official national identity by reconstituting it on an Islamic-cultural basis and because they constituted an alternative, nonstate political subject that assumed the authority to represent the nation.

Islamist interventions also attempted to normalize Islamism as a new national ideology, but this project was cut short as a result of pressures and protests by secularist circles, particularly the military, that culminated in the National Security Council decree against political Islam in 1997.

Islamic Modernism and the Emergence of the AK Party

Under the Refah Party, Islamic discourse turned into an Islamist political project that contested the authority of secularism, but retained the nationalist, homogenizing, and authoritative systems of state control intact and uncontested. It is this fusion of Islamic discourse with modern systems of control that became a concern not only for secularist circles, but also for some Islamist circles as well. In this respect, it is significant that Islamist intellectuals such as Ali Bulaç have been warning the Islamist movement against the dangers of nationalism and modernity and suggesting that it remain a social movement that works toward the expansion of democratic rights and freedoms in civil society.[1]

As the Refah Party became a popular party, more than doubling its support base during the early 1990s, it also found it necessary to veer its ideological stance toward the center of the political spectrum. However, this resulted in increasing tensions within the party, mostly between the conservative and fundamentalist line, which took an antagonistic and uncompromising stance toward secularism and the republic, and the moderate line, which endorsed compromise and dialogue with secularist circles. This latter line, organized around the Istanbul city administration under the leadership of Mayor Erdoğan, grew more powerful during Erdoğan's incumbency as his popularity soared in Istanbul. In order to facilitate dialogue with secularism, the Istanbul city administration under Erdoğan diverted substantial resources to organize forums, panels, conferences, and seminars to publicly debate secularism and the role and status of Islam within the current constitutional system with other social forces, particularly secularist circles. The response of secularists to these invitations has been marked by consistent and stark rejection. An adamantly secularist journal, *Devinim*, published a special issue on this topic titled "Compromise Is Not Possible with Reactionaries!" The author of the lead article noted, "They use terms like Islamic intellectual and ask us to go into dialogue with them. There can be no such thing. An intellectual cannot be Islamist, and an Islamist cannot be an intellectual. The reason is very clear. An Islamist wants the state to be governed according to the principles of Islam, whereas an intellectual is secular."[2]

This reasoning, which has resonated through secularist discourse, refuses to acknowledge Islamism as a legitimate political contender with which constitutional norms may be negotiated. Secularist circles were convinced from the onset that Islamist interventions in the public sphere could serve only the goal of forcefully taking over the state and establishing an Islamist regime based on the Shariat, similar to the situaton in Iran. Within this secularist discourse, a mere piece of cloth in the form of a headscarf came to be perceived as a direct threat to the security of the state and the existence of the secular system.

Islamists' interventions may not have reached their goal of transforming society as they envisioned, but their overall effect has been to open up the principle of secularism to negotiation. The advancement of an alternative nationalist ideology that projected a different sense of nationhood with a radically different understanding of national history resulted in unsettling the power and normalized status of secularism in the public sphere and forced it to be perceived as just another ideological position. In other words, Islamist interventions served to reveal that secularism is neither natural nor a fact of public life, but indeed another forged and partial principle that is quite negotiable and contestable. It was particularly this effect of Islamist interventions, which had unsettled the authority of secularism, that the state responded to with an ultimatum issued in February 1997.

On 28 February 1997, the National Security Council (NSC) issued a decree calling for measures to be taken against "reactionism" and toward the enforcement of secular principles and a tighter control on religious institutions and organizations. During the following month, the NSC held meetings with various bureaucrats, politicians, representatives of nongovernmental organizations, and the media, briefing them on the current threat posed by Islamic fundamentalism and the measures that needed to be taken against this threat. Basically, the military was instructing "civil society" how to carry out the vision and objectives of the military so as to crush the rise of political Islam, but without directly intervening itself. For this reason, the 28 February decree has been referred to as the "mild intervention" or "postmodern coup."[3] It is important to note that a majority of these civil society associations more than enthusiastically complied with the requests of the military.

The indirect intervention of 1997 was the closing of all venues for the formal negotiation of constitutional principles. The military explicitly established itself as the ultimate overseer of the secular system, which would not be opened up to negotiation or contestation. The ban on the headscarf, which was enforced under the tutelage of the military, was the articulation of intolerance toward contestations of secularism.

What was particularly unacceptable to secularist circles and the military leading up to the February 1997 decree was that the leaders of the Refah/Fazilet Party were frequently making antagonizing statements against the founding ideology of the republic, particularly secularism, and resorted to a rhetoric that used Islam as a mobilizing force. The party leadership around Necmettin Erbakan went so far as to make public statements in which they told the electorate that voting for the Refah Party was a precondition to becoming a true Muslim. Note that this call was in outright defiance of the authority of official Islam and therefore a stark rejection of the basic postulate of secularist ideology that sanctions only the Directorate of Religious Affairs to speak on behalf of and represent Islam. These statements of the Refah Party leaders were later used against them when they were tried and sentenced, resulting in the shutdown of the Refah Party by the Constitutional Court in 1998 and the barring of both Erbakan and Tayyip Erdoğan from active political involvement until 2003.

Even though Erbakan and Erdoğan shared this common fate, there were important differences in their views. While Erbakan represented the conservative older generation of leaders within the party, Erdoğan was the leader of the younger moderate wing that was in power in the Istanbul city administration, which later separated from the Refah Party to found the Adalet ve Kalkınma (AK) (Justice and Development) Party in 2001. During his mayoralty in Istanbul, Erdoğan frequently stated that their party's duty was to serve not just their supporters but the larger public, regardless of their political opinions. Erdoğan presented their cause as one of democratization and autonomy with regard to civil society, instead of resorting to claims of being the only true representatives of Muslims in Turkey, as the Refah Party leadership was doing. In stating their policy objectives and their justifications, rather than turning to the Koran and the sacred sources of Islam, they invariably resorted to a liberal discourse, demanding from the secular state a recognition of basic individual rights and liberties, particularly freedom of conscience, which involved more autonomy for the practice and knowledge of religion in Turkey.

This difference in the rhetorics of the Refah Party leadership and the moderate wing that gathered around Erdoğan became more pronounced after the NSC decree of 28 February 1997. This decree set off a soul-searching phase among the ranks of the Refah/Fazilet Party, especially among the younger generation. After 28 February, the antisecularist remarks of the Refah Party leaders toned down substantially, and they started to openly endorse secularism. They claimed that it was the state that was actually antisecular because it was directly meddling in religious affairs and was not recognizing freedom of conscience. They claimed that the Fazilet Party was the truly secular party because it was in favor of a true separation of the affairs of the state from religious affairs. However, this rhetorical maneuver was not sufficient to ease the growing dissatisfaction within the party. The growing discontent with the oldfashioned undemocratic methods of leadership and policies that unnecessarily antagonized the secular state and the military culminated in the separation of the moderate wing from the Fazilet Party to establish the AK Party.

The AK Party's electoral success during the November 2002 general elections only a year after it had separated from the Fazilet Party marked the beginning of a new era not only in Turkish history but also globally in terms of the place and status of Islam within modern secular systems. The clear victor in these elections was the AK Party under the leadership of Tayyip Erdoğan. The Refah/Fazilet Party's successor, the Saadet Party under Erbakan's leadership, received only 2.5 percent of the vote. Obtaining 34 percent of the general vote, the AK Party won a majority of the seats in parliament, allowing it to form a government on its own. In fact, the AK Party's victory was so substantial that it had the two-thirds majority necessary to make amendments to the constitution. In other words, for the first time in the history of Turkey, a political party with Islamist origins had come to power with a sufficient majority to change the constitution. Hence, it would be possible, at least hypothetically, for the AK Party to, say, remove the secularism clause from the constitution. However, such an option was never even uttered within the ranks of the AK Party, and its leader, Prime Minister Erdoğan, has stated at every opportunity that they are a secular party and are adamantly against the use of religion for political purposes. As soon as the AK Party came to government, the first task they undertook was advancing Turkey's long-held dream to become a member of the European Union (EU). Of course, since the EU membership process necessitated that the military cease to interfere in politics, it was a most reliable guarantee that the military would not be taking any action against the AK Party government.

The global significance of the AK Party government was that this was going to be the first experience of an Islam-based political movement coming to power with an overwhelming majority in a strictly secular system, without facing military intervention or other restrictions to its government. Hence, secularist circles not only in Turkey but in the whole world would be watching the outcome of this genuine experiment in what an Islam-based political party could do with a modern-secular system when it could enjoy being in power without the restraints of a coalition partner or the fear of a military intervention.

The founders of the AK Party under the leadership of Erdoğan left the Refah/Fazilet Party in order to pursue a more liberal, less confrontational political line by endorsing secularist ideals, downplaying Islamism, and giving priority to economic liberalization and development. They refused to be associated with political Islam in any way and frequently made public declarations that the worst damage to Islam is brought about by its politicization, thereby indirectly condemning the policies of the former Refah/Fazilet Party. They even rejected labels such as "Muslim Democrat" or "Islamic Democrat" that were ascribed to them by the secular media, because they wanted to project a new public image that was dissociated from Islam as far as possible. The headscarf again emerged as a symbol of political ideology, but this time the AK Party used it to mark its difference from the Refah/Fazilet Party, which had used it as the banner of their political movement. On numerous occasions Erdoğan openly stated that the headscarf issue was not the AK Party's concern, that Turkey had much more pressing problems, and that the party refused to be distracted by such trivial matters.

That the AK Party's political lineage reached back to the Refah Party's moderate wing partially explains why the AK Party government had no difficulty in continuing some of the important economic and foreign policies initiated by previous secular governments, such as economic liberalization, membership in the European Union, and fighting with corruption. In fact, the AK Party government has been putting more effort into the implementation of these policies than did their predecessors, mainly because they want to prove to secularist circles in Turkey and to the rest of the world that an Islam-based political party can be equally efficient to a secular party, if not more so, in solving Turkey's main economic, political, and social problems. They are deeply motivated to prove wrong accusations brought against Islamists that they are backward, uncultured, and hostile to Western ideals such as democracy, individual rights and liberties, and economic liberalism. Motivated by such a cause, the AK Party government has been working doubly hard toward advancing modernist and liberal ideals such as economic liberalization, privatization, putting a brake on populist and clientalist policies that have been one of the main causes of the crisis in the public sector, decentralization of the state, democratization, and, most important, furthering Turkey's candidacy for membership in the European Union.

This public repositioning of the AK Party has certainly played a key role both in its electoral success, winning a considerable number of secular votes, and especially in the cautious acceptance of its position by the military. The military not only acquiesced to the AK Party's government and program but actually declared unconditional support for its policy toward advancing Turkey's pending candidacy for membership in the European Union.

This said, however, the AK Party's unofficial newspaper, *Yeni Şafak*, continues to endorse a liberal-Islamist perspective in which economic and political liberalism is combined with conservative social values and a sense of national identity and culture that takes Islam as its essential defining value.[4] In other words, even if the AK Party has publicly disassociated itself from political Islam, Islamism still dictates the intellectual foundations of its ideology, which is especially evident in the understanding of national culture and identity projected in *Yeni Şafak*. Furthermore, the wives of a majority of AK Party parliamentarians and cabinet members are wearing the Islamic headscarf and attire, including the first lady as well as Erdoğan's daughters. This has caused some tension at official receptions, where the presence of veiled women has caused some unrest among secularist circles. This unrest culminated in a more serious crisis during the official annual Republic Day reception held on 29 October 2003 and hosted by President Ahmet Necdet Sezer when he refused to issue invitations to the wives of AK Party parliamentarians because he would not accept the presence of the Islamic headscarf in public spaces. Even though a majority of the AK Party parliamentarians refused to attend the reception in protest, all members of the cabinet and Prime Minister Erdoğan attended without their wives. This incident demonstrates that the issue of secularism and the place and status of Islam in Turkey are far from being resolved in the near future.

It is possible, therefore, to interpret the AK Party's full incorporation into the secular political system as another victory of secularism in successfully assimilating a rival political ideology. Indeed, secularism still enjoys an unchallenged status in the public sphere. After all, what had made Erdoğan, who, only a couple of years before the election, had been removed from office as Istanbul's mayor and sentenced for conspiring against the secular principles of the state, turn around and publicly endorse the principle of secularism was no doubt the repressive and assimilative measures taken against political Islam not only by the military but also by civilian forces including university administrations, intellectuals, and the secular media. Such measures seem to have made it clear to Islamist circles that they would have to find ways to operate and advance their ideology within the parameters of political conduct set by official secularist ideology. However, it also seems that these restrictions motivated some Islamist circles to find innovative ways to merge Islamic thought and practice with secularism and modernity, further advancing the emergence of Islamic modernism.

Notes

1 *Europe* is used here to include the Anglo-Saxon world.

2 Dilip Parameshwar Gaonkar, "On Alternative Modernities," *Public Culture* 11, no. 1 (1999): 1–18.

3 Gaonkar, "On Alternative Modernities," 17.

4 One of the most comprehensive collection of studies on Turkish modernity is Sibel Bozdoğan and Reşat Kasaba, eds., *Rethinking Modernity and National Identity in Turkey* (Seattle: University of Washington Press, 1997). A majority of the articles in this volume endorse the idea that modernization has been imposed "from above."

5 In both academic and intellectual discourse, what are seen as political, social, and cultural "anomalies," such as state authoritarianism, the rise of political Islam, separatist Kurdish nationalism, the musical genre called *Arabesk* associated with lower-class urban culture, and general problems of urbanization, are predominantly attributed to the failure of the official modernization project due to its imitative nature, imposed as it was as a top-down process by the state. For example, Ayşe Kadıoğlu maintains that the authoritarianism of the Turkish state resulted from the top-down imposition of Turkish modernity that could only be sustained by an authoritarian state, in "The Paradox of Turkish Nationalism and the Construction of Official Identity," *Middle Eastern Studies* 32, no. 2 (April 1996): 177–93.

6 Şerif Mardin, "The Just and the Unjust," *Daedalus* (Summer 1991): 116.

7 For a detailed and well-illustrated account of the transformation of official state ideology into a "secular religion," see Sibel Bozdoğan, *Modernism and Nation Building: Turkish Architectural Culture in the Early Republic* (Seattle: University of Washington Press, 2001), 286.

8 *Atatürk'ün Söylev ve Demeçleri* (Atatürk's speeches and lectures), vol. 3, 91, quoted in Mehmet Sarıoğlu, *"Ankara" Bir Modernleşme Öyküsü (1919–1945)*, ("Ankara": A story of

modernization [1919–1945]) (Ankara: TC Kültür Bakanlığı Kültür Eserleri, 2001), 103. All Turkish-to-English translations are the author's unless otherwise noted.

9 For an account of the shift in the conceptualization of modernity during the 1950s, see Nilüfer Göle, "Engineers: Technocratic Democracy," in *Turkey and the West: Changing Political and Cultural Identities*, ed. Metin Heper, A. Öncü, and H. Kramer (New York: I. B. Tauris & Co., 1993), 199–218.

10 The Refah Party was the main Islamist political party in Turkey that increased its support base geometrically within a decade, a trend that brought the party to power in 1996. After a decree issued by the National Security Council against the rising threat of political Islam in 1997, the Refah Party was forced to move out of power, and it ceased to exist in 1998. It reemerged immediately after under a new name, Fazilet (Virtue) Party, which became the main opposition party in the parliament after the 1999 general elections. In 2001 the Fazilet Party also ceased to exist, but reorganized again under the name Saadet (Felicity) Party. At this juncture, the moderate wing representing the younger generation left the party and founded the Adalet ve Kalkınma (AK) (Justice and development) Party under the leadership of Recep Tayyip Erdoğan and came to power as a majority government following the November 2002 elections.

11 William E. Connolly, *Political Theory and Modernity* (New York: Basil Blackwell, 1988), 2.

12 Designating Islamism as traditional, antimodern, or anti-Western has become a firmly established norm in the popular media in Turkey as well, to such an extent that the word *modern (çağdaş)* is used as a synonym of secularism and to designate a position that is directly opposed to Islam. Yet obviously this specification is not an invention of Turkish secularist circles. As Edward Said has shown in *Orientalism* (New York: Vintage Books, 1978), this designation is the direct product of Orientalist discourse. The proliferation of books and articles with titles such as "Islam and Modernity" or "Islam and the West" in the 1990s alone suggests that this discourse, which has established Islam and modernity as diametrically opposed and hierarchically ordered categories, still rules, albeit in new forms.

13 Bruce B. Lawrence, *Defenders of God: The Fundamentalist Revolt against the Modern Age* (Columbia, SC: University of South Carolina Press, 1995), xiv.

14 Ibid., 2.

15 Ibid., 229.

16 Martin E. Marty and R. Scott Appleby, "Introduction: A Sacred Cosmos, Scandalous Code, Defiant Society," in *Fundamentalisms and Society: Reclaiming the Sciences, the Family and Education*, ed. Martin E. Marty and R. Scott Appleby (Chicago: University of Chicago Press, 1993), 3.

17 For a detailed account of the Nur movement, see Şerif Mardin, *Religion and Social Change in Modern Turkey: The Case of Beduizzaman Said Nursi* (Albany: State University of New York Press, 1989).

18 For example, one of the most popular orders, the Nakşibendi, had very close links with ANAP (the Motherland Party), which was the secular neoconservative ruling party in the 1980s. Its founder and leader and Turkey's former prime minister and president, the late Turgut Özal, was known to be a member of this order.

19 Arslan and other intellectuals, such as Ali Bulaç, mentioned here, have expressed

these views most comprehensively in the quarterly *Bilgi ve Hikmet* (Knowledge and virtue), which was published in the 1990s.

20 Ali Bulaç, "Bir Arada Yaşamanın Mümkün Projesi: Medine Vesikası" (A possible project of living together: The Madina Document), *Bilgi ve Hikmet* 5 (Winter 1994): 3–15.

21 See, for example, Ömer Çelik, "İnsanın Modern Kimliği: Evrenselcilik, Irkçılık ve Cinsiyetçilik" (Man's modern identity: Universalism, racism and sexism), *Bilgi ve Hikmet* 4 (Fall 1993): 9–23, or Ali Bulaç, "Tasarlanmış Fenomenler Dünyasında Akıl, Nefis ve Kimlikler" (Mind, self and identities in the world of constructed phenomena), *Bilgi ve Hikmet* 4 (Fall 1993): 24–45. Note that Ömer Çelik later became a member of the parliament from the AK Party and one of Prime Minister Erdoğan's top consultants in 2002.

22 Roxanne L. Euben, "Mapping Modernities, 'Islamic' and 'Western,'" in *Border Crossings: Toward a Comparative Political Theory,* ed. Fred Dallmayr (New York: Lexington Books, 1999), 30.

23 The AK Party won 34 percent of the general vote, earning the party a clear majority in the parliament. Whereas the Saadet (Felicity) Party, which was established by the older generation of leaders of Refah/Fazilet, won only 2.5 percent of the vote.

24 See, for example, Binnaz Toprak, "Islamist Intellectuals: Revolt against Industry and Technology," in *Turkey and the West: Changing Political and Cultural Identities,* ed. Metin Heper, Ayşe Öncü, and H. Kramer (New York: I. B. Tauris & Co., 1993), 237–57.

25 Michael Meeker, "The Muslim Intellectual and His Audience," in *Cultural Transitions in the Middle East,* ed. Şerif Mardin (New York: E. J. Brill, 1994, 153–88), 164.

26 Several authors have qualified Turkish modernity as "imitative" or "cosmetic." See, for example, Ayşe Kadıoğlu, "The Paradox of Turkish Nationalism," and Çağlar Keyder, "Whither the Project of Modernity? Turkey in the 1990s," in Bozdoğan and Kasaba, *Rethinking Modernity,* and Nilüfer Göle, *The Forbidden Modern: Civilization and Veiling* (Ann Arbor: University of Michigan Press, 1996).

27 Even though official national history takes the onset of the republic in 1923 as a new beginning and a sharp break from the Ottoman past, the quest for modernity and a search for a path on which Turkey could comfortably situate itself was an uninterrupted process throughout the nineteenth and twentieth centuries.

28 The assumption that modernity and nationalism displace religion is made not only by studies that take the classical modernization perspective. More sophisticated works on nationalism, such as Benedict Anderson's *Imagined Communities* (New York: Verso, 1983) or Ernest Gellner's *Nations and Nationalism* (Ithaca, NY: Cornell University Press, 1983), make the claim that modernity and nationalism were made possible as a result of the decline of religions.

29 "The other Turkey" was a term coined by a secular journalist, Serdar Turgut, to refer to sections of the population who have been left out of the modernization process. The term was appropriated by the Refah Party circles during the 1994 elections when they claimed to represent the interests of this "other Turkey." *İzlenim* (Impression) 6 (9 April 1994).

30 *Modernity and Ambivalance* (Ithaca, NY: Cornell University Press, 1991), 272.

31 Michel Foucault, "What Is Enlightenment?" in *The Foucault Reader,* ed. Paul Rabinow (New York: Pantheon Books, 1984), 32–50.

32 In the special issue of *Public Culture* on alternative modernities, Gaonkar also uses Foucault's account as the point of departure for studying non-Western modernities. For an insightful review of Foucault's understanding of modernity, see Gaonkar, "On Alternative Modernities."

33 Bauman, *Modernity and Ambivalence*, 10.

34 Marshall Berman, *All That Is Solid Melts into Air: The Experience of Modernity* (New York: Penguin Books, 1988), 6.

35 Ibid., 14.

36 Connolly, *Political Theory and Modernity*, 2.

37 Deniz Kandiyoti, "Gendering the Modern—On Missing Dimensions in the Study of Turkish Modernity," in Bozdoğan and Kasaba, *Rethinking Modernity*, 1997, 117.

38 It is Anne Norton's work on popular culture and the U.S. Constitution that has inspired me to take the written constitution as the constitution of a nation. Anne Norton shows how daily activity and the proliferation of the signs of the nation in daily life are indeed about the making and remaking of the U.S. Constitution and its constitutive principles, namely liberalism. *The Republic of Signs: Liberal Theory and American Popular Culture* (Chicago: University of Chicago Press, 1993).

39 Norton, *Republic of Signs*, 1.

40 Judith Butler develops the notion of speech as a "performative act" that constitutes subjectivities and political agency in *Excitable Speech: A Politics of the Performative* (New York: Routledge, 1997).

41 Ibid.

42 Throughout the text I use *interpellate* and *interpellation* to mean "hailing or calling a subject into being." As is discussed at length in chapter 1, this meaning comes from the Althusserian notion of interpellation, which refers to hailing as a speech act by which a subject is brought into existence. Louis Althusser, *Lenin and Philosophy* (New York: Monthly Review Press, 1971), 170–77. For a thorough account of interpellation as a speech act, see Butler, *Excitable Speech*, 24–28.

1. PEFORMATIVE POLITICS AND THE PUBLIC GAZE

1 Jürgen Habermas, *The Structural Transformation of the Public Sphere*, trans. Thomas Burger (Cambridge, MA: MIT Press, 1989), 36.

2 Ibid., 35–37.

3 Craig Calhoun, "Introduction: Habermas and the Public Sphere," in *Habermas and the Public Sphere*, ed. Craig Calhoun (Cambridge, MA: MIT Press, 1992), 13.

4 Jürgen Habermas, "The Public Sphere: An Encyclopedia Article (1964)," *New German Critique* (1973): 49.

5 Jürgen Habermas, "The European Nation-State: On the Past and Future of Sovereignty and Citizenship," *Public Culture* 10, no. 2 (1998): 408.

6 Habermas, *The Structural Transformation*, 38–39.

7 Nancy Fraser, "Rethinking the Public Sphere: A Contribution to the Critique of Actually Existing Democracy," in *The Phantom Public Sphere*, ed. Bruce Robbins (Minneapolis: University of Minnesota Press, 1993); Seyla Benhabib, *Democracy and Difference: Contesting Boundaries of the Political* (Princeton, NJ: Princeton University Press, 1996); Jean L. Cohen, "Critical Social Theory and Feminist Critiques: The Debate with Jürgen Habermas," in *Feminists Read Habermas: Gendering the Subject of Discourse*, ed. Johanna Meehan (New York: Routledge, 1995).

8 Oskar Negt, *Public Sphere and Experience: Toward an Analysis of Bourgeois and Proletarian Public Sphere*, trans. P. Labanyi, J. O. Daniel, and A. Oksiloff (Minneapolis: University of Minnesota Press, 1993).

9 Calhoun, "Introduction," 34–36, in "The Black Public Sphere," special issue, *Public Culture* 7, no. 1 (Fall 1994).

10 See, for example, Joan Landes, "The Public and the Private Sphere: A Feminist Reconsideration," in *Feminists Read Habermas*, ed. Meehan; Michael Warner, "The Mass Public and the Mass Subject," in *Habermas and the Public Sphere*, ed. Calhoun; Lauren Berlant, "National Brands/National Body: *Imitation of Life*," in *The Phantom Public Sphere*, ed. Robbins.

11 Landes, "The Public and the Private Sphere."

12 Berlant, "National Brands/National Body"; Warner, "The Mass Public."

13 Habermas, "The Public Sphere," 50.

14 Warner, "The Mass Public," 381–82.

15 Ibid., 377.

16 *Sabah*, 30 November 1997.

17 *Sabah*, 7 August 1997.

18 Warner, "The Mass Public," 383.

19 Berlant, "National Brands/National Body," 176.

20 Habermas, *The Structural Transformation*, 159–80.

21 This discussion draws on Bourdieu's work on the constructions of class distinction, in Pierre Bourdieu, *Distinction: A Social Critique of the Judgement of Taste*, trans. R. Nice (Cambridge: Harvard University Press, 1984).

22 The notion of "everyday life" as a discursive space wherein techniques of power proliferate is extensively discussed in Michel de Certeau, *The Practice of Everyday Life* (Berkeley: University of California Press, 1984).

23 de Certeau, *The Practice of Everyday Life*, 34–40.

24 Warner, "The Mass Public," 398.

25 Ibid., 399.

26 Michel Foucault, *Power/Knowledge: Selected Interviews and Other Writings, 1972–1977*, ed. C. Gordon (New York: Pantheon Books, 1977), 148.

27 Michel Foucault, *Discipline and Punish: The Birth of the Prison*, trans. A. Sheridan (New York: Vintage Books, 1979), 201.

28 I am using *artist* to refer to the creator of the painting so that the person will not be confused with the painter depicted in the painting.

29 Michel Foucault, *The Order of Things: An Archaeology of the Human Sciences* (New York: Vintage Books, 1970), 15.

30 Althusser, *Lenin and Philosophy*, 170–77.

31 Foucault, *The Order of Things*, 15.

32 Judith Butler, *Gender Trouble: Feminism and the Subversion of Identity* (New York: Routledge, 1990), 145 (emphasis in the original).

33 Stephen Kinzer, "In Defense of Secularism, Turkish Army Warns Rulers," *New York Times*, 2 March 1997.

34 Habermas, "The Public Sphere," 53.

35 Foucault, *Discipline and Punish*, 201.

36 Ibid., 217.

37 Foucault, *Power/Knowledge*, 156.

2. CLOTHING THE NATIONAL BODY

1 See, for example, Nira Yuval-Davis and Floya Anthias, eds., *Woman-Nation-State* (London: Palgrave Macmillan, 1989), and various chapters in Tamar Mayer, ed., *Gender Ironies of Nationalism: Sexing the Nation* (New York: Routledge, 2000).

2 See, for example, Emma Tarlo, *Clothing Matters: Dress and Identity in India* (Chicago: University of Chicago Press, 1996); Patricia A. Cunningham and Susan Voso Lab, eds., *Dress and Popular Culture* (Ohio: Bowling Green State University Popular Press, 1991); Ruth Barnes and Joanne B. Eicher, eds., *Dress and Gender: Making and Meaning in Cultural Contexts* (Providence, RI: Berg Publishers, 1992).

3 Helen Callaway, "Dressing for Dinner in the Bush: Rituals of Self-Definition and British Imperial Authority," in *Dress and Gender*, ed. Barnes and Eicher, 239.

4 Ibid., 246.

5 Note that in Sunni Islam prayer is one of the five obligations of being a true Muslim. It is done five times a day and involves bending and kneeling several times.

6 Abdurrahman Arslan, "Vakit-Nakit/Zaman-Mekan ve Halılar" (Time-cash/Time-space and carpets), *Nehir* (River) 19–20 (May 1995): 51.

7 "New veiling" is a term used by Arlene MacLeod to describe the type of Islamic attire that developed in the early 1980s in Egypt, which is specifically urban and middle class and is not a continuation of a traditional style of Muslim dress. See Arlene MacLeod, *Accomodating Protest: Working Women, the New Veiling, and Change in Cairo* (New York: Columbia University Press, 1991).

8 Cihan Aktaş, *Kılık, Kıyafet ve İktidar: 12 Mart'tan 12 Eylül'e* (Clothing, apparel, and power: From 12 March to 12 September) (Istanbul: Nehir Yayınları, 1991), vol. 1, 170–73.

9 Nira Yuval-Davis, *Gender and Nation* (London: Sage Publications, 1997), 23.

10 For an insightful account, see Malek Alloula, *The Colonial Harem* (Minneapolis: University of Minnesota Press, 1986).

11 Nora Şeni, "Fashion and Women's Clothing in the Satirical Press of Istanbul at the End of the 19th Century," in *Women in Modern Turkish Society*, ed. Şirin Tekeli (London: Zed Books, 1995), 25–45.

12 Donald Quataert, "Clothing Laws, State, and Society in the Ottoman Empire, 1720–1829," *International Journal of Middle East Studies* 29, no. 3 (August 1997): 407.

13 Ibid., 409.

14 Ibid., 413.

15 Şeni, "Fashion and Women's Clothing," 26.

16 Ibid., 26, 36.

17 Nilüfer Göle, *The Forbidden Modern: Civilization and Veiling* (Ann Arbor: University of Michigan Press, 1996); Meyda Yeğenoğlu, *Colonial Fantasies: Towards a Feminist Reading of Orientalism* (Cambridge, England: Cambridge University Press, 1998); Tekeli, ed., *Women in Modern Turkish Society*; Deniz Kandiyoti, "Gendering the Modern: On Missing Dimensions in the Study of Turkish Modernity," in *Rethinking Modernity and National Identity in Turkey*, ed. Sibel Bozdoğan and Reşat Kasaba (Seattle: University of Washington Press, 1997), 113–32.

18 Yeğenoğlu, *Colonial Fantasies*, 132.

19 Quoted in ibid., 133.

20 Sarah Graham-Brown, *Images of Women: The Portrayal of Women in Photography of the Middle East, 1860–1950* (New York: Columbia University Press, 1988), 218–21.

21 Göle, *The Forbidden Modern*, 65.

22 Aktaş, *Kılık, Kıyafet ve İktidar*, vol. 1, 179.

23 Deniz Kandiyoti, "End of Empire: Islam, Nationalism, and Women in Turkey," in *Women, Islam, and the State*, ed. Deniz Kandiyoti (Philadelphia: Temple University Press, 1991), 41.

24 Graham-Brown, *Images of Women*, 220.

25 For detailed information on this period, see Şirin Tekeli, *Kadınlar ve Siyasal Toplumsal Hayat* (Women and social political life) (Istanbul: Birikim Yayınları, 1982); Kandiyoti, "End of Empire"; and Yeşim Arat, "The Project of Modernity and Women in Turkey," in *Rethinking Modernity*, ed. Bozdoğan and Kasaba, 95–112.

26 Nilüfer Göle, "The Gendered Nature of the Public Sphere," *Public Culture* 10, no. 1 (Fall 1997): 65.

27 Tekeli, *Kadınlar ve Siyasal Toplumsal Hayat*, 210–13.

28 Quoted in Aktaş, *Kılık, Kıyafet ve İktidar*, vol. 1, 171–72.

29 Aktaş, *Kılık, Kıyafet ve İktidar*, vol. 1, 172.

30 Quoted in Yeğenoğlu, *Colonial Fantasies*, 133.

31 Yeğenoğlu, *Colonial Fantasies*, 132.

32 In "The Project of Modernity," this point is discussed in detail by Yeşim Arat, who contrasts the generation of women of the early republican period, who are devotedly defensive about secularism, with the later generation of women, who are taking a more critical stance toward secularist reforms of the period. See also Kandiyoti, "End of Empire."

33 The reason for the closure of the federation was that a particular decision reached by the federation during the Twelfth Congress of the International Federation of Women held in Istanbul that year, which favored disarmament, contradicted foreign policy objectives of the state. Kandiyoti, "End of Empire," 41–42.

34 Ibid., 43.

35 For example, Nilüfer Göle argues that "Republican men called on women to be active agents in the building of a modern nation," thereby constituting women as political agents, in "The Gendered Nature," 67.

36 Quoted in Aktaş, *Kılık, Kıyafet ve İktidar*, vol. 1, 143.

37 Quoted in Yeğenoğlu, *Colonial Fantasies*, 133.

38 Ibid., 136.

39 Quoted in Zeynep Kezer, "The Making of a National Capital: Ideology and Socio-Spatial Practices in Early Republican Ankara" (Ph.D. dissertation, University of California, Berkeley, 1999), 212.

40 This information was provided by my late grandmother, Celile İnan, whose picture at a horseback riding club, wearing riding pants and boots, had appeared in a German magazine in 1936. Also, Sarah Graham-Brown mentions that such images of Turkish women were indeed circulating in European publications at the time, in *Images of Women*, 218.

41 Quoted in Aktaş, *Kılık, Kıyafet ve İktidar*, vol. 1, 175.

42 Ibid., 176.

43 Ibid.

44 Among numerous examples, a recent one is an article that appeared in the *Economist* on 10 August 2002, "Islam and the West: Europe's Muslims," 10. The only photograph accompanying the piece was that of a veiled woman, whose eyes were

glancing suspiciously toward the distance. The caption read, "Islam is now firmly established in Western Europe. Don't be afraid of it."

45 Ayşe Zengin, "Namus Kavramı ve Örtü" (The notion of honor and the covering), *Milli Gazete*, 17 June 1996.

46 Sibel Eraslan, interview by the author, 13 September 1996.

47 Ömer Torlak, "Çalışma Hayatı ve Kadının Mahremiyeti" (Working and woman's privacy), *Yeni Şafak*, 14 May 1997.

48 "Türban Kapatma Gerekçesi" (The turban is a reason for closure), *Sabah*, 5 March 1998.

49 MacLeod, *Accomodating Protest*, 109–12.

50 Quoted in Cihan Aktaş, *Kılık, Kıyafet ve İktidar: 12 Mart'tan 12 Eylül'e* (Istanbul: Nehir Yayınları, 1990), vol. 2, 131.

51 The 1980 coup and the following military regime was an intervention that mainly targeted to put an end to the highly polarized political divide between the left and the right, which had dominated all domains of public life during the 1970s. In this respect, the dress code was directed toward the removal of the marks of rightist and leftist identities in the public sphere, which involved the wearing of specific styles of mustache and hair. The ban on the beard elicited a reaction from among left-wing intellectuals and was not perceived as a secularist measure against a mark of Islam.

52 Aktaş, *Kılık, Kıyafet ve İktidar*, vol. 2, 130–31.

53 The word *sıkmabaş* is among the pejorative words used by secularist circles to refer to the religious headscarf. It means "a tightly wrapped head." *Cumhuriyet*, 8 January 1987.

54 Adile Oduncu, "Are There Negroes in My Country?" *Kadın ve Aile* (June 1986): 6–9, excerpted from JPRS-WER-86-122, 18 December 1986.

55 See note 53 regarding *sıkmabaş*. *Çarşaf* is often used to refer to the black garment that covers the whole body, including the head. Whereas the headscarf and new veiling are rarely, if ever, black, the black *çarşaf* is never worn by university students and is associated with extreme conservatism.

56 Higher Education Council press release, *Cumhuriyet*, 31 December 1986.

57 *Milliyet*, 8 January 1987.

58 Oktay Akbal, "Bu Tutumla, Bu Kafayla" (With this attitude and this mentality), *Cumhuriyet*, 11 January 1987 (emphasis in the original).

59 *Cumhuriyet*, 7 January 1987.

60 "İslamcı Akımlar Ne İstiyor?" (What do Islamist movements want?), *Cumhuriyet*, 11 January 1987; *Cumhuriyet*, 17 January 1987.

61 *Cumhuriyet*, 19 January 1987.

62 For a detailed review of these incidents, see Aktaş, *Kılık, Kıyafet ve İktidar*, vol. 2.

63 "Türban Yasağı Anayasada Var" (The ban on the turban is in the constitution), *Sabah*, 2 February 1997.

64 Yasar Kaplan, *Akit*, 2 September 1996.

65 *Milliyet*, 23 March 1998.

66 Hüseyin Besli, "Kadının Medyatik Değeri" (The value of woman in the media), *Istanbul Bülteni* 2, no. 29 (23 October 1995): 14–15.

67 Davut Dursun, "İslam, Kadın ve Modernlik" (Islam, woman, and modernity), *Nehir* 8 (June–July, 1994): 68.

68 Turkish Daily News, 18 July 1997, Turkish Probe issue 236.
69 Hüseyin Besli, "Kapı Gıcırtısı" (The squeaking of a door), İstanbul Bülteni 2, no. 29 (23 October 1995): 15.
70 For a detailed account of Islamic fashion shows, see Yael Navaro-Yashin, The Faces of the State: Secularism and Public Life in Turkey (Princeton, NJ: Princeton University Press, 2002), 90–113.
71 Kemal Öztürk and Osman Özsoy, "Meydanlardan Podyumlara Tesettür" (Islamic dress from demonstrations to fashion shows), Yeni Şafak, 1 July 1995.
72 Only civil marriages are recognized under the secular civil code.
73 Said Nursi is the founder of the Nur movement, one of the largest Islamic orders in Turkey. For a detailed account of the teachings and life of Said Nursi, see Şerif Mardin, Religion and Social Change in Modern Turkey: The Case of Bediuzzaman Said Nursi (Albany: State University of New York, 1989).
74 The Aczmendi leader, Müslüm Gündüz, was frequently making speeches about the need to abolish the republic and replace it with an Islamic state. After his arrest, he called for an Islamic revolution in Turkey. He also claimed that he did not officially get married to his wives because he did not believe in the secular laws and institutions of the republic.
75 "Medya Devleti mi Hukuk Devleti mi?" (A state of law or a state of the media?), Milli Gazete, 4 January 1997; "Bir Takım Adamlar Kameralarla . . ." (Some men with their cameras . . .), Yeni Şafak, 3 January 1997.
76 Later in her book Fadime Şahin explains that she was actually raped by the leader of this order, Ali Kalkancı, who then threatened her into an unofficial religious marriage. Fadime Şahin, Fadime Şahin'in Anıları: Sahte Tarikatların Perde Arkası (Fadime Şahin's memories: Behind the curtains of the false orders) (İstanbul: Ad Yayıncılık, 1997).
77 "Tesettürün Kurtarıcılığı" (The liberating power of the new veiling), Yeni Şafak, 30 June 1997.
78 It should be noted here that the media conveniently overlook the fact that one of the reasons such mystical orders and Islamic practices are covert in the first place is because they were outlawed.
79 Covering is a word commonly used to refer to the headscarf, the veil, and also bedsheets. "Örtünün Altında Ne Var?" (What is underneath the covering?), Radikal, 12 January 1997.
80 "Tesettürün Kurtarıcılığı," Yeni Şafak, 30 June 1997.
81 Aktüel is a popular weekly, heavy in visual content, that includes political, social, and entertainment news reports, research articles, and gossip columns. Fadime Şahin was the subject of the cover story in the 22 January 1997 issue.
82 The photograph alleged to be that of Fadime appeared in Sabah on 30 November 1997. In a later interview, Fadime Şahin denounced such claims. Hürriyet, 23 December 1997.
83 Hürriyet, 25 December 1997.

3. CITIES, SQUARES, AND STATUES

1 Nurettin Can Gülekli, Anıtkabir Rehberi (Anıtkabir guide) (Ankara: Türk Tarih Kurumu Basımevi, 1973), 30.
2 Cited in Mehmet Özel, Ankara (Ankara: Kültür Bakanlığı Yayınları, Türk Matbaacılık Sanayi AŞ, 1992).

3 Zeynep Kezer, "The Making of a National Capital: Ideology and Socio-Spatial Practices in Early Republican Ankara" (Ph.D. dissertation, University of California, Berkeley, 1999), 134.

4 Ibid., 213–15.

5 Cited in İnci Yalım, "Ulus Devletin Kamusal Alanda Meşruiyet Aracı: Toplumsal Belleğin Ulus Meydanı Üzerinden Kurgulanma Çabası" (The means of legitimation of the nation-state in the public sphere: Efforts to construct social memory in Ulus Square), in *Başkent Üzerine Mekan-Politik Tezler: Ankara'nın Kamusal Yüzleri* (Spatio-political theses on the capital: The public faces of Ankara), ed. Güven Arif Sargın (Istanbul: İletişim Yayıncılık, 2002), 198.

6 Ibid., 201.

7 Carole Pateman, *The Disorder of Women: Democracy, Feminism and Political Theory* (Stanford, CA: Stanford University Press, 1989), 49–53.

8 The construction of the monument started in 1944 and ended in 1953. On 10 November 1953, Atatürk's body was brought to and buried in a special chamber within the mausoleum.

9 Gülekli, *Anıtkabir Rehberi*, 11.

10 Afife Batur, "Anıtkabir," *Cumhuriyet Dönemi Türkiye Ansiklopedisi* (Encyclopedia of Turkey in the republican period) (Istanbul: İletişim Yayınları, 1983), vol. 5, no. 1392.

11 Ibid.

12 Kezer, *The Making of a National Capital*, 141–42.

13 Ahmet Demirhan, *Izlenim* 6 (9 April 1994), 6–8.

14 For example, several articles appearing in a special issue of *Türkiye Günlüğü*, no. 27 (March–April 1994), written by academics and journalists taking different positions on the political spectrum, mark 27 March 1994, the election day, as a major historical landmark in Turkish history.

15 Ergun Yıldırım, "MNP'den MSP'ye Refah Partisi: Gelişimi, Felsefesi ve Projeleri" (The Refah Party from MNP to MSP: Its development, its philosophy, and its projects), *Nehir* 6 (March 1994, supplement).

16 One of the major exhibitions organized by the Turkish History Foundation, a secular organization, on the occasion of the Habitat II conference was the "Istanbul: World City" exhibition. This qualification was also used throughout the *National Report and Action Plan* prepared for the Habitat II conference. Likewise, Istanbul is often cited as "a global metropolis" in the publications of the Islamist city administration. See, for example, *Istanbul Bülteni* 44 (March 1996): 20.

17 Oktay Ekinci, *Bütün Yönleriyle Taksim Camisi Belgeseli* (The Taksim Mosque documentary from all angles) (Istanbul: Çağdaş Yayınları, 1997).

18 *Yeni Yüzyıl*, 1 February 1997.

19 Ekinci, *Bütün Yönleriyle Taksim Camisi Belgeseli*.

20 *Cuma* 6, no. 313 (12 September 1996).

21 Mustafa Karahasanoğlu, "Cuma'dan" (From Friday), *Cuma* 6, no. 313 (12 September 1996): 1.

22 *Milliyet Gazetesi*, 29 May 1994.

23 Hüseyin Besli, Director of the Media and Public Relations Office of the Istanbul Metropolitan Municipality, interviews with the author, July 1996.

24 Akif Beki, "The Representation Crisis at the Turkish Front of Habitat II," *Turkish Daily News*, 5 April 1996.

25 Ibid.

26 Mayor Erdoğan preferred to use the word *parallel* rather than *alternative*, because, he said, he did not want to give the impression that the city was opposed to the official UN conference. The city participated fully both in the organization of the conference and as a participating member of the NGO Forum. Cited in *Habitat Days,* 30 May 1996, 3.

27 Beki, "The Representation Crisis."

28 "Habitat II İstanbul Büyükşehir Belediyesi Faaliyet Programı" (Habitat II Greater Municipality of Istanbul activity report), Greater Municipality of Istanbul, 4 April 1996.

29 *Habitat Days,* 30 May 1996, 2.

30 This theme is repeated in various issues of *Habitat Days.* See, for example, Mustafa Kutlu, "The Spirit of a City," *Habitat Days,* 31 May 1996, 4.

31 Ibid.

32 For example, Nazif Gürdoğan, "Virtuous Cities as Future States," *Habitat Days,* 2 June 1996; Kutlu, "The Spirit of a City"; Aykut Köksal, "The Protection of Historical Values," *Habitat Days,* 3 June 1996.

33 Bilal Eryılmaz, "Globalization and the Future of Cities," *Habitat Days,* 5 June 1996.

34 Bilal Eryılmaz, "Old Istanbul as a Multicultural City," *Habitat Days,* 10 June 1996.

35 Nabi Avcı, "The Blues, The Greens and the Other Istanbul," *Habitat Days,* 2 June 1996.

36 The official Web site of the Metropolitan Municipality of Istanbul, "Cumhuriyet Döneminde Istanbul" (Istanbul during the republic), http://www.ibb.gov.tr/ index.htm, link to "Istanbul'un Tarihi" (Istanbul's history), accessed 10 December 1997. Note that even though several articles on this Web site that made references to Istanbul as the capital of the "Ottoman-Islamic civilization" were removed when Mayor Erdoğan was removed from office in 1998, this particular page remained active as of October 2003.

37 The official Web site of the Metropolitan Municipality of Istanbul, "Kültür Hizmetleri" (Cultural services), http://www.ibb.gov.tr, accessed 10 December 1997. This link was removed from the site when Mayor Erdoğan was removed from office in 1998.

38 Davut Dursun, "Hangi Istanbul" (Which Istanbul?), *Nehir* 18 (March 1995): 14–15.

39 Ibid.

40 Akif Çankırılı, "Istanbul: Yitik Şehir" (Istanbul: The lost city), 16–17; Muharrem Es and Hamza Al, "Göç, İstanbul ve Kentlileşme" (Migration, Istanbul, and urbanization), 22–25.

41 The official Web site of the Metropolitan Municipality of Istanbul, "Kültür Hizmetleri" (Cultural Services).

42 The official Web site of the Metropolitan Municipality of Istanbul, "Dünya Şehri Istanbul" (Istanbul the world city).

43 Hüseyin Besli, interview.

44 *Sabah Gazetesi,* 23 July 1995.

45 "Bir Şişe Cola'da Kopartılan Fırtına" (So much fuss over a bottle of Coke), *Istanbul Bülteni,* 1 August 1995, 7.

46 When I first visited Çamlıca, there was a drawing on the wall at the entrance of the coffee house that clearly depicted such an arrangement. This drawing was later

replaced by a proper painting depicting the same, which was then moved to decorate one of the walls of the restaurant.

47 Mehmet Şefik Aydın, Chief Assistant Director of Çamlıca Premises, interview with the author, 9 August 1996.

48 Arda Aydoğan, Director of Cemal Reşit Rey Concert Hall, interview with the author, 5 August 1996.

49 Şenol Demiröz, Director of Cultural Affairs, Greater Municipality of Istanbul, interview with the author, 10 May 1996.

50 Haydar Sanal, *Mehter Musikisi (Mehter music)* (Istanbul: Milli Eğitim Basımevi, 1964).

4. PERFORMING THE NATION

1 Benedict Anderson, *Imagined Communities* (New York: Verso, 1983), 26.

2 Ibid.

3 Ibid., 33.

4 This demand is raised in several articles covering the 29 May celebrations. See, for example, *Milli Gazete*, 30 May 1995, or *Yeni Şafak*, 31 May 1996.

5 Ana Maria Alonso, "The Effects of Truth: Re-presentations of the Past and the Imagining of Community," *Journal of Historical Sociology* 1, no. 1 (March 1988): 35.

6 The idea of "writing the nation into being" in the more general sense is implied by studies on the construction of national identities in national literatures, including Anderson's *Imagined Communities* and several articles in *Nation and Narration*, ed. Homi Bhabha (New York: Routledge, 1990). More specifically, Anne Norton draws attention to the U.S. Constitution as "the Declaration [that] spoke the nation into being." Anne Norton, *Republic of Signs: Liberal Theory and American Popular Culture* (Chicago: University of Chicago Press, 1993), 9. Likewise, drawing on the work of Michael Warner (*The Letters of the Republic: Publication and the Public Sphere in Eighteenth-Century America* [Cambridge, MA: Harvard University Press, 1990]), Prasenjit Duara draws attention to the written constitution as the objectifying document through which "the people" are written into being. Prasenjit Duara, *Rescuing History from the Nation: Questioning Narratives of Modern China* (Chicago: University of Chicago Press, 1995).

7 Duara, *Rescuing History*, 33.

8 Homi K. Bhabha, "DissemiNation: Time, Narrative, and the Margins of the Modern Nation," in *Nation and Narration*, ed. H. K. Bhabha (New York: Routledge 1990), 300.

9 Homi K. Bhabha, *The Location of Culture* (New York: Routledge, 1994), 147.

10 John R. Gillis, "Memory and Identity: The History of a Relationship," in *Commemorations: The Politics of National Identity*, ed. J. R. Gillis (Princeton, NJ: Princeton University Press, 1994), 7.

11 Lyn Spillman, *Nation and Commemoration: Creating National Identities in the United States and Australia* (New York: Cambridge University Press, 1997), 113.

12 Prasenjit Duara, "Historicizing National Identity, or Who Imagines What and When," in *Becoming National*, ed. Geoff Eley and R. G. Suny (New York: Oxford University Press, 1996), 159.

13 The word *gazi* is an honorary military title with Ottoman references.

14 Turkish History Committee, *The Outline of Turkish History* (Istanbul: Kaynak Yayınları, 1996), 466–67. Emphasis in the original.

15 Gillis, "Memory and Identity," 8.

16 Ibid.

17 Gillis, "Memory and Identity," 11.

18 Duara, "Historicizing National Identity," 152.

19 Ann Anagnost, *National Past-Times: Narrative, Representation, and Power in Modern China* (Durham, NC: Duke University Press, 1997), 2.

20 Studies on nationalism that have highlighted the constructed nature of national identities, such as Benedict Anderson's *Imagined Communities*, Ernest Gellner's *Nations and Nationalism* (Ithaca, NY: Cornell University Press, 1983), and Eric Hobsbawm and Terence Ranger's *The Invention of Tradition* (New York: Cambridge University Press, 1983), have been prone to interpretations that read *invention* as *fantasy*, *construction* as *forgery*, or *imagination* as *illusion*. However, these readings overlook a crucial component of nationalist discourse: namely, that its claims to homogeneity and singularity serve to mask not a made-up or false history, but rather its multiplicity and indefiniteness.

21 Gellner, *Nations and Nationalism*, 56.

22 Suna Kili, *Türk Devrim Tarihi* (History of the Turkish revolution), 3rd ed. (Istanbul: Tekin Yayınevi, 1982), 66–69.

23 For example, *Yeni Şafak*, 30 May 1997.

24 *The Outline of Turkish History*, 445.

25 Sezai Karakoç, "Bir Fetih Günü" (A day of conquest), *Fatih ve Fetih* (The conqueror and the conquest) (Istanbul: Metropolitan Municipality of Istanbul, Directorate of Cultural Affairs Publications, 1995), no. 17: 8.

26 Sezai Karakoç, "Istanbul'un Fethi" (The conquest of Istanbul), *Fatih ve Fetih*, 58.

27 The official Web site of the Metropolitan Municipality of Istanbul, "Istanbul'un Fethi," http://www.ibb.gov.tr/guzistanbul/tarihreh/fetihvelst/htm, accessed 15 December 1997. This particular link was discontinued when Mayor Erdoğan was removed from office in 1998.

28 See, for example, *Akit*, 31 May 1995; *Milli Gazete*, 29 May 1996.

29 *Milli Gazete*, 31 May 1996.

30 *Akit*, 29 May 1996.

31 See Olivier Roy, *The Failure of Political Islam*, trans. C. Volk (Cambridge, MA: Harvard University Press, 1994).

32 *Istanbul Bülteni*, 15 December 1996, 7.

33 The official Web site of the Metropolitan Municipality of Istanbul, "Kültür Hizmetleri" (Cultural Services).

34 Directorate of Cultural Affairs, Metropolitan Municipality of Istanbul, *Welcome to Istanbul*, videocassette prepared by the Istanbul city administration for the Habitat II conference, 1996.

35 There are several references to the victory won against the "West" in 1453 in most of the documents reviewed here. See, for example, *Izlenim* 1, no. 5 (April 1994): 27.

36 Kili, *Türk Devrim Tarihi*, 123.

37 Tanıl Bora, "Fatih'in Istanbul'u: 'Islam Şehri' ile 'Dünya Şehri' arasında İslamcıların İstanbul rüyası" (Fatih's Istanbul: The Istanbul fantasy of Islamists amid the "Islamic city" and the "global city"), *Birikim* 76 (August 1995): 45.

38 Akif Çankırılı, "Istanbul: Yitik Şehir" (Istanbul: The lost city), *Nehir* 18 (March 1995): 17.

39 Dursun, "Hangi İstanbul" (Which Istanbul?), *Nehir* 18 (March 1995): 14–15.

40 Ibid., 15.

41 *Lahmacun* is a popular Turkish pizzalike meat pastry that has Arab origins, as the name suggests.

42 "Istanbul'daki Güneydoğu" (The Southeast in Istanbul), *Istanbul Bülteni,* 13 November 1995, 10. The "Southeast" referred to in the title of this paragraph was a politically correct (or, rather, politically allowed) word used at the time to designate the Kurds. Until Turkey's candidacy for European Union membership started in 2002, the existence of Kurds as a distinct ethnic group and of Kurdish as a distinct language were not recognized by the state. Official state discourse, especially under pressures from the military, referred to the Kurds as the "Southeasterners" and the Kurdish issue as the "Southeastern question." As is evident in this paragraph, the urban lower class was identified with recent migrants to the city from rural areas and smaller Anatolian cities. In the 1990s the rapid increase of Kurdish migrants resulted in the identification of "lower class" with Kurds, thereby adding an ethnic dimension to class issues.

43 *Akit,* 31 May 1995.

44 *Milliyet,* 30 May 1997.

CONCLUSION

1 Ali Bulaç, "Modern Devletin Totaliter ve Ulus Niteliği" (The totalitarian and national nature of the modern state), *Bilgi ve Hikmet* 3 (Summer 1993): 3–15.

2 Nejat Gülen, "Gerici İle Uzlaşma Olmaz!" (Compromise is not possible with reactionaries!), *Devinim* 10 (November 1994): 8.

3 This term was coined by Cengiz Çandar in his columns in *Sabab.*

4 This Islamist discourse was developed around the mid-1990s mostly in the daily *Yeni Şafak,* whose columnists and writers were also working as consultants or aides for the Refah Party's Istanbul city administration under Tayyip Erdoğan's mayoralty, and some of them became AK Party parliamentarians after the 2002 elections.

Select Bibliography

Alloula, Malek. *The Colonial Harem*. Minneapolis: University of Minnesota Press, 1986.

Althusser, Louis. *Lenin and Philosophy*. New York: Monthly Review Press, 1971.

Anagnost, Ann. *National Past-Times: Narrative, Representation, and Power in Modern China*. Durham, NC: Duke University Press, 1997.

Anderson, Benedict. *Imagined Communities*. New York: Verso, 1983.

Appadurai, Arjun. "Disjuncture and Difference in the Global Cultural Economy." *Public Culture* 2, no. 2 (1990): 1–24.

Barnes, Ruth, and Joanne B. Eicher, eds. *Dress and Gender: Making and Meaning in Cultural Contexts*. Providence, RI: Berg Publishers, 1992.

Bauman, Zygmunt. *Modernity and Ambivalance*. Ithaca, NY: Cornell University Press, 1991.

Benhabib, Seyla. *Democracy and Difference: Contesting Boundaries of the Political*. Princeton, NJ: Princeton University Press, 1996.

Berlant, Lauren. "National Brands/National Body: *Imitation of Life*." In *The Phantom Public Sphere*, ed. Bruce Robbins, 173–208. Minneapolis: University of Minnesota Press, 1993.

Berman, Marshall. *All That Is Solid Melts into Air: The Experience of Modernity*. New York: Penguin Books, 1988.

Bhabha, Homi K., ed. *Nation and Narration*. New York: Routledge, 1990.

————. *The Location of Culture*. New York: Routledge, 1994.

Bourdieu, Pierre. *Distinction: A Social Critique of the Judgement of Taste*. Trans. R. Nice. Cambridge, MA: Harvard University Press, 1984.

Bozdoğan, Sibel. *Modernism and Nation Building: Turkish Architectural Culture in the Early Republic*. Seattle: University of Washington Press, 2001.

Bozdoğan, Sibel, and Reşat Kasaba, eds. *Rethinking Modernity and National Identity in Turkey*. Seattle: University of Washington Press, 1997.

Butler, Judith. *Gender Trouble: Feminism and the Subversion of Identity*. New York: Routledge, 1990.

————. *Excitable Speech: A Politics of the Performative.* New York: Routledge, 1997.

Calhoun, Craig, ed. *Habermas and the Public Sphere.* Cambridge, MA: MIT Press, 1992.

Çınar, Alev. "Refah Party and the City Administration of Istanbul: Liberal Islam, Localism, and Hybridity." *New Perspectives on Turkey* 16 (Spring 1997): 23–40.

————. "National History as a Contested Site: The Conquest of Istanbul and Islamist Negotiations of the Nation." *Comparative Studies in Society and History* 43, no. 2 (April 2001): 364–91.

Connolly, William E. *Political Theory and Modernity.* New York: Basil Blackwell, 1988.

Dallmayr, Fred, ed. *Border Crossings: Toward a Comparative Political Theory.* New York: Lexington Books, 1999.

De Certeau, Michel. *The Practice of Everyday Life.* Berkeley: University of California Press, 1984.

Duara, Prasenjit. *Rescuing History from the Nation: Questioning Narratives of Modern China.* Chicago: University of Chicago Press, 1995.

Foucault, Michel. *The Order of Things: An Archaeology of the Human Sciences.* New York: Vintage Books, 1970.

————. *Power/Knowledge: Selected Interviews and Other Writings, 1972–1977,* ed. C. Gordon. New York: Pantheon Books, 1977.

————. *Discipline and Punish: The Birth of the Prison.* Trans. Alan Sheridan. New York: Vintage Books, 1979.

Gellner, Ernest. *Nations and Nationalism.* Ithaca, NY: Cornell University Press, 1983.

Gillis, John R., ed. *Commemorations: The Politics of National Identity.* Princeton, NJ: Princeton University Press, 1994.

Göle, Nilüfer. *The Forbidden Modern: Civilization and Veiling.* Ann Arbor: University of Michigan Press, 1996.

————. "The Gendered Nature of the Public Sphere." *Public Culture* 10, no. 1 (Fall 1997): 61–81.

Graham-Brown, Sarah. *Images of Women: The Portrayal of Women in Photography of the Middle East, 1860–1950.* New York: Columbia University Press, 1988.

Habermas, Jürgen. "The Public Sphere: An Encyclopedia Article (1964)." *New German Critique* (1973): 49–55.

————. *The Structural Transformation of the Public Sphere.* Trans. Thomas Burger. Cambridge, MA: MIT Press, 1989.

Heper, Metin, A. Öncü, and H. Kramer, eds. *Turkey and the West: Changing Political and Cultural Identities.* New York: I. B. Tauris, 1993.

Hobsbawm, Eric, and Terence Ranger, eds. *The Invention of Tradition.* New York: Cambridge University Press, 1983.

Kandiyoti, Deniz. "End of Empire: Islam, Nationalism, and Women in Turkey." In *Women, Islam, and the State,* ed. Deniz Kandiyoti, 22–47. Philadelphia: Temple University Press, 1991.

Kandiyoti, Deniz, and Ayşe Saktanber, eds. *Fragments of Culture: The Everyday of Modern Turkey.* New York: I. B. Tauris, 2002.

Lawrence, Bruce B. *Defenders of God: The Fundamentalist Revolt against the Modern Age.* Columbia: University of South Carolina Press, 1995.

Lewis, Bernard. *Islam and the West.* New York: Oxford University Press, 1993.

MacLeod, Arlene E. *Accommodating Protest: Working Women, the New Veiling, and Change in Cairo.* New York: Columbia University Press, 1991.

Mardin, Şerif. *Religion and Social Change in Modern Turkey: The Case of Bediuzzaman Said Nursi.* Albany: State University of New York, 1989.

Marty, Martin E., and R. Scott Appleby, eds. *Fundamentalisms and Society: Reclaiming the Sciences, the Family, and Education.* Chicago: University of Chicago Press, 1993.

Meehan, Johanna, ed. *Feminists Read Habermas: Gendering the Subject of Discourse.* New York: Routledge, 1995.

Navaro-Yashin, Yael. *The Faces of the State: Secularism and Public Life in Turkey.* Princeton, NJ: Princeton University Press, 2002.

Negt, Oskar. *Public Sphere and Experience: Toward an Analysis of the Bourgeois and Proletarian Public Sphere.* Trans. P. Labanyi, J. O. Daniel, and A. Obsiloff. Minneapolis: University of Minnesota Press, 1993.

Norton, Anne. *The Republic of Signs: Liberal Theory and American Popular Culture.* Chicago: University of Chicago Press, 1993.

Pateman, Carole. *The Disorder of Women: Democracy, Feminism, and Political Theory.* Cambridge, England: Polity Press, 1989.

Robbins, Bruce, ed. *The Phantom Public Sphere.* Minneapolis: University of Minnesota Press, 1993.

Roy, Olivier. *The Failure of Political Islam.* Trans. C. Volk. Cambridge, MA: Harvard University Press, 1994.

Said, Edward. *Orientalism.* New York: Vintage Books, 1978.

Spillman, Lyn. *Nation and Commemoration: Creating National Identities in the United States and Australia.* New York: Cambridge University Press, 1997.

Tekeli, Şirin, ed. *Women in Modern Turkish Society.* London: Zed Books, 1995.

Warner, Michael. "The Mass Public and the Mass Subject." In *Habermas and the Public Sphere,* ed. Craig Calhoun, 377–401. Cambridge, MA: MIT Press, 1992.

Yeğenoğlu, Meyda. *Colonial Fantasies: Towards a Feminist Reading of Orientalism.* New York: Cambridge University Press, 1998.

Yuval-Davis, Nira. *Gender and Nation.* London: Sage Publications, 1997.

Index

ALEV ÇINAR teaches in the Department of Political Science at Bilkent University, Ankara, Turkey.